SAMURAI WARRIORS

Based on twelfth-century *yoroi* preserved at the Itsukushima Shrine Museum, Miyajima (Hiroshima Prefecture), this mounted figure, depicting the crossing of Uji River by Yoshitsune's troops in 1184, gives a good idea of the appearance of a well-to-do samurai at the height of the Gempei War. His armour is of a similar design to that shown in Plates 1 and 4, but the angle of view reveals the extent of the leather breastplate, which was fastened over the body of the armour, only the right side of the 'box' being separate (see Plate 6 for details). Also visible is the *tanto*, or dagger, and the wooden reel tied on to the belt which carried a spare bowstring. The tying cords of the *kote* are shown as they run along the length of the arm. The helmet bears a very ornate pair of *kuwagata*, or 'antlers', set off by a grinning *oni*. Note that this samurai has adopted the protruding *eboshi* as padding for the helmet.

The horse is adorned in typical samurai fashion, with an arrangement of silken tassels still observable in the eighteenth century. The heavy *abumi*, or stirrups, are of iron, lacquered inside, on which the foot rests flat.

STEPHEN TURNBULL

SAMURAI WARRIORS

ILLUSTRATIONS BY JAMES FIELD

PHOTOGRAPHS BY STEPHEN TURNBULL

BLANDFORD PRESS
POOLE·NEW YORK·SYDNEY

First published in the U.K. 1987 by Blandford Press,
Link House, West Street, Poole, Dorset, BH15 1LL.

Distributed in the United States by
Sterling Publishing Co., Inc.,
2 Park Avenue, New York, N.Y. 10016.

Distributed in Australia by
Capricorn Link (Australia) Pty Ltd
PO Box 665, Lane Cove, NSW 2066

British Library Cataloguing in Publication Data

Turnbull, S.R.
  Samurai warriors.
  1. Samurai —History
  I. Title
  305.5′2   DS827.S3

         ISBN 0 7137 1767 X

Typeset by Best-set Typesetter Limited, Hong Kong
Printed in Great Britain by
Purnell Book Production Ltd
Member of the BPCC Group

To the author's mother, Joyce M. Turnbull,
and the artist's wife, Sally Field

Contents

Acknowledgements

Until the publication of this book, non-Japanese-speaking readers have been denied an authoritative account of the development of the costume and equipment of the Japanese samurai as it relates to changes in military history, such as has been produced by scholars like Yoshihiko Sasama. Several of Sasama's indispensable works, especially his *Zukai Nihon Katchu Jiten* (1973), and *Zuroku Nihon no Katchu Bugu Jiten* (1981) have been consulted initially on points of detail for this work, but in every case the resulting illustration or description has been taken from source, making *Samurai Warriors* totally original. It draws upon 20 years of research into samurai history, armour and weapons and, using exclusively Japanese sources, paints a picture of the samurai in words, photographs and via specially commissioned artwork that is unique outside Japan itself.

Such use of rare materials could not have been entertained without the help and support of many individuals and organisations. In this context particular mention must be made of Mrs Nahoko Kitajima of Moriguchi City, Osaka, and her colleague Mr Nishikawa; and also Mr Yukito Kaiki and Miss Nobuyo Ichifugi, of Kanazawa. Much valuable information was also supplied by the helpful staff of the Tokyo Offices of the Prefectures of Yamanashi, Shizuoka, Gifu, Shiba, Ishikawa and Aichi. Museums and collections that opened their doors to us include the Nagashino Castle Preservation Hall, the Minatogawa Shrine Museum, Kobe, the Ieyasukan at Okazaki, the Gifu City Historical Museum, the Sanada Museum, Matsushiro, Ueda Castle Museum, Osaka Castle Museum, Hamamatsu Castle Museum, the Nampian Kannon-ji at Kawachi-Nagano, the Memorial Hall at Nakamura Park, Nagoya, and the Takeda Museum at the Erinji, Enzan, in addition to well-known national collections such as the Tokyo National Museum.

This book is the product of a partnership. Quite the most enjoyable and rewarding aspect of its production has been to place my research beside the considerable artistic talents of James Field. It has proved to be a fruitful co-operation, and I know James joins with me in saying the biggest 'thank-you' to our wives, Jo Turnbull and Sally Field, without whose happy tolerance none of what follows would have been possible.

Stephen Turnbull

1

Heian Period

The samurai were the knights of Medieval Japan. Like their counterparts in Europe, they began as a military élite and became a social élite, their prize being the triumph which their swords had won for them. The history of the samurai is very much the history of Japan itself, so for convenience we will follow a chronological sequence based on the traditional divisions of the Japanese historical eras. The 'Heian Period' (during which the word 'samurai' is first used) derives from the name by which the capital city, Kyoto, was known at the time: 'Heian-kyo' or the city of heavenly peace.

The Early Warriors

There is no doubt as to when the samurai officially ceased to exist as a separate class. The decisive date must be 1876, when the wearing of swords was forbidden to all except the national conscript army of the new Japan. What is at issue is how the samurai began. Exactly how did a military élite emerge? This is a problem of Japanese history that has still not been adequately explained. In terms of the long history of the Japanese people the samurai are comparative newcomers. The word itself hardly pre-dates the eleventh century AD and follows a millennium of years of war. *Samurai* means, literally, 'those who serve', implying the rendering of honourable military service by an élite to an overlord, which is effectually what the samurai existed to provide until the time when the class was abolished in the 1870s. These three factors: military prowess, élitism and service to another, are the keys to identifying the origin of the samurai.

Ancient records give us some clues as to the samurai antecedents. Within the *Nihongi*, the *Chronicles of Japan*, compiled sometime during the first decades of the eighth century AD, may be found the term *bugei*, or 'martial arts', so no doubt some degree of military specialism existed in the armies of the period, whether they were under the control of the central government or local officials. The early history of Japan was as much a time of conflict as any of the 'samurai centuries' that followed.

In the year AD 672 we are given a hint of one role which the future samurai were to make very much their own, that of the mounted archer, a form of warfare, which, it would appear, was already achieving an élite status. In AD 671 the Emperor Tenchi died, his death causing one of those succession disputes with which samurai history is littered. Emperor Tenchi had apparently promised the throne to his brother, who had declined the honour and subsequently become a monk, so that on Tenchi's death his son ascended to the throne. This was, however, only within a month of the uncle renouncing the world, and the opportunity to take up that which he had recently discarded must have proved very tempting. As a result the brother left the monastery and revolted against his nephew. What is interesting from a military point of view is that he made good use of the rapid striking power of a force of mounted archers. The coup was successful, and he ascended the throne as Emperor Temmu. The accounts of Temmu's coup, and the achievements of his reign, come from the above-mentioned *Nihongi*, which was compiled under the jurisdiction of Temmu's daughter, so its claims for Temmu's military accomplishments may have to be regarded with some scepticism. Nevertheless, this is the first written account of the mounted archer in action, a model of military accomplishment that was to be the mark of the élite samurai.

Rivalry such as this between Imperial princes was far less common as a reason for war than the continuing need for campaigns against the aboriginal inhabitants of the Japanese islands, the Ainu. The old accounts make it quite clear that the suppression of these people was seen almost as a moral duty and an act of spreading civilisation, as it is referred to in the *Chronicles* as *emishi no seiobatsu* or 'punishment of the emishi'. *Emishi*, which

PLATE 1   *A samurai of the time of the Later Three Years' War*

In contradiction to its title, this war lasted from 1083 to 1087, and was one of the several 'little wars' in which the Minamoto clan rose to prominence by defeating rebels.

The samurai wears a suit of armour of the classic *yoroi* style, laced with thick silken cords. The *yoroi* is the typical samurai armour of the time and is derived from Asiatic styles of lamellar armour, whereby an armour plate is made up of several small plates fastened together in some way, rather than using single large plates of metal or leather. The plate of a *yoroi* would be made by binding a row of scales together with leather thongs, then lacquering the whole to make a waterproof, light and tough protection. A number of these plates would then be fastened together by cords, overlapping slightly in concertina fashion. The *yoroi* is the style which we will meet time and time again as we go through samurai

history. The box-like body-armour, or *do*, hangs from the shoulders and is fastened around the waist. Only the plate under the right arm is separate. There is a leather covering, beautifully patterned, on the front of the armour, called the *tsurubashiri*, which gives the appearance of a breastplate. The two appendages, called the *sendan-no-ita* and the *kyubi-no-ita*, which hang in front, are designed to protect the cords holding the armour from severance by swordstrokes.

For an indication of what this armour would look like from the rear, consult the illustration on p. 20.

The helmet worn with a *yoroi* was made from a number of iron plates riveted together. We can see the large rivet heads left protruding from the helmet surface, in the style known as a *hoshi-kabuto*. His hair has been gathered into a pigtail on top of his head inside an *eboshi* cap, which protrudes through the *tehen*, the

hole formed where the ends of the helmet plates meet, thus providing a padding for the weight of the helmet. He wears a *kote*, or armoured sleeve, on his left arm only, thus leaving the right freer for drawing a bow, for at this period in Japanese history the samurai was essentially a mounted archer. His sword is suspended from a belt beside a *tanto*, or dagger.

The figure is based on an illustration in the *Gosannen no eki emaki* (Scroll of the Later Three Years' War) in Tokyo National Museum, with additional details of the armour being taken from a *yoroi* of the period preserved in the Oyamazumi Shrine Museum, Omishima (Hiroshima Prefecture). The common soldier beside him has much simpler armour called *do-maru*, or 'body-wrappers', made of similar lamellar construction.

A map showing the general outline of Japan and its main islands, and also its position in relation to the Asiatic mainland.

is probably a variant of the Ainu word for 'man', was used in the sense of 'barbarian', implying the disdain of a civilised state, much as the word was used by the Romans against the Celtic tribes of Europe. *Emishi* was actually the politest term their enemies used for them, as the indigenous population are elsewhere variously referred to as 'earth spiders'.

The *emishi* proved to be stubborn fighters and early Emperors very soon made a habit of recruiting pacified *emishi* for their armies, a practice that had on occasions already been adopted by rebels against the throne, for whom these discontented and rebellious people were an obvious source of

12

Prince Yamato-Takeru, slayer of serpents and semi-mythological hero of early Japan. Yamato's career, as the brave individual warrior, sets the tone for the most cherished ideals of the samurai. His statue is in the Kenroku-en Gardens, Kanazawa.

support. They proved to be worthy of their hire, and many of the military traditions which later became associated with the samurai had their origins in these warriors. Even the curved sword, so much a symbol of the samurai, probably owes its origin to the weapons carried by *emishi* who were recruited as guards for the Imperial Court in the latter part of the ninth century. But, most important of all, it was the *emishi* campaigns, which were fought against soldiers who were familiar with their territory, that provided the practice for the wars of later years when the samurai would take on their own kind in struggles for the fertile lands of Japan.

For an explanation of the élite nature of the samurai we must look elsewhere than the barbarian *emishi*. There was a clearly defined tendency for certain families to acquire reputations for military excellence from the earliest centuries. Examples are the Otomo in the eighth century, who held the post of hereditary palace guards, and the Sakanoue in the ninth, but it is not until the tenth century that we see tl̄ emergence of 'warrior houses' of samurai. The formation of these units, based on the possession of land rather than patronage, was the most important social development during these early years. Typically, such a unit would be based around a central familial core, often with aristocratic connections. In many cases there was an actual lineage from a scion of the Imperial House, an honoured ancestor who had left Kyoto for the distant provinces to open up new rice-lands, pacify barbarians, and generally make a name for himself. The members were bound together by ties of loyalty and reward. These 'warrior houses', or 'clans' (either translation gives the reader a good mental picture of their fundamental nature), prospered best in areas remote from the capital, where they were able to grow at the expense of rivals and had the constant threat from the *emishi* to keep them in trim.

These developments are illustrated by the revolt of Taira Masakado in AD 935. Masakado, as his name implies, came from a branch of the Taira clan, which was to achieve great power in the following century. His rebellion, which went as far as Masakado proclaiming himself as a rival Emperor, produced a serious challenge both to the ruling house and to the other law-abiding members of the Taira family. It was in fact his own clan which was instrumental in bringing about his death in AD 940. *Konjaku Monogatari*, the twelfth-century chronicle which covers the rebellion, includes in its narrative some important guidelines as to how the idea of an élite samurai class was emerging and what its values were. One theme that comes over is the move towards a certain exclusivity of the samurai class, membership of which is a privilege so universally accepted that it is felt necessary to make some comment when this factor is absent. One example is the comment on a particular samurai that 'although he did not belong to a

---

PLATE 2   *A provincial samurai, in a poor quality armour, ca 1160*

The samurai who fought for the Minamoto cause in the early campaigns of the Gempei War were regarded as rough and vulgar characters by the more sophisticated Taira clan. This plate, which is based on a section of the *Heiji Monogatari Emaki* in the Museum of Fine Arts, Boston, Massachussetts, is an attempt to realise such a rough, unshaven warrior. His heavy helmet (copied from an extant specimen in the Oyamazumi Shrine Museum, Omishima, Hiroshima Prefecture) with its wide *fukigayeshi* (turnbacks) and *shikoro* (neckguard) has a minimum of decoration, the finish of the metal bowl being a natural coating of rust. His suit of armour is the simple *do-maru*, lacking the leather breastplate of his betters, but he enjoys a better protection than a common footsoldier by wearing two large *sode* or shoulder-plates. His pole-arm is a very plain *naginata*, which he is carefully sheathing after use. Note that, even though his main weapon is not the bow, he wears no armour on his right sleeve, in true samurai tradition. His armour is laced with leather thongs.

A warrior from the period between the fifth and seventh centuries AD wearing a *tanko*, the solid plate form of body-armour that preceded the adoption of lamellar styles. This statue is in the Gifu Historical Museum.

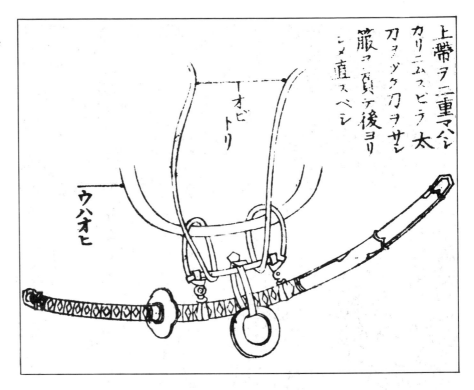

warrior house, he was courageous and accomplished in the Way of Bow and Arrow'. This latter phrase, *kyusen no michi*, otherwise rendered as *kyuba no michi*, 'The Way of Horse and Bow', is the obvious precursor of the much later *bushido*, 'The Way of the Warrior', and implies the existence of certain standards of conduct and accomplishment which are by rights the prerogative of an élite, though not, as yet, the élite's exclusive possession. A further example is found in the *Shoyuki*, the diary of the venerable old Fujiwara Sanesuke (957–1046). Here Sanesuke refers disparagingly to a distant relative called Fujiwara Norimoto, who killed one of his own vassals. 'Norimoto enjoys the martial arts', writes Sanesuke, 'but people do not approve. He is not of warrior blood.'

The struggle for land is a fundamental theme throughout samurai history. Sometimes it was gained by outright warfare, but territory could often be acquired by being granted a high office of state with lands attached, and the conflicts for such appointments could be as bitter as direct campaigns for the acquisition of territory. Taira Masakado's revolt occurred because he was refused the important office of *kebiishi*, an appointment concerned with the arrest and punishment of criminals. An order given by the *kebiishi* carried with it the full weight of Imperial authority and many warrior houses gained their early reputations by delivering the heads of criminals to Kyoto and collecting rewards such as provincial governorships. To become a provincial governor made a samurai into a petty prince, taking his considerable share of the produce of the lands entrusted to his care. *Kebiishi* was thus a coveted position.

Provincial governors were not always benevolent. One notorious example is Taira Korehira, son of the vanquisher of Masakado, who at various times was granted governorships of the provinces of Ise, Mutsu, Dewa, Izu, Shimotsuke, Sado, Kozuke and Hitachi. Not that he governed any of them very well. His successor in Hitachi complained that the people were starving and Korehira eventually ended his disappointing career by making open war against his kinsman Muneyori. For this he was apprehended and was exiled to the island of Awaji in the Inland Sea.

The Classical Samurai

The most important series of events in the history of the samurai was the process by which these élite, land-owning fighters transformed their condition from being the servants of Emperors and quellers of rebels and barbarians to being the *de facto* government of Japan, reducing the Emperor to a mere figurehead under their military dictatorship. This revolution happened during the latter part of the twelfth century AD, and is centred around a civil war between two clans, the Minamoto and the Taira, called the Gempei War.

Both the Minamoto and the Taira descended from branches of the Imperial family. Both had ancestors whose valiant exploits had set the standard against which their samurai measured their own accomplishments, and both were enormously ambitious. Each clan held numerous rice-lands and provided a focus for the adherents who served them as farmers and samurai and occasionally married into the family. The strength of the Taira was concentrated in the West of Japan. Their 'family temple' was the beautiful Itsukushima Shrine built out onto the sea of the island of Miyajima in the Inland Sea. They had great influence at Court, bought by years of service to succeeding Emperors.

PLATE 3   *A warrior monk from Mount Hiei, ca 1170*

A prominent feature of the warfare of eleventh-and twelfth-century Japan was the use of armies of *sohei*, or warrior monks, by the great Buddhist foundations of Kyoto and Nara. The *sohei* shown here wears a costume typical of these fierce fighters. The long white monk's robe, which is gathered at the ankles, is augmented by a simple footsoldier's *do-maru* armour, consisting of a tube-like corselet of lacquered leather or iron plates laced together with leather or cord thongs. It has seven *kusazuri*, or skirt pieces. On top is worn a thin black, gauze-like outer robe, and the sword hangs outside it, through the deep slashes at the waist. The traditional headgear was either a knotted towel around the shaven pate, or the elaborate headcowl shown in this illustration, which reached almost to nose level and was tied behind the head. He carries the traditional weapon of the warrior monks – the *naginata* – and is depicted standing outside one of the hundreds of shrines on Mount Hiei, to the North-West of Kyoto. The main foundation of Mount Hiei, the Enryaku-ji, was a Buddhist temple, but the mountain was also sacred to a Shinto deity, Sanno, the Mountain King, hence the *torii* gateway behind him.

The picture is based on several sources, notably the scrolls *Tengu Zoshi emaki* (Tokyo National Museum) and *Kasuga Gongen Reikenki* (Imperial Household Collection).

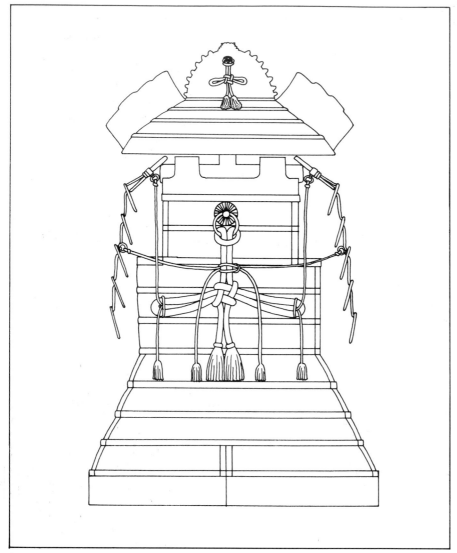

The *agemaki* bow
The decorative *agemaki* bow was the means whereby the various parts of a *yoroi* armour were held together at the rear. It was suspended from a ring on the upper plate of the back, and the various cords, shown in the first drawing, connected it to the *sode* (shoulder-plates), thereby holding them back to allow the arms free movement. The second and third drawings show how the *agemaki* was formed from one long cord.

The Minamoto's power lay in the less-civilised East where there were still *emishi* to fight. Their family temple was the striking Tsurugaoka Hachiman Shrine in Kamakura, dedicated to Hachiman, the Shinto God of War. These 'Eastern Warriors' were spoken of disparagingly by the more sophisticated West and, in the early days of the clans' struggle, the differences were probably quite marked. The troops of Minamoto Yoshinaka (1154–1184), for example, were regarded as rough mountain men, whose appearance and manners alone alarmed the people of the capital and did much to erode his support. Yoshinaka's own uncouth and ambitious presence eventually led to his death at the hands of his cousin Yoritomo.

By contrast the Taira samurai are often portrayed as accomplished poets and refined courtiers. Nor was this far from the truth, for by the 1170s the

20

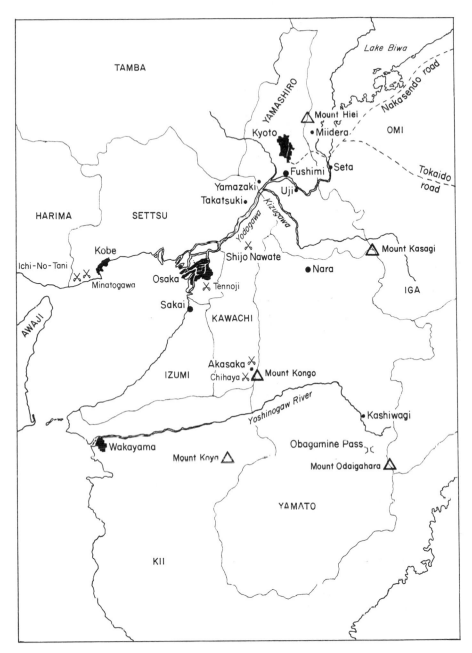

The 'Home Provinces' of Japan. Until modern times this central area of Japan between Kyoto and Osaka, bordered to the north-east by Lake Biwa, and to the south by the mountains of the Kii peninsula, was the pivot around which much of Japanese history revolved.

Taira had risen to a point of political pre-eminence by the straightforward process of marrying their daughters to Imperial princes. There was nothing particularly revolutionary about this – the Fujiwara clan had been doing it for centuries, and the Taira was merely the first other family to try the same game. It meant, however, that the Taira, in the person of the clan head, Taira Kiyomori, an astute politician, had gained political power by using and manipulating existing political institutions which they served as loyal samurai. It was the Minamoto who were to provide the samurai revolution.

The early samurai battles of the Gempei War are notable for the presence of a third force – contingents of warrior monks, or *sohei*. Several of the great monasteries of Kyoto and Nara maintained armies for defence in the lawless times, and would readily use them against rival temples or samurai armies. The fiercest coterie of warrior monks belonged to the Enryaku-ji, the main temple on Mount Hiei, which lies to the North-East of Kyoto, an area regarded as the abode of several very powerful *kami*, the Shinto word for a spiritual divinity. Mount Hiei also provided a natural fortress, and a standing army of several thousand monks, and we will see regular references to support being sought from the warrior monks of Mount Hiei as late as the sixteenth century. They were formidable warriors, though unreliable as allies, for they always put the interests of their temples first. In their early disputes the fear of the *kami* they represented was often enough to frighten the Imperial Court into granting their demands. They would march on Kyoto carrying the sacred *mikoshi*, or portable shrine, in which the *kami* was supposed to dwell. If the Imperial Court would not grant their wishes, which were usually concerned with land rights or prestige, the *mikoshi* would be left in the city street until a different decision was reached. Few samurai had such fear of the monks, but they would earn great approbation for standing up to them.

The war between the Taira and the Minamoto was a struggle for supremacy into which all social classes were drawn. The first Taira/ Minamoto struggle in which the monks fought was the First Battle of Uji in 1180. The veteran warrior, Minamoto Yorimasa, raised the flag of rebellion against the Taira while he was still based in Kyoto – a very risky operation. His monkish support came from the temple of Onjo-ji, or Miidera, which lies at the foot of Mount Hiei and had a long history of stubborn independence from the Enryaku-ji on the summit. When Yorimasa's plot

PLATE 4   *A general being dressed by a page in a fine* yoroi, *ca 1180*

This plate provides a direct comparison between the military costume of the highest and lowest ranking samurai of the Gempei War Period. The *taisho* (general) is completely armed except for his helmet. Note that instead of the hair being gathered into a pigtail it has been let down. The stiff *eboshi* cap will be removed before the helmet is placed on to the head. This may indicate that the helmet has a separate lining. The *yoroi* armour is little different from that shown in Plate 1, except that it is more richly ornamented with gilt fittings, as befits the wearer, and is based on an extant specimen in the Oyamazumi Shrine Museum, Omishima (Hiroshima Prefecture). His *yoroi-hitatare*, or armour robe, is richly embroidered and ornamented with pom-poms. His attendant is tying the general's quiver securely round his waist in such a position that arrows may be easily withdrawn with the right hand. The arrows are held in place in the basket-like quiver by twisted cords that are wound round the quiver's back. As the general is of such exalted rank he has been depicted wearing footwear while indoors! The interior design is based on the contemporary Genji Monogatari Scroll.

The attendant's costume, which appears to change little for four centuries, is based on the simple *do-maru* we noted on the warrior monk. His black *eboshi* cap, tied with cords, is of similar design to the general's. When going into battle it would be augmented by the face-mask seen in Plate 5. His small shoulder-protectors are of padded cloth, possibly strengthened within by metal or leather plates. As he is not an archer he wears two *kote* (armour sleeves) which are simple cloth bags with metal plates sewn on at strategic places.

was discovered he and his warrior monks decided to retreat South, across the Uji River, to join forces with the warrior monks of the Kofuku-ji at Nara. The Uji River, which flows out of Lake Biwa to join the Yodo River, entering the sea near Osaka, has always been a natural moat to Kyoto, and the two bridges at Seta and Uji were strategic prizes for any army wishing to take the capital or, as in Yorimasa's case, safeguard his flight from it. The Taira forces followed in pursuit, so the Minamoto tore up the planking of the Uji bridge and prepared to make a stand until the Nara monks could join them. After much fierce fighting, and gallant acts of swordsmanship while balanced on the beams of the broken bridge, the Taira samurai succeeded in crossing the river and Yorimasa, completely surrounded, committed suicide.

The act of suicide when faced with certain defeat is a well-known tradition concerned with samurai warfare. Suicide could also be taken as an alternative to execution, as a means of apologising for a wrong deed while saving one's honour and, more rarely, as a highly dramatic act of protest. Yet suicide was never an automatic act. We frequently hear of samurai fleeing, withdrawing and, occasionally, surrendering, though the latter is very often followed by the suicide of the captive. As we shall see in the following pages the omission of suicide is sometimes more surprising than its commission.

Minamoto Yoshitsune

A large part of the accounts of the Gempei War is taken up by descriptions of the long campaigns of Minamoto Yoshitsune, the Minamoto's ablest general, and one of the most famous samurai who ever existed. He is best known for his battles against the Taira, but he began his career by defeating his cousin, the rough man from the mountains, Minamoto Yoshinaka.

Yoshinaka had in fact served the Minamoto cause well, by defeating the Taira at the Battle of Tonamiyama (or Kurikara) in 1182, where he had succeeded in forcing the Taira army into a dead-end valley by stampeding a herd of cattle, enraged by tying lighted torches to their horns. As a result he succeeded in being the first of the Minamoto to enter the capital in triumph, where his men behaved very badly. It was probably Yoshinaka's very success that set his cousins against him, rather than any genuine concern for the inhabitants whom his men had abused. Yoshitsune was sent to the West to chastise him and met Yoshinaka's force at the Uji River. Unlike Yorimasa in 1180, however, who was fighting off an attack from the capital, Yoshinaka attempted to use it in reverse. But once again a successful crossing was made and Yoshinaka withdrew with a handful of followers, until his horse crashed through the ice of a frozen paddy field. As Yoshinaka turned in the saddle an arrow hit him in the face. Two samurai ran up and struck off his head.

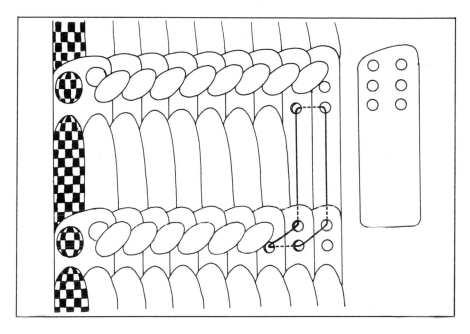

With Yoshinaka's personal ambitions out of the way the main branch of the Minamoto could concentrate on the defeat of the Taira, who had possession of the child Emperor, grandson of Taira Kiyomori. To be seen to be acting in the name of the Emperor, even if he was virtually a hostage, was an important guarantee of support. The other great strength of the Taira was their command of the sea. They had their own fleet and a network of bases along the Inland Sea. On three occasions they withstood attacks from Yoshitsune while based either on the sea or very near to it. The first was the Battle of Ichi-no-tani in 1184. Ichi-no-tani was a stockade-type fortress on the shore of the Inland Sea near to the present-day city of Kobe. It was defended on two sides by palisades, while the third was open to the sea where the escape craft lay, and the rear was defended by steep cliffs. Yoshitsune's attack shows his imagination and daring. While two groups of samurai attacked from the sides, he led a picked band of men down a precipitous path at the rear and took the Taira completely by surprise. There was no wild panic for the boats – samurai honour would not have permitted that. Instead a number of individual combats took place on the shore, several of which, such as the death of the young Taira samurai, Atsumori, quickly entered the pantheon of samurai heroics as being perfect examples of the death of the brave, lone warrior – an image cherished throughout samurai history. But the bulk of the Taira escaped, taking with them the child-Emperor Antoku, whose capture was their main aim.

A few months later Yoshitsune pursued them to Yashima on the island of Shikoku. Here the battle was fought in the shallows which divided the then island of Yashima from Shikoku. It was fiercely contested, but one celebrated incident which occurred during the fighting shows that the tradition of the samurai as an élite mounted archer was still as strong as

25

ever. During a lull in the fighting the Taira had tied a fan to the mast of one of their ships and challenged the Minamoto to shoot it down, hoping thereby to encourage them to waste their ammunition. The challenge was accepted by Nasu Munetaka, a young samurai retainer of the Minamoto, who took careful aim as the fan fluttered in the breeze and shattered it with his first shot, which greatly improved the Minamoto morale.

The Battle of Yashima was as indecisive as Ichi-no-tani had been, as the child Emperor was once again spirited away by sea. But it served to illustrate that the Minamoto were determined to pursue the Taira wherever they led. The final reckoning came in April 1185, when both armies met in a sea battle at Dan-no-Ura in the Straits of Shimonoseki, the narrow gap of water that divides Honshu from Kyushu. The fighting was long and hard, and a sea battle only in the sense of two armies using ships as fighting platforms for archers and swordsmen, for there is very little of naval manoeuvring to be discerned. Dan-no-Ura ended with the utter defeat of the Taira, and one of the largest mass suicides in samurai history as the Taira reeled from an overwhelming attack. The child-Emperor Antoku was drowned and the replica Sacred Sword, one of the three items that comprise the Japanese Imperial Regalia, was lost forever. So terrible was the eclipse of the Taira clan at Dan-no-Ura that many legends grew up concerning ghosts, seas of blood, and crabs with the spirits of samurai within them. It is still regarded as one of the most decisive battles in Japanese history.

Minamoto Yoshitsune, however, was not the clan member who benefited from the defeat of its rivals. His elder brother Yoritomo was head of the clan, and it was Yoritomo who was to take over where the Taira had left off, and found a dynasty to rule the country in the name of the Emperor. Where Yoritomo's achievement differed from that of the Taira, however, was that instead of making use of existing institutions of Imperial government, and marrying daughters into the family, Yoritomo founded a new system of hereditary military government under a dictator known as the *shogun*, a word that is nowadays as familiar as *samurai*. In 1192 Minamoto Yoritomo became the first Minamoto Shogun, ruling by means of a Shogunal government or *bakufu*. The Minamoto triumph was complete, as was the total ascendancy of the samurai military élite.

PLATE 5   *A footsoldier in a* do-maru, *ca 1184*

This common footsoldier is taken directly from an illustration in the scroll *Kasuga Gongen Reikenki*. He is on guard duty outside a samurai headquarters in Kyoto. His costume is very similar to that of the footsoldiers in Plates 4 and 6 except that he wears a metal face-protector that covers the forehead and cheeks, and provides some defence against a sword slash. His shoulder-protectors are covered by a dyed leather similar to that used for the 'breastplate' of a samurai's armour. Details of the scenery are taken from the Heiji Monogatari Scroll.

2

Kamakura Period

The establishment of Minamoto Yoritomo's Shogunate, or *bakufu*, marks the beginning of the 'Kamakura Period' in Japanese history, from 1192 until 1333, as the city of Kamakura was the seat of the Shogun and thus the administrative capital of Japan.

The Fall of the Minamoto

The Kamakura *bakufu* was never all-powerful, in spite of the dramatic way it had been formed, and had to face a continued resistance to the Shogunal power from the Imperial family. As we shall see, it was to be the power of an Emperor that finally brought about its downfall. There is one other remarkable feature about the Kamakura Period: that the Minamoto, the family whose triumph seems so complete in 1192, should so soon be vanquished as thoroughly as they had destroyed the Taira.

In view of the tremendous achievement of Yoritomo in raising his family to the highest position in the land, it is strange that their dynasty should turn out to be so short-lived. Apart from the earlier destruction of Yoshinaka, the first feuding within the family was Yoritomo's personal rivalry with his brothers Yoshitsune and Noriyori, whose military skills had helped him gain the position of Shogun. Both were driven from office and pursued to death. Perhaps fittingly Yoritomo himself enjoyed only 7 years as Shogun, dying in 1199, at the age of 52, when he was thrown from a horse while returning in state from a public ceremony. His death was accidental, untimely, and threw the whole *bakufu* into confusion. His 18-year-old son Yoriie immediately succeeded to his late father's civil offices, but there was a long delay in having him appointed Shogun. Many Kamakura officials had expressed genuine concern about the young man's ability to govern, but in fact the whole of the government had been so thoroughly shaken by Yoritomo's unexpected death that it was left to his widow, Masa-ko, to form a provisional government together with her father Hojo Tokimasa.

Masa-ko comes over as a very strong-willed woman. She had entered the religious life on her husband's death, as was the custom of the times, but her vows do not seem to have diminished her political skills and ambi-

One of the most historic places associated with the samurai is the Tsurugaoka Hachiman Shrine at Kamakura. It is always thronged with visitors. It is dedicated to Hachiman, the God of War, and was particularly honoured by the Minamoto clan, although this picture illustrates two tragic aspects of the history of that great samurai family. In the foreground is the dancing platform where Shizuka Gozen, the lover of the fugitive Minamoto Yoshitsune, was forced to dance for Yoshitsune's brother, Yoritomo, the first Shogun of Japan. Shizuka defiantly sang a song in praise of Yoshitsune, an act which enraged the dictator, and when she gave birth to a male child he had the baby murdered. To the left is a very large, and very old gingko tree, which may well be the actual one behind which lurked the assassin of the third and last Minamoto Shogun, Sanetomo, one snowy day in 1219.

tions, for she is referred to as *ama shogun*, the 'Nun Shogun'. Her provisional government, however, was not a success in bringing about the unity the country required and, when Yoriie was eventually proclaimed Shogun in 1202, little had been done to assist the headstrong young man in his rule of the warriors. Then Yoriie became gravely ill and within a year had been forced to retire, sick and humiliated, from the post of Shogun. He withdrew totally from public life and entered a monastery, only to be assassinated in 1204, probably at the instigation of his grandfather, Hojo Tokimasa.

Yoriie had a son, but the Hojo influence in the *bakufu* was so strong that his succession was passed over in favour of Yoriie's younger brother Sanetomo, who was then only 12 years old. Sanetomo became the third and last Minamoto Shogun and, as he was a minor, a Regent was necessary, a role Hojo Tokimasa was ready to fulfil. Tokimasa therefore became the first of a long line of *shikken*, the Hojo Regents, who ruled behind a nominal Shogun for a century and a half.

But even with the power of the Minamoto so dramatically curtailed, Sanetomo was doomed to enjoy for a very short time the honours of office. In the New Year of 1219 Sanetomo proceeded to the Tsurugaoka Hachiman Shrine in Kamakura to give thanks to Hachiman, the patron deity of the Minamoto, for the favours which his clan had received. As he was walking down the snow-covered steps of the shrine, a figure jumped out from behind a gingko tree and stabbed him to death. He was 26 years old. Legend has embellished the facts of his murder, which was as much a tragedy for Japanese culture as it was for the family of Minamoto.

Sanetomo was a noted poet, and legend tells of how he was warned of the threat to his life, but declined his attendant's suggestion that he should wear armour under his robe. Instead he wrote a farewell poem, and left a lock of his hair behind as a memento.

His nephew Kugyo, whose succession had been ignored, was the natural suspect for instigating the murder plot, and the deed provided the perfect excuse for having him, the last in the Minamoto line, executed. This was the final act of the blood-letting that makes the clan of Minamoto sound like the subjects of Greek tragedy. For the next 100 years power was kept by the 'Nun Shogun's' family, the Hojo, who had so thoroughly eclipsed them.

The Jokyu War

The establishment of the Shogunate may have weakened the Imperial power, but little could negate the magic in the name of the divine Emperor, and we see throughout samurai history successive Emperors of Japan, sometimes manipulated and reduced to ceremony, sometimes defiant and proud, but always exerting the charisma that comes from unquestioned legitimacy. The fall of the Minamoto showed the comparatively weak base of any alternative ruler.

The great problem which faced the rule of the Hojo *shikken* was to find a succession of suitable candidates for Shogun, in whose names they could rule as Regent, so it was almost inevitable that the Imperial family should

---

PLATE 6 *Hojo Yasutoki, in 'half-armour', inspects heads after the Jokyu Rebellion, 1221*

From ancient times the surest proof that a samurai had performed the task with which he had been entrusted was for him to return to his master bearing the severed head of the enemy. Elaborate rituals grew up over how heads were presented, prepared and examined. The business of preparing severed heads was traditionally done by the women of the clan, and there exist accounts of how the heads were washed, drained of blood and mounted on a spiked wooden board. The hair would be neatly combed from the mess which battle would have caused and tied with white paper into the traditional samurai pigtail. The heads would be anointed with perfume by waving an incense burner under them, and cosmetics applied to recreate the colours they would have possessed in life. The

final touch was provided by tying a slip of paper to each pigtail, giving the name of the dead samurai, the name of the samurai whose 'trophy' the head had become, and any other relevant details. In the case of a shaven-headed monk the absence of a pigtail meant that a hole had to be made in the ear-lobe to take the identifying document!

Head-viewing ceremonies could be very elaborate, as they were an important part of public relations. By head-viewing, a victorious general was given the opportunity of commenting upon an ally's achievements and making a forcible point to newly subordinate clans of the folly of opposing such a glorious band of samurai.

This plate is a reconstruction of the head-viewing ceremony that must have taken place following the

collapse of ex-Emperor Go-Toba's Jokyu Rebellion of 1221. The victorious general, Hojo Yasutoki, sits on a tiger-skin rug on a camp stool in 'undress armour', which shows what was worn under the main body-armour of the *yoroi*. The extent of the sleeve bag on the left arm is clearly seen, and also how the separate portion of the *yoroi* fitted under the right arm. His *eboshi* is a courtier style, which is much larger than that normally worn under a helmet. The footsoldiers wear simple body-armours.

The label on the monk's head reads 'The head of a brave warrior monk: Hojo Yasutoki'. The other labels credit their trophies to Yasutoki's uncle, Hojo Tokifusa, who also took part in the downfall of Go-Toba's rebellion.

try to take advantage of this potential weakness whenever possible, and the early thirteenth century provided such a challenge in the person of the ex-Emperor Go-Toba. The Emperor Go-Toba had succeeded to the throne in 1184, at the age of 4, and soon learned the lesson of all Emperors that true power only came about following abdication, when they could rule behind the scenes, freed from the long round of religious ritual, which, as living god, the Emperor was required to perform. He was still too young to become such a Retired, or 'Cloistered' Emperor when Go-Shirakawa died in 1192, and 1192 was also the year when Yoritomo achieved the Shogunate, reducing all Imperial power to a very low ebb. He eventually managed to abdicate in 1198, and tested his new powers by appointing his infant son, Tsuchimikado, to the vacant throne without asking permission from Kamakura. Yoritomo was much annoyed, but before he could assert his Shogunal authority he had suffered the fatal accident which was eventually to destroy the Minamoto clan. Go-Toba played a careful game through the troubled years of Yoriie and Sanetomo and was, in fact, on very good terms with the latter, as he shared his love for poetry, but when Sanetomo was murdered Go-Toba realised that the Hojo's need for a puppet successor to the Shogunate might provide an opportunity for the throne to assert itself more strongly than it had for half a century.

The first suggestion the Regent Hojo Yoshitoki made was that one of Go-Toba's own sons should become Shogun. Go-Toba refused the apparent honour, as he saw the potential danger that could arise if there was a succession dispute when an Imperial prince was Shogun. He then turned down a candidate from the Fujiwara family and, in fact, managed to frustrate for several years every one of the Hojo's attempts to have a Shogun appointed. In the meantime he openly courted the favour of any rival samurai families who might one day join him in armed struggle against the Shogunate for the restoration of Imperial power. There were a number of clans in the Western half of the country who could be persuaded to support him. Some were the remnants of the once mighty Taira, others mere opportunists who had suffered from the Minamoto or Hojo ascendancy. But they were only one factor in Go-Toba's scheme. The other involved seeking support from that most dangerous and unreliable of weapons: the warrior monks.

The armed clergy had been very peaceful during Yoritomo's lifetime. The first Shogun had been generous with his gifts towards rebuilding temples

---

PLATE 7 *A samurai commander awaits the Mongol Invasion in 1274*

His armour has altered to no appreciable degree since the time of the Gempei War, evidence that, until the coming of the Mongols, there was little to challenge any samurai assumptions about the nature of warfare. He is seated on an armour box, into which his *yoroi* would be packed for careful storage.

damaged during the Gempei War, but in common with every other faction in the land they had become rebellious when the Shogunate was seen to be weakening. In 1219 the old rivalry between the Enryaku-ji and Miidera once more flared into life, and the Kofuku-ji of Nara also began to rediscover its warlike traditions. A land dispute provided the excuse for the Mount Hiei monks to try their mettle against Go-Toba, and in the manner which had been so successful with his predecessors they descended on Kyoto to lay their grievances before the throne with threats and riot. But times had changed. Instead of being cowed by the threats of divine vengeance Go-Toba scattered their incursion by a well-timed assault from the palace samurai. However, in further contrast, he followed up this lesson not with a revenge attack on the Enryaku-ji, but with a carefully worded call to arms against the Shogun on the Emperor's behalf, asking them to unite against the warriors from the East who had shown so little respect for the monks' militant and religious tradition.

Go-Toba began an open revolt against the *bakufu* on 6 June 1221, when by solemn decree the Regent Hojo Yoshitoki was declared to be an outlaw. Three days later a further statement was made decreeing the whole of the Eastern half of the country to be in a state of rebellion. Both announcements were designed to catch Kamakura unawares, but a relay of fast messengers had managed to warn Yoshitoki of the former proclamation by the day the latter was issued, and he immediately took steps to assure himself of the loyalty of neighbouring samurai. His support was solid, and plans were quickly made.

Their first consideration was one of defence, of closing the passes of Ashigara and Hakone, in the Mount Fuji area, to prevent any advance on Kamakura by the Tokaido Road. But bolder spirits argued that attack would be the better response to the Imperial forces, so a plan was drawn up involving a march on Kyoto by means of the three practical routes: the Tokaido along the Sea Coast, the Nakasendo through the central mountains, and a wide sweep off the Nakasendo going round Lake Biwa to approach Kyoto from the north. This third column met with the most resistance. There were still several clans in the Hokurikudo region who had not accepted Kamakura rule, and the Hojo forces were held for a while at Tonamiyama, the site of Yoshinaka's fierce battle in the Gempei War, but this fighting in Echizen Province proved to be the only serious resistance Kamakura faced and, by the time the Hokurikudo column had fought its way down from the mountains, the capital was already in *bakufu* hands. The Imperial troops were largely inexperienced and had little will to fight the warriors from the East, whose fathers' reputations had preceded their advance Westwards. Many of the defenders fled from their positions in Mino and Omi Provinces, putting their trust in the natural moat of the Uji River, so for the third time in half a century the two bridges of Uji and Seta echoed to the din of war. But this time there were no warrior monks to stride nimbly with their *naginata* across the broken planking, for in spite of all Go-Toba's pleas the *sohei* of the Enryaku-ji remained on Mount Hiei,

This illustration from the *Gunyoki* is one of several recommended ways of displaying a severed head. Note the carefully delineated positions of the hands, the identification label, and the spiked wooden board.

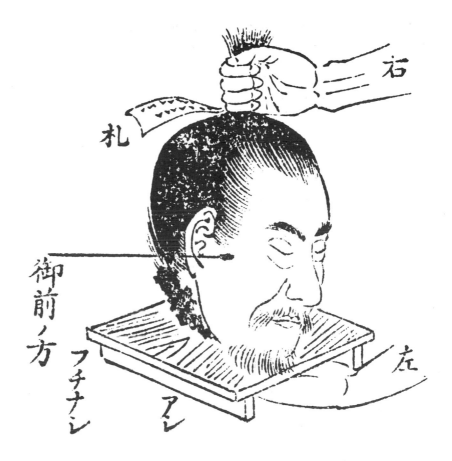

and it was an almost totally secular force that attempted to hold the line on 5 July. The fighting of this, the Third Battle of Uji, lasted all through a hot summer's day, but by nightfall Hojo Yasutoki's men had taken Seta, in spite of heavy losses, and the road to Kyoto was open.

Hojo Yasutoki (who was Yoshitoki's eldest son) made a grand entrance on the following day, 6 July, his scouts having prepared the city for his arrival. Unfortunately many of the retreating troops, and some of the Hojo's advance guard, had burned and looted as they went, and the Imperial capital presented a sorry spectacle when the *bakufu* army received the surrender of Go-Toba.

Thus ended the brief Jokyu Rebellion, so called from the era name of Jokyu (1219–1221). The *bakufu's* triumph was due largely to its boldness in advancing. Had their original consideration of a defensive strategy been put into effect it is quite likely that Go-Toba's support would have continued to grow to an extent dangerous to the Shogunate. In the event Go-Toba was exiled and the *bakufu* confiscated the largest area of defeated enemies' lands since the fall of the Taira. The Minamoto may have passed away, but even without the figurehead of a Shogun to lead them, the Hojo *shikken* proved that the institution of warrior government which Yoritomo had established was sufficiently sound to withstand even a challenge from

35

an ex-Emperor. It was to be 50 years before any other military threat arose and, when it came, it was very different from anything the samurai had faced before.

The Mongol Invasions

The attempts to invade Japan made in the thirteenth century by the Mongol Emperor of China, Kublai Khan, are unique events in Japanese history. The ferocity with which the attacks were launched, the strength and bravery of the resistance, and the final, sudden and spectacular end of the Mongol fleet by a typhoon fill some of the noblest pages in the history of the samurai.

Kublai Khan, it must be admitted, had reasons for invading Japan other than mere personal ambition. The pressing demands of various civil wars had caused *bakufu* officials in Kyushu responsible for maintaining law and order to turn a blind eye towards a frequent abuse of their authority – overseas piracy. The coastal areas of China and Korea were frequently ravaged by Japanese pirates and Kublai Khan's first letter to the Japanese government was simply a request that such activities be curtailed. It was only when he received no reply to this demand that his theme became one of demanding tribute from the Japanese people. It was fortunate for Japan that it faced the challenge under the Hojo Regent Tokimune, the seventh of the *shikken* and a capable and resourceful samurai. It was also free from civil strife so it was possible to make a positive response to the threat.

PLATE 8   *Kusunoki Masashige defends Chihaya castle, 1333*

The mid-fourteenth century is dominated by the epic struggle of the War Between the Courts. This plate depicts the greatest hero of that war, the loyal samurai, Kusunoki Masashige (1294–1336). He is shown conducting operations in the forests around Mount Kongo, where he established his bases of Akasaka and Chihaya, and defied the Kamakura *bakufu*. His defence of Chihaya, in particular, is regarded as one of the three classic sieges of samurai history when defenders withstood enormous odds and never capitulated.

Kusunoki Masashige is wearing what is basically a *yoroi* armour, but with several developments. First, the *yoroi* has lost something of its stiff, box-like appearance and fits the body more closely, like a footsoldier's *haramaki*. It still has the *tsurubashiri*, the leather 'breastplate', and Masashige's is very beautifully decorated. An *agemaki* bow would connect all the pieces from the rear.

The helmet's *shikoro* is now much flatter, which would allow the wearer to turn his head more easily, while its greater sweep still allows good protection. His helmet bowl is neater. The conical rivets have disappeared, and it is ornamented by a particularly fine set of *kuwagata*.

It is in his leg protection that we notice the greatest difference. The *suneate* are much heavier and extend up higher to surround the knee. The thighs are now protected by an early form of *haidate*, or thigh-guards, which are of exactly similar construction to the plates of the body-armour, and fasten behind the leg. Bearskin boots have given way to the more practical *waraji*, straw sandals, and *tabi*, the traditional Japanese sock with a divided toe.

The long, red-lacquered bow is well represented here, for even though horsemanship is irrelevant in the wooded mountains, the samurai is still an archer. Note the waterproof quiver, and the arrow being brought to the bow from the righthand side, in the Japanese style of archery.

The figure is based on the modern statue of Kusunoki Masashige at the Kanshin-ji near Chihaya, where Masashige's head is buried, and painted scrolls kept at the Nampi-an Kannon-ji, also near Chihaya. Details of his body-armour are taken from a *yoroi* of the period preserved in the Kasuga Shrine at Nara which is supposed to have been owned by Masashige. Details of accessories and leg-armour are taken from a sketch by Sasama.

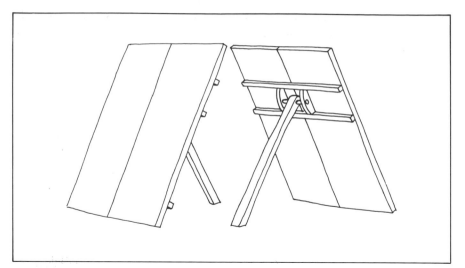

The wooden shield
This type of wooden shield was used throughout the samurai period. It was planted in the ground, and provided protection for missile troops. Contemporary illustrations often depict them with *mon* painted on the front.

The first attack came in 1274. The Khan swelled his army with subservient Koreans and packed them into several hundred ships. They first attacked Tsushima, the island mid-way between Japan and Korea, where the garrison of 200 men under So Sukekuni, grandson of Taira Tomomori, who was drowned at Dan-no-Ura, fought bravely until they were overwhelmed. The next island, Ikishima, suffered a similar fate. Their attempt on the Japanese mainland (in fact the large Southern island of Kyushu) took place near the present-day city of Hakata. The Japanese resistance was fierce, in spite of several surprises that the Mongols were able to inflict on the defenders, for their military traditions were totally different from the samurai. The Japanese were used to a style of warfare that laid great emphasis on individual combat, while the Mongols controlled, by drum and gong, huge bodies of troops packed together in phalanxes, and fired arrows in huge random showers. There were no noble opponents to challenge to individual combat, just an anonymous alien horde of Mongols, Chinese and Koreans. Their enemies also had some form of fire-bomb, flung by catapult, which is illustrated in a painted scroll of the period. The samurai very quickly adapted to all these new threats and their fighting skills forced the Mongols into a tactical withdrawal. A storm caught the fleet as it left, causing much damage, and the first invasion came to a end.

The Mongols returned in 1281 with a much bigger armada. By this time coastal defences had been strengthened, including the building of a long stone wall, and the Japanese also managed to harass the fleet as it approached the coast. They sailed out in little ships and mounted daring hit-and-run raids under the cover of darkness. On one occasion thirty samurai swam out to a ship, cut off the heads of the crew, and swam back. Apart from the direct damage the raids were able to inflict, these raids also had the considerable benefit of forcing the Mongol fleet to remain for long periods lying safely offshore in the stifling heat of summer. As the days wore on, the typhoon season approached and, on 15 August 1281, the Japanese prayers were answered when a fierce storm, the *kami-kaze*, blew up. It surpassed in intensity the storm that had damaged the fleet in 1274 and smashed the Mongol fleet so totally that they never returned.

Few episodes in Japanese history are as proudly recalled as the defeat of the Mongols. To the defeat of the Mongols we owe the phrase *kami-kaze* (divine wind), an expression which came to have such a different meaning in 1945, when it linked the threat of an American invasion with the failed attempts of 1274 and 1281, inspiring a new generation to resist an assault on the homeland. It has in it all the finest elements of Japanese tradition. There are noble samurai, united against a common enemy, and fired by a common spirit which later manifests itself in the cataclysm of the holy typhoon. For once in their history the samurai are not fighting each other, but become Japanese before anything else.

The War of Emperor Go-Daigo

The defeat of the Mongols saw the samurai united as never before, yet within two generations they were to be divided on the most fundamental issue of their tradition: that of the legitimacy of their divine Emperor. The attempts of a young Emperor, Go-Daigo, to rule, rather than merely to reign, caused a schism in the Imperial House, and a long civil war.

The destruction of the Mongol fleet may have been a military victory for the *bakufu*, but one long-term result was to produce severe economic strain on the government. No one could be sure that the Mongols would not return, so they faced the need to be prepared against foreign invasion for half a century. Rewards also had to be paid to samurai who had fought in the wars, and there were no freshly conquered lands to redistribute, as would have been the case in a civil war. Numerous claims were made. One samurai even had a long narrative scroll painted depicting his exploits as an aid to his demands. Temples and shrines too, mindful of the miraculous intervention of the *kami-kaze*, put in claims for reward as a mark of appreciation of their spiritual efforts. Hojo Tokimune, whose leadership had proved such an inspiration to the samurai, died in 1284, and his successors failed completely to inherit his abilities and drive. As at the time of Jokyu, the Imperial family saw the *bakufu*'s weakness as their opportunity.

From 1318 the incumbent of the throne had been the Emperor Go-Daigo, or 'Daigo the Second'. He had succeeded at the age of 30, and made it quite clear that he was a proud and ambitious man. It is difficult to tell at what stage Go-Daigo began to think of achieving his aim of absolute control by overthrowing the *bakufu*, but there is circumstantial evidence from the very beginning of his reign. On the day of his accession he sent his son, Prince Morinaga, to be a monk at Mount Hiei. There can have been no reason for removing his heir from the mainstream of politics other than to use him as a way of gaining support from the warrior monks, and this was confirmed in 1328 when he promoted Prince Morinaga to be Abbot of Mount Hiei. Prince Morinaga, an accomplished samurai warrior, is referred to as 'The Prince of the Great Pagoda' in the *Taiheiki*, the great war chronicle of the time.

In 1321 Go-Daigo abolished the hallowed tradition of the Cloistered Emperor, making clear his determination to rule directly as Emperor. Contemporary chroniclers speak well of the reforms he introduced, and contrast the lack of action the *bakufu* took against them with their speedy reaction to Go-Toba's similar attempts at independence of thought and action. There was an equally sluggish reply when the *bakufu* received hard evidence that Go-Daigo was preparing to challenge the *bakufu* rule by force. When they eventually sent an army from Kamakura, Go-Daigo had full knowledge of their approach and sufficient time to plan accordingly. As well as courting Mount Hiei he had made generous offerings to the Buddhist institutions of Nara, a wise move, considering that the *bakufu* controlled a much higher proportion of the land than had been the case under Go-Toba. In fact the governors of over half the provinces in Japan were Hojo kinsmen, so armed support from monks would be crucial.

Go-Daigo's plots were revealed to the *bakufu* in September 1331, and Go-Daigo left Kyoto for the safety of the Todai-ji in Nara. He took with him the symbols of his sovereignty – the Imperial Regalia, or at least that part of them he was able to secure. As the legitimacy of the Imperial claimant was inseparable from the question of the possession of the 'Crown Jewels', it is worth spending a little time discussing what these regalia are. They consist of three objects: the Mirror, the Sword and the Jewels. The Mirror and the Sword that are actually transmitted from one Emperor to another have been, from ancient times, replicas of the originals, which are kept respectively at Ise and the Atsuta Shrine near Nagoya. In 1185, as noted previously, this 'replica' Sword was lost at the Battle of Dan-no-Ura and, in 1210, another replica had to be made. But to all intents and purposes these replicas were treated as if they were the real thing. They were, after all, the actual objects that had passed from hand to hand as the legitimate sign of kingship. The Imperial Jewels, however, were never copied, and it was with the original Jewels, and the other 'official copies' that Go-Daigo fled to Nara.

The Todai-ji monks expressed concern that they could not withstand an attack by the *bakufu*, so Go-Daigo moved on to Kasagi, a mountain some 600 feet high overlooking the Kizugawa. It, too, was the home of warrior monks, who welcomed him and strengthened their position against an expected attack. The *bakufu* forces however first concentrated their attacks on Mount Hiei and 'The Prince of the Great Pagoda', and overcame their initially slow response to the crisis by forcing Prince Morinaga to flee for his life, thus isolating Go-Daigo at Kasagi. While the attacks continued on Kasagi, the *bakufu* made moves in the political sphere and tried to negotiate, hoping to persuade Go-Daigo to abdicate and enter a monastery.

When he refused to do so the drastic decision was made to raise another member of the Imperial family to the throne. Go-Daigo had therefore been officially deposed, but he still had the Regalia, so the actual enthronement ceremony had to be postponed until the items were recaptured.

It is at this point in the war that we first hear the name of Kusunoki Masashige, a samurai whose skill in warfare, and above all his loyalty to the legitimate Emperor, make him the model of perfection for all samurai. Little is known of his background, except that he was from an obscure warrior family in Kawachi. He suddenly enters history as Go-Daigo's staunchest supporter, and fights for him from a stronghold called Akasaka in Kawachi, a fortified encampment ('castle' is a misleading description) in the Western foothills of Mount Kongo. Here he was joined by Prince Morinaga, who helped Kusunoki defend it against a determined attack by the *bakufu*. The loyalists were short of troops and soon only the terrain frustrated the attackers' attempts. The 'castle' fell on about 20 November 1331 but, instead of making a last-ditch stand and an honourable suicide, Kusunoki Masashige and Prince Morinaga both escaped, the latter to a monastery in Nara where, according to legend, he hid in a large wooden chest. But bad news awaited them. On his way to join them in Akasaka, Go-Daigo had been captured and taken to Rokuhara, the *bakufu* headquarters in Kyoto. A few months later, in 1332, he was exiled to the island of Oki. It appeared to all that Go-Daigo's revolt had been crushed as thoroughly as that of Go-Toba, and that further resistance was useless.

Had it not been for Kusunoki Masashige and Prince Morinaga this latest attempt at Imperial restoration would indeed have been over. However, Prince Morinaga, who had by now abandoned his monkish habit and returned to the life of the son of the legitimate sovereign, based himself with an army of warrior monks in the mountainous district of Yoshino, far to the South of Kyoto, and sent out calls to arms to any samurai clans who would support him. Meanwhile his former comrade in arms, Kusunoki Masashige, continued to demonstrate how successful a continuing resistance to the *bakufu* might be. He built a new stronghold at Akasaka, Kami-Akasaka, higher up the mountain than the previous one, and inflicted such damage on the *bakufu* armies attempting to take it that orders were issued for the execution of the Prince and Kusunoki, rescinding previous commands merely for their capture.

The resistance greatly surprised the *bakufu*. Early in 1333 three armies left Kamakura to chastise the Imperial rebels. The first, commanded by a Hojo kinsman called Aso, was to attack Kami-Akasaka along the Kawachi road. The second, under Osaragi, was to attack Yoshino. Both were ultimately successful, though Kami-Akasaka only fell when its water supply was cut, and Prince Morinaga fled to Koya-san, a remote and peaceful monastery, the centre of the Shingon sect of Buddhism. The two victorious *bakufu* armies then joined the third force (under Nagoshi) for a full-scale assault on Kusunoki's newest fortification at Chihaya, to which he had withdrawn.

Chihaya was also on Mount Kongo but much stronger than Kami-Akasaka and, to the *bakufu's* amazement and chagrin, held out against every attempt to take it. The great army of the Hojo was practically immobilised in front of this makeshift mountain fortress. All of Kusunoki Masashige's skills were brought to bear in enticing the enemy to attack him in places where the terrain, with which Kusunoki's men were familiar, proved as much of a hindrance as the loyalists' arrows. Huge boulders were balanced on cliff edges, ready to be dislodged into a pass full of *bakufu* soldiers. The *bakufu* samurai were tempted into night attacks and picked off at will. Pits were dug across paths, felled trees provided almost insurmountable obstacles and, with every day that the *bakufu* spent frustrated in the forests round Chihaya, more and more samurai clans were shown that Kamakura could be challenged, and encouraged to try their hand.

In fact Chihaya was never captured and its continuing existence inspired the exiled Go-Daigo to return in the Spring of 1333. He landed in Hoki Province, on the Japan Sea coast West of Kyoto, and the local response to his return so alarmed Kamakura that the *bakufu* sent to oppose him two of their ablest generals: Nagoshi Takaie, a Hojo kinsman, and Ashikaga Takauji, who was descended from Minamoto stock and leader of one of the wealthiest families in the East.

They set out separately from Kyoto but, on his way to Hoki, Nagoshi was attacked by a guerrilla army similar to Kusunoki's under Akamatsu Norimura and was killed. His troops fled back to Kyoto, where they were absorbed by Takauji, who now had sole command of all the *bakufu* forces in Western Japan. Takauji realised what an opportunity had come his way. Unlike any other of Go-Daigo's supporters his Ashikaga family had the lineage which would enable them to accept the position of Shogun from a captive, or merely grateful, Emperor. Takauji's future lay with Go-Daigo, not the Hojo Regency. Kusunoki's defence of Chihaya was daily exposing the weakness of the Hojo state, so, declaring himself to be for the Emperor, Ashikaga Takauji turned from a pursuit of Go-Daigo and launched his army against the *bakufu's* Kyoto headquarters at Rokuhara. The surprise element was total and he succeeded in capturing the city for the rightful Emperor. Go-Daigo, still apparently in possession of the Imperial Jewels, returned in state to his throne. He generously allowed the Hojo-nominated Emperor to abdicate peacefully and retire to estates Go-Daigo made available to him, and set about restoring his previous position.

When the news of the *bakufu's* collapse in the West reached Chihaya, the siege was abandoned and many of the samurai went over to the Imperial camp. The Hojo strength was now largely confined to Eastern Japan and its doom was almost complete. In June 1333 a warrior called Nitta Yoshisada joined the Imperial supporters. He collected other opportunistic clans about him in Kozuke Province and descended from the mountains on to the *bakufu* capital of Kamakura. He divided his army into three and the columns slowly forced their way through the narrow passes that act as a natural defence for the city. Nitta Yoshisada is credited with obtaining

Samurai warrior, armed with a sword. His quiver is covered with a cloth bag to protect the arrows from rain. (From the *Gunyoki*)

Footsoldier archer, wearing a *do-maru*. (From the *Gunyoki*)

divine intervention from the Sun-Goddess, who, in response to Yoshisada's offering of his sword, caused the sea to roll back so that his army could attack Kamakura from the coastal route. After 5 days of fighting through the man-made tunnels and cuttings of Kamakura, the last of the Hojo *shikken*, along with several hundred of his men, withdrew to a small Buddhist temple, where they committed suicide as Kamakura blazed about them.

The fall of Kamakura marked the end of the Hojo Regency and the eclipse of Kamakura as the administrative capital. From now on the focus would be the Imperial capital of Kyoto. Go-Daigo's restoration of the Imperial power was complete.

Footsoldier archer, wearing a *do-maru* and carrying a bow. (From the *Gunyoki*)

3

Early Muromachi Period

The return of authority to Kyoto marks the beginning of the 'Muromachi Period' in Japanese history, because the seat of the subsequent Ashikaga *bakufu* was a palace on Muromachi Avenue in Kyoto. It is convenient to subdivide this long span of time into shorter units, the first of which may be regarded as ending with the Onin War in 1467, when the capital itself was the battlefield.

The Triumph of the Ashikaga

The destruction of Kamakura in 1333 confirmed Go-Daigo as supreme ruler – for a time. The Hojo *shikken* may have disappeared for ever, but the institution of *bakufu* rule, the government of the samurai by the samurai and largely for the samurai, had attractions that only began to be appreciated once it had ended. The crisis for Go-Daigo came when he was required to make rewards to the samurai warriors who had served him so well. There were many claimants and problems of finance similar to those that had undermined the Hojo after the Mongol Wars. Many were disappointed. None had more to gain than Ashikaga Takauji, and none was more dissatisfied with his reward.

Ashikaga Takauji, as we noted in the last chapter, was of Minamoto

---

PLATE 9   *A footsoldier in a stockade in the Yoshino Mountains, 1348*

The samurai of the War Between the Courts were supported, as samurai had always been, by large numbers of footsoldiers. In this plate we see one such footsoldier taking guard from a parapet of a fortress high in the mountains of Yoshino, where the Southern Emperors held sway. His body-armour is a *hara-ate*, a very rudimentary form of protection, which consists of the front section of a samurai's *do*, without any unnecessary appendages, to which are attached three short skirt pieces, or *kusazuri*, the longer of which is central to protect the groin area. The *hara-ate* had no back-plate and was tied diagonally at the rear by stout straps, which appear to be well padded across the shoulders.

He wears two simple *kote* on his sleeves and, as it is summer, he wears a rough pair of shorts and simple, heavy cloth *suneate* or shin-protectors. Bare feet are considered adequate by this hardy warrior.

His headgear is still the traditional *eboshi* cap and the metal face-protector. His *naginata* has a particularly fierce-looking blade. The figure is based on a sketch by Sasama, and the details of the *hara-ate* on contemporary illustrations.

Girl
with
Wildflowers

With the arrival of Schoonmaker's apprentice, Iris becomes, if not happier, at least less self-conscious, because Caspar doesn't seem to notice her sorry looks. To be sure, Iris knows that she's not the insult to the human form that huge Ruth, with her withered arm and spilling spit, can seem; but Iris also knows that she's not a proof of a divine presence in a corrupt world.

The best she has been able to wish for, most of her days, is to be unnoticeable.

Every morning the Master draws Iris, and then he begins to paint her, quick studies that he won't allow her to see. He incorporates any meadow flowers that Ruth brings. "What does the form or the color matter," he mumbles, "when what is required is the freshness of the blossom?"

He shifts onto larger canvases. When he has a form he admires, he begins to work more slowly, thinning his colors with oil so as to keep them wet and malleable days at a time. Every afternoon when the light changes, though—he can sense it to the instant, by some canniness that Iris can't fathom—he throws down his brushes and sends Iris from the room.

Sometimes Caspar hangs about in the shadows of the studio. From him Iris picks up the habit of watching how the Master works. How he pets a surface with the softest of splayed-bristled brushes. "A blush to emphasize the reflected light," he murmurs.

Iris can't see—she's not allowed to look at the image— but Caspar sucks in his breath and says, "That shrill yellow jagged line—a bold inaccuracy, but so revealing!" The Master grimaces, but Iris can tell he is pleased.

Though it embarrasses Iris to think about it, from a corner Caspar occasionally attempts drawings of her too. He hides his work from Iris and the Master. One morning the Master has had enough of this coyness. "How am I to teach you if I can't see your errors?" the Master grouses.

Caspar replies, "You teach me through your own errors."

"And what errors might they be?" The tone is so ominous that Iris breaks her pose to lean and see the Master's scowl.

"In this studio you've painted God and His companions," says Caspar, "and in the next room you've portrayed the degenerate. Your two obsessions. So what you hope to accomplish by—this once—painting in the middle of the moral spectrum—?" He nods at Iris and at the canvas Iris can't look at. "I admire your self-denial, your sacrifice, to forsake your grand subjects for the mundane—"

He's needling the Master, though Iris hasn't the wit to work out how. The Master says, "God preserve me! The abuses I put up with, from those who gobble at my own table and warm their backsides at my own hearth!" He snatches a stout cloak from a peg. "I'm locked here with curs and idiots," he says, "while the babble of children and a foolish housewife poisons the air. Get out of my way." He leaves the house for the first time since the Fishers have arrived. Margarethe, hearing some of this from the kitchen, goes to the door and watches him stride down the lane.

He isn't an old man. He walks briskly and with purpose, striking his blackthorn staff against the cobbles. Dogs retreat, children stand still, and the women of the lane mutely nod greetings, showing pious disapproval.

"Oh, Caspar," says Margarethe, "we will all be thrown out on our heads, and then what?"

"Nonsense," says Caspar cheerily. "He doesn't walk enough. He gets bad-humored. He'll be better when he gets back. This is part of my job, don't you see? I have to annoy him enough to keep him involved with the world. Otherwise he would latch the shutters and hide inside his paintings and never emerge. It's a steady trial for him, this habit of black spirits and black bile, and retreating from the world because of it."

"Does he request this of you?" says Margarethe.

"What he requests and what he needs are often separate things," says Caspar.

"Who assigned you to decide the difference?"

"Love assigned me," says Caspar, surprised at the ques-

tion. "You are a mother, you know what love requires on behalf of your family."

Margarethe says, pompously, "Obedience and silence."

Caspar says, "Charity, and a cudgel about the shoulders from time to time."

The Master being gone, Margarethe allows herself to sit in the sun on the stoop next to Iris. Iris is given a bowl of late summer peas to shell. Margarethe rinses lentils. Ruth brings her toy. She squats in the ungainly position taken by small children at play or by folks relieving their bowels in a ditch.

Caspar says to Iris, "Well, he won't be back for hours. He's gone off to see his betters, his cronies."

"He has no friends but us, I thought," says Iris.

"He could have a wide circle of friends if he paid them as much attention as he pays his paintings," says Caspar know-ingly. He likes to publish his opinions. "Schoonmaker is thought of fondly by the best artists of the city. But he keeps apart, ashamed that his work is less well regarded than theirs."

"Tell me," says Iris, brave to approach a subject now that the Master is away, "tell me: Is there a changeling child in Haarlem?"

"Gossip is stronger than gospel sometimes," says Caspar. "They say there is: Clara, the daughter of the man who has commissioned the Master's current work."

"Clara!" says Iris. "That's the name of the child who gave Ruth the small windmill. She's no changeling."

"Don't ask me for the truth, for cats lie in the sun, and dogs lie in the shade, and I lie whenever and wherever I can get away with it." He grins saucily. "She's a hidden child to Haarlem's prying eyes, so few can prove it or deny it. But the rumor mongers would have it so. And the Master would swear it in court if it would get him a decent commission."

"You talk with too much freedom of your Master's concerns," says Margarethe stiffly. Caspar laughs. "I'm serious," she goes on. "You're a servant here, as we are; what license allows you to squawk such an opinion against him?"

"Youth," says Caspar, pointing a finger at himself.

Margarethe purses her lips. "Youth is a liability to be outgrown as quickly as possible."

They are a match for each other, Caspar and Margarethe. Iris is amazed.

"Come," says Caspar. He leaps up and tugs Iris's hand. "Do you want to see the paintings he has done of you?"

"I forbid it!" cries Margarethe.

"Oh, what's the harm?" says Caspar. Iris is surprised and bothered by Caspar's touch, and if only to break away from him, she jumps up as if in assent. She hands her bowl to Ruth, who settles the windmill inside it, up to its little wooden neck in emerald peas.

"Iris, will you imperil our position here?" asks Margarethe.

Iris can't answer her mother. Caspar has Iris again by the faintest of touches. Walking backward, he draws her into the studio. "Why shouldn't we learn by studying the Master's work; it's why we're here, isn't it?" says Caspar.

"I am here being silent and helpful," says Iris, to be truthful, "not to learn."

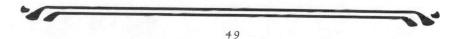

"No master restricts learning, or he is no master," says Caspar. At last he drops Iris's hand—she feels immense disappointment. Sudden hollowness. Ridiculous!

Caspar pivots heavy panels from their careful angles, drying here, there; he finds the one he is looking for, and pushes it out into a waning shaft of sunlight that falls in one corner of the room.

"A study of . . ." says Caspar. Words fail him then.

Iris puts her hands to her mouth.

Margarethe has been unable to maintain her posture of superiority. Out of interest or a motherly tendency to chaperone, she has followed them into the chamber.

"Oh," says Iris, "oh."

"It is a good likeness," says Margarethe at last.

"It is severe," Caspar concedes.

"It is severe, and true," says Margarethe. "Iris is plain to look at. Painfully plain. Don't exaggerate her physical virtues, Caspar; it does no good in the end. She must accept it like the rest of us."

Iris on the canvas is well painted, to be sure; even Iris can see that. The colors are magic: a field of black lit with topaz, against which human figure and sprays of wildflowers glow in uncompromising light. The girl is a study in human ordinariness. Yes, it stops shy of grotesquerie; that would be Ruth, or worse. But the eyes are flat, lacking in intelligence; the lips pursed, practicing resentment; the brows furrowed, the chin weak, the nose large. It is entirely Iris, or the Iris that she can guess at when she catches her own image in mirror or puddle or window glass. But it isn't the Iris whose hand almost throbbed with a terrified life of its own when Caspar grabbed it. It isn't the Iris who tends to Ruth when her mother has had enough. It is another Iris, a smaller one, secured on canvas thanks to ivory, olive, and smudged umber.

"Do you see what he is doing?" says Caspar.

"Oh, wipe your eyes, you make yourself worse," says Margarethe roughly, and thrusts a rag at her younger daughter.

"Do you see his efforts, do you understand?" says Caspar.

Ruth comes in, pointing at the canvas with surprise. Even she sees the likeness. Oh, hell's unholy agents!

"He's taken and flattened all that is attractive in you," says Caspar. "It's like a lie that has enough resemblance to truth to convince for a brief moment. But you must not take it for gospel. He has used the—the *grammar* of your features to spell out a sentence. Do you know what it says?"

Iris can't speak.

Margarethe grunts, "It says that with all we have been through, we're lucky to be eating every day, and sleeping safe under a roof. We're lucky if we're not being hunted down by some brimstone-breathing fiend from hell. That's all it says. Come, girls."

"It says," Caspar insists, "it says nothing about luck, nothing about Iris, nothing about girls. It says only one thing. It says: Aren't the flowers beautiful?"

Iris isn't sure she can hear the dreadful painting say anything of the sort.

"Don't you see?" says Caspar. "Here is a clutch of wildflowers ripped from the meadow, and here's a peasant girl paused to catch her breath. They're the same thing; they're about simple values, which are natural, not artificial or cultivated—"

"You embarrass everyone, keep still," says Margarethe. "You're making it worse. Caspar, what good have you done us?"

"She likes to look," says Caspar. "Don't you know this about your daughter?"

"She can scarcely look, her eyes are streaming with silly tears." Margarethe doesn't move to hold her daughter. Iris knows that isn't her mother's way. But Margarethe's voice is cold in her daughter's defense, and for a moment that is warmth in itself.

"Stop this nonsense," says Caspar. "You're an apprentice as much as I am, Iris. Don't look at yourself on the canvas. Look at the painting of the Master. It doesn't matter whether he gets the commissions from the titled families of Europe. He's a genius, though none know it but we in this room. Look at the painting: *here* is your luck. You are a part of a small masterpiece. You will live forever."

Caught forever as a slab-cheeked pike!

Iris runs from the room and stands on the other side of the open doorway, her sides heaving as if they will split.

Margarethe doesn't follow her. She says to Caspar, "You've broken a household law of the Master's. I'll advise him to release you from your bondage to him. You've done damage to his intentions, as if the damage you've done to my daughter's spirit isn't enough."

Caspar says, "Oh, hush. You don't have the power to recommend a thing to him, and he doesn't have the power to release me even if he wanted. As for Iris, she'll come to thank me, in time, for the eye needs education, and she has an eye. You're more the fool to be so blind to it."

"And an 'eye,' as you call it, will find such an ugly girl a husband?" says Margarethe. "When the time comes, an 'eye' will help her be happy at her chores at hearth and table, at well and garden, in the bed and over the graves of her children? You, for all your airs, are young enough to be almost entirely stupid."

"An eye will help her love the world better, and isn't that why we live?"

"And who will love her?" says Margarethe. "I think it won't be you, young Caspar."

She has cut him. Iris, out of sight, knows it, because for once he is silenced. Margarethe mutters beneath her breath about the portrait of Iris with poking sprays of gold and amethyst flowers. "Raw cruelty, but raw honesty," she avers.

Ruth is the one who lumbers out of the room, following the trail of muffled sobs, to comfort her sister by bringing along the pretty plaything, the windmill. It doesn't comfort Iris, but she twirls the arms anyway, trapped into being pleased, for stupid Ruth's sake.

Half a Door

Caspar's strategy to lift the Master's spirits has worked. The next morning Schoonmaker is in fine form. He rouses the girls and Margarethe with a comical song, and Caspar stumbles from the bed, bleary-eyed and crazy-haired, groggy and grateful at once.

"Hilarity at this hour? It's hardly Dutch," says Caspar. "This can't be Holland. Where are we, Padua, Rome, Marseilles?"

Iris rubs her eyes and thinks once again: Yes, where are we? Where in the world, or out of it?

"Get yourselves in breeches, wash your face, you," says the Master, "and Iris, no sitting today. Take your sister to the meadow, now—"

"They haven't had a morsel," says Margarethe. "It's cold in the meadow at this hour. Hoarfrost in the lane, and even the doves in the eaves have chilly throats—"

"—let them take bread with them, and stay there till they're sent for. They can run races to warm up. I'm expecting important company this morning. There'll be no sitting today."

"I will not sit for you again," says Iris in a small voice.

"Tomorrow is time enough," says the Master.

"Never again," says Iris, more loudly. Caspar blushes and ducks his head into a clean shirt, and stays there, like a turtle retracted in its shell.

"What manner of revolution is this?" says the Master, hardly listening. "Margarethe, I'll need your help at my ablutions. Are you skilled at clipping beards?"

"Give me the knife and expose your throat, and we'll find out," says Margarethe.

"Everyone so cheery this morning," says the Master hastily. "Well, no matter. My own blemished self will have to serve. What *are* you chattering about, Iris?"

"I've seen how you paint my face," says Iris. She has thought the words out, and struggles to say them in an even voice. "You view me with humor and contempt. You've made me look the fool. I already look the fool in my own eyes. I won't be put forward to look the fool to the world."

"So, you've broken my law, and peered at the paintings the moment my back is turned?" The Master's voice is distant-thundery soft.

"It was Caspar's suggestion," says Margarethe, shooting the young man a look. He twists in his shirt comically.

"Oh, Caspar," says the Master, contempt and dismissal intermingled. "One expects nothing better of him. Caspar, come out of that shirt, you ass. I'll have your head on a platter by noontime if you don't stop your games. Iris, I have more to do today than to kiss away tears of hurt feelings. Off with you, girls, off, off! A patron is coming by, and the floors,

Margarethe, must be swept and the paintings arranged to be seen in the best daylight."

Iris is pushed aside, her brave thoughts spoken but unheard. The Master has other matters on his mind.

"We should run away," says Iris fiercely to Ruth. They hold hands and leave the noise of aggressive housecleaning behind them. Along the lane a crippled old dame comes poking with the aid of two sticks. Her back is gnarled nearly double, and her horny hands are tied to the canes so she can't drop them.

"Looking for that painter fellow," she screeches at Iris, "the one who likes old crippled crabapple trees like me. I'm the Queen of the Hairy-Chinned Gypsies, and I can blow smoke rings out my bottom. Where is he? Tell me, or I'll curse you into the bottom of a well, where you'll have no one but frogs to hear your confession."

Ruth, who is timid of most people, keeps behind Iris, no doubt frightened by the crone's bread-loaf chin, with its thin growth of pig-bristle white whiskers. Iris isn't scared, though; for some reason she thinks about the dame hidden in the shadows near the quay that first day. The one who had said to Margarethe, "You tell your own way!" Iris says, "I'll tell you where the Master lives, if you'll magic *him* into the bottom of a well!"

"Change him into a slug and hit him with my shoe," says the crone agreeably. "After he paints me and pays me first. Immortality calls, so who am I to keep myself to myself? Tell me where to find him."

"If you promise," says Iris. The crone leers. Oh, to it,

then. "The house just beyond, with the big window and the half door."

"Queen of the Gypsies, Hen to the Cheated Chicks, Dame of the Damned, Sow to the Suffering Sucklings, Midwife to the Changelings, Mother Abbess to the Whores, of whom you'll never be one, you ugly thing. Better go turn yourself in at some convent already, and save yourself the trouble. Bless you, child, and stand aside. I start lunging and I can't stop."

The crone moves off, more like a splayed-leg bug skittering along the surface of a pond than a Queen. *Midwife to the Changelings*, thinks Iris. Can you tell us then about Haarlem's changeling child?

Iris wants to follow. She'd love to see a curse lowered on the Master. To watch him reduced to a slug! She doesn't dare. Instead, she takes Ruth's hands and they hurry along. Iris mutters, "We should go back to the quay and find the boat on which we came, and head back to England. We're not at home here among crazy painters. I hate this madhouse. I hate him. Why would anyone want to see such a painting? Do you think the patron is coming to see that very painting? Take your fingers out of your mouth, you look a mess."

The meadow is still full of the same late flowers, though they now are browning, bug-chewed, going to seed. Iris can hardly bring herself to sit there, because she feels she is imitating the painting: ill-favored young woman shown up by the commonest of weeds.

Once Ruth is settled, happily, with bread to gnaw, Iris climbs the boughs of the apple tree as she has before, and makes her way into the second tree that affords a view over the city walls. She watches the Master's household, to see what kind of guest might take it into his head to visit. There's no sign of the Queen of the Hairy-Chinned Gypsies. Probably turned away from the door with a wooden shoe planted in her smoky behind. The Master is in no mood for diversions today.

Iris doesn't have long to wait. Almost before the rest of Haarlem is awake and about its business, a gentleman comes striding from the better district, along the lane to the Master's house. He wears a tall hat with a buckle so brightly polished that it gleams even from this distance, and he sports a cape with a more than generous cut. A lace collar settles on his shoulders like the sepals of a rose, cradling his ruddy countenance. It's an intelligent face, made the more pointed by a well-trimmed goatee and flourishes of mustache. Next to him, thinks Iris with pleasure, the Master looks a bloody potato eater.

The gentleman stands outside the door of the Master's household for a moment, contemplating the situation. Perhaps he knocks. The door swings open, and there's Caspar, more neatly attired than Iris has yet seen him. Iris hasn't settled on her feelings about Caspar after yesterday. She'd rather not despise him, but somehow he seems in collusion with the Master at her expense. How little she matters in this household!

Caspar ushers the guest inside, and the bottom half of the door swings closed, to keep stray cats and pigs and rude dwarves from wandering in.

Iris says to Ruth, "Why should we be sent to pasture like a pair of disobedient goats?"

Ruth just chews her bread.

"I've given what I had to give, whether I wanted to or no; why shouldn't I learn what is made of me?" says Iris. "Who is he to send us packing?"

Ruth falls back against the grass, enjoying the sun on her face.

"Don't eat lying down, you choke, you know you do," says Iris. "Ruth, sit up." Ruth sits up, fussing.

"I'll be back for you. If the cows come just yell at them. You can yell when you want to," says Iris. "Will you be all right?"

Ruth shrugs.

Iris leaves. It's only a matter of moments, now that she's familiar with the terrain, before she is slowing to a tiptoe and approaching the house, bent over so as not to be seen. She creeps up to the door. It's a warm day for mid-autumn, or maybe the Master wants as much ambient light as he can get; the top half of the door is still open. Iris crouches against the bottom half, her arms hugging her knees, listening. The front studio is just inside, and the Master is issuing his thoughts in a public voice. Bravado, thinks Iris, but it doesn't really disguise his fear.

She's pleased at his discomfiture. Still, she'd rather he be a dead slug on the floor.

She listens and tries to sort out the occasion. Apparently, the visitor is looking at paintings; the Master and Caspar are setting one painting after another up in the best light. There are Annunciations and Lamentations and Nativities;

there are Saints Basil, Nicholas, and John the Baptist. "And patrons, in their holiest of aspects," says the Master, "I can do women with veils, I do lace as in this study of Catherine of Cleves, and pearls of the finest luster. Notice the skin tone, cherry underpainted with a fine olive-blue, an achievement in both grinding and application that is not common knowledge among my peers—"

"Young von Rijn of Amsterdam has superior flesh tones," murmurs the guest, "and his handling of light, even for a youth, is remarkable. He paints the light of holiness itself. One can't imagine how it is done. Grace of God, one guesses."

"God works through pigment and varnish, just like the rest of us," says the Master with as generous a sigh as he can muster. "May we all aspire to the achievements that Rembrandt von Rijn will accomplish. In the meantime, let's keep ourselves to the matters at hand. Now, Caspar, show Heer van den Meer the studies of flowers that he requested. Let my woman take that flask for you—Margarethe! Please— and here—are you comfortable, take the bench—here— Caspar, a little this way—just so. Voilà."

"Mercy," says Heer van den Meer in a noncommittal tone.

"Exactly," says the Master, bravely.

"One can hardly attend to the flowers," says Heer van den Meer. "Who is the unfortunate child? Is she a composite from your wicked imagination?"

"She's as clever as she is homely," says the Master. "Who can know how God chooses to work His way in this world?"

"I think there was never a girl of Holland so plain."

"She is mostly of England. They are homely there."

"England, say you? How does she come to sit for you?"

"My bosom bursts with charity for the unlucky," sighs the Master. "Such a big heart. It's my curse. A commission from you would help me keep her fed."

"Keep her off the street, you'd do us a service," murmurs Heer van den Meer. There's a little hollow laughter, and Iris hears her mother blandly say, "Will that be all, gentlemen?"

There is silence. "Of course, I'm also impressed by the flower pieces of Hans Bollongier," says the guest. "It was his work that gave me the notion—"

The Master says hurriedly, "Now, good sir, don't be distracted by the novelty of the girl. It's the paintings of flora you wanted to see. I've set off the commonest of flowers with the commonest of faces, so you can judge my touch, my palette, my skill at arrangement. Beauty shines out even in the coarsest of materials if they're arranged well. Not to put thoughts in your head, of course."

"Of course not," says van den Meer.

Another silence. Iris aches to peer over the ledge of the door, but she doesn't dare. Why doesn't the Master show the patron his secret gallery of misfits, dwarves, and other magic folk?

"Does the child know Dutch as well as English?" says van den Meer.

"You are here to look at paintings!" says the Master.

"She does, sir, she does," interrupts Margarethe. "I am her mother."

"And I *am* here to look at paintings," says van den Meer. "Very well. Is this painting dry enough to move in a cart?

It's a fine painting, you know, it's very fine. I like what I see. You mustn't fight the tides of change so; life needn't be so hard. There are fortunes to be made, there is slow recovery from the endless wars with Spain to be achieved, there is a place for all of us in the good times ahead, but you must not grasp with such lack of dignity at things of the past. Yes, bring the painting to my home, tomorrow if the weather be good. Yes," says van den Meer, "bring the painting, bring the child as well."

There is a pause. "Why the child?" says the Master. "She's a sullen enough thing. Do you mean to assess my skills by mounting subject and portrait on a stage side by side? She won't do it."

"She'll do what she's told—" begins Margarethe.

"She won't do it because I'll tell her not to do it," says the Master firmly.

But van den Meer only laughs. "I want nothing of the child's looks, who could?" he says. "But if she's a clever soul who can speak both Dutch and English, she might be of use to my household. Don't worry. The ones who hold the purse strings will look at your painting and they won't care about the model. But as long as you're coming, bring the girl to my house, well scrubbed and courteous, and we'll see what happens. It may solve a domestic problem and keep my good dame happy. In the meantime, I have little else to say. You've carried out your assignment well, and I hope that you'll be engaged at the next stage of our venture. Here is coin to the amount we settled upon. Turn the picture to the wall now; no one should have to look on that longer than necessary."

He laughs, but none of the others join in. There is the sound of a canvas being shifted.

"And, you, lad," says van den Meer, making ready to leave, "how do you like it here, living in the neighborhood of such a brilliant talent?"

"I am blinded, sir," says Caspar. "A change from time to time would do me good. If there is some small work to be done in your household—"

"I don't need a boy," says van den Meer, "you wouldn't do. Tomorrow, then."

Iris races back to collect Ruth, her shoes on the stones ringing out a kind of alarm. However blank and smoky her childhood, however angry she is at the Master, however uncertain her feelings about Caspar, the idea of solving any-one else's domestic problems seems suddenly a far more gloomy prospect. Where is the Queen of the Hairy-Chinned Gypsies when you need her? *I'd* be a changeling if I could, thinks Iris; turn me into a flounder, a sparrow, a dormouse. Better yet, turn me into an insensible chair with a broken rush seat, a nail on the hoof of a horse! Turn me into sad thick Ruth! Anything or anyone that is too dull to be able to think about herself. It's the endlessly thinking about yourself that causes such heart shame.

Van den Meer's Household

"**I** don't see why I should go. I won't be paraded as a freak."

"There is every reason for you to go."

"Why?"

"There's no reason for you to know the reasons. Don't be insolent."

Iris has her hair brushed, her apron tied, her hands examined for dirt. She twists as much as she dares, and Margarethe slaps her when enough has become enough. Iris's cheeks sting, but she doesn't cry out. Margarethe, as if ashamed, turns away to the low worktable by the kitchen window. "Now wrap this bit of pastry in a cloth and present it to whoever greets you, and thank them well, in English and in Dutch, for their kindness."

"I don't know what kindness you are talking about." Iris doesn't turn her head, but she looks at her mother at an angle, like a bird. "What makes you think I would recognize a kindness if I saw one?"

"Ungrateful child!" cries Margarethe. She approaches her daughter with disbelief. "Do you know what it means to feed a family, and I with no living husband, father, brother, or son to turn to? Do you have any idea how near we are to throwing ourselves on the mercies of the Church or the city fathers? To have had to go from house to house begging for work—for you, stupid witless thing, it is a game. For me, this is my life, a horrid thing. God plagues the mothers of the world with worry, from His own sweet Mary to the meanest fishwife of the harborside!"

"I don't care," says Iris.

Margarethe draws in her breath and narrows her eyes. "You are too young to know how women must collaborate or perish," she hisses. "Why should I keep you from that knowledge, what good does it do for you or for me? If you aren't willing to behave and earn a coin when you can, whatever this van den Meer wants you for, I won't answer to the amount of food that makes its way to Ruth's bowl every night."

Iris bites her lower lip and clenches her small hands together.

"You go and be clever, for that's how you are made. Be a help to your mother and your sister, and stand back, child, from considering your own foolish thoughts. There's no time in this world to indulge in those. Do you hear me? I say, do you hear me?"

"My ears hear you," says Iris.

"Get away with you, then, and do as you are bid."

Iris waits on the stoop. Ruth crawls up and puts her head

in Iris's lap. Iris strokes Ruth's hair, which is badly in need of brushing. Out of habit, Iris searches for lice, and thinks about striking Ruth in the face, to punish her for being so slow of mind and useless.

Though she hates Ruth—she *hates* her—Iris will not see her big sister go hungry.

Her mother, now—another story. How agreeable to see Margarethe pilloried in the stocks and whipped by virtuous citizens. Of whom Iris would be the first to volunteer.

Around the corner of the house come the Master and Caspar, managing the offending canvas between them. They have hired a cart from a neighbor. They fumble like bump-kins, misjudging the height of the step and the depth of the cart. Iris imagines finding a knife from the kitchen and rush-ing up to slash the canvas to ribbons. But she doesn't destroy the Master's work, since so much hangs in the balance. Mar-garethe's threat is an effective one.

Eventually, the donkey braying in impatience, the cargo is safely covered with a cloth. The Master, Caspar, and Iris wave good-bye to Ruth, who puts her finger in her nose.

All the way through the city streets Iris keeps close to Caspar. She's forgiven him his part in tempting her to view the painting; how could her own sorry looks possibly be Cas-par's fault? Besides, with so much else to fear, she can't afford to keep her distance from his good humor. See how he prances! Head high, hair tossed in the sea breeze like a horse's mane, eyes darting left, right, settling on Iris to make sure she is keeping up, turning away to note a weathervane, a whitewashed chimney, a friendly lad grinning from a window.

The Master keeps his head down and his collar up. Iris suspects this isn't so much to guard against the wind, as the weather still hasn't turned bitter, but to protect against the gazes of Haarlem neighbors. Or maybe he's guarding against the fact that there are few glances turned his way, few who really care whether he is coming or going.

Into the Grotemarkt. How orderly is this magical world through which ugly girls may trudge! Iris hears a ring, almost a musical tapping, like a clock striking. It's a man sitting on the cobbles, his legs stretched out on either side of him, hitting stones in place with a hammer. And is that an echo, off the magnificent facade of the Stadhuis? No, it's another man at the same task on the far side of the market square. Every little part of this world must be pounded into place. The whole world a huge ticking clock that tells God's story of charms and punishments.

They reach their destination. It's a house that fronts on the Grotemarkt, the very house against which Ruth leaned that first day—the house of the strange child. The so-called changeling child.

Van den Meer must be a man of means. The broad-shouldered home has a walled garden beside it. In plum-red brick interrupted by gray lateral stones, the house looms up two full stories, with a step gable pinching two abbreviated attics. At this late afternoon hour the sun doesn't strike the front of the house, and the windows facing the marketplace are like panels of black water. The building looks august and—what is it—cautious? Like a house of secrets, like a cage of smoke.

No, thinks Iris, it is something about those dark windows—there in the topmost one, is that a face disappearing? As if unwilling to be seen by the approaching company? Is it the obscure child? Why does everything hide its true face here?

The Master hasn't noticed this. He doesn't even pause to look for the path to the kitchen yard. He hands the reins of the donkey to Caspar and walks up to the door, which is almost level with the cobbles. He knocks briskly.

"Yes, yes, but come in," says a man's voice, sounding busy, irritated. "I'll send the stable boy around to take the donkey, and he can get some fellows to carry the study of flowers."

"Caspar will help to make sure the painting isn't knocked in transport," replies the Master.

Oh, be knocked in transport, thinks Iris.

"And let the girl come in. That's it, don't waste my time. Step right in. What is your name?"

Except for the Master, Iris isn't used to being addressed directly by gentlemen. She ducks her eyes to the steps and almost walks into the doorpost. When she tells her name, she mumbles, and the Master has to repeat it.

"Well, I am Heer van den Meer. I have no time to deal with you yet. Can you manage to sit quietly while a company of gentlemen talk? Or do you need to run and play outside?"

She can't think which would be more horrible, so she doesn't answer.

"Well, come and sit, then," says van den Meer. "Through to the salon."

They enter the grandest room that Iris has ever seen. Well-carved and oiled chairs and cupboards stand against walls hung with patterned fabric. Upon a shelf sits a succession of silver bowls; another shelf boasts an abundance of mugs. In shadow or light, everything is patterned: vases, picture frames, candlesticks, porcelain. In the center of the room stands a table draped with a rich carpet of a sort that Iris has never seen before. In lozenges, stripes, curlicues, cartouches. Sage-green, cream, three shades of red, and that blue!

Iris's fingers are clean. She'd like to drive them through the pile and learn if the colors feel different from each other.

Van den Meer points to a small chair in a corner, and there Iris sits. She's forgotten to hand him the pastry Margarethe sent as a gift.

Caspar and some servants bring in the painting and prop it up on a sideboard. Iris tries to blur her eyes so that she can enjoy the splendor of the room without having to look at her portrait. There are other paintings to see. One particularly, over a veneered hutch of some sort, shows a capable young woman in yellow and black silks. The way the skirts billow reminds Iris of a bumblebee. A blond woman in silks and shiny ornaments *belongs* in this kind of a house, not an ugly girl with wildflowers.

Van den Meer leaves the Master and Caspar alone for a few minutes. Iris can hear him barking instructions to the kitchen staff for refreshments to be served in an hour: a platter of lobsters and a bowl of lemons—some greens, soaked to remove sand—a pitcher of beer and a pitcher of water and a pile of freshly ironed linens so the guests might clean their soiled hands. Everything is to be well presented, and can there be a kitchen child to wave a fan above the fish, keep the flies and the cat away?

The kitchen child is gone, he is told, along with that worthless cook who has complained of the plague and left for Rotterdam.

"I have a girl in the salon, she'll do," says van den Meer, and Iris knows he means her.

The guests arrive. A dozen bearded men, stout and prosperous, in ruffles, laces, and the freshest of stockings. Many of them sweep hats with billowing feathers into the air as they greet one another. Van den Meer takes each gentleman up to the Master, making introductions in tones both grave and merry. Each gentleman is promenaded before the painting of Ugly Girl with Wildflowers. Each gentleman comments. Before long there is too much noise for Iris to hear the remarks on the comically plain maiden. She's glad about this.

Glad too that neither the Master nor van den Meer draws attention to her, sitting in the corner.

Caspar pulls up a stool and perches near her. "Are you petrified?" he says.

She won't answer.

"They are entrepreneurs," he says. "They know nothing about art except how to buy it. They are like bears wandering in from the eastern forests. Think of them as growling, uneducated beasts that some magician has dressed in laces and sashes."

She has to stifle a giggle, and tears stand in her eyes then, only because Caspar cares enough to talk to her.

Caspar glances at her, raises his eyebrows, and plows on. "In fact, the guests actually *are* bears," says Caspar. "Van den Meer is their prince regent. Look at his hands. They aren't hands, really, they're just paws that someone has clipped the fur from. See how clumsy he is?"

She stares. Surely he's only jesting? But oh, van den Meer *is* clumsy, patting the newest guest on the back!

"The bears are too stout from a summer of foraging for berries in the woods, and trout in the streams. They can't even bend at the waist! Look how shallowly they bow to one another."

Iris has to stuff her knuckle in her mouth to keep from gasping aloud.

"*I* met the Queen of the Hairy-Chinned Gypsies," she begins. But now van den Meer raises his voice and calls the room to attention. Caspar is no more a full-fledged member of this association than Iris is. He settles his hands in his lap and listens.

Iris listens too. This isn't the kitchen Dutch that she has been taught by Margarethe. It's sprinkled with words from other lands, France, Friesland, perhaps, and certainly a remark or two in English. A few words from bear language? The gentlemen seem to have no problem attending and understanding.

Van den Meer doesn't talk right away about the Master or his painting of Ugly Girl with Wildflowers. He talks instead about flowers in general and the native appetite for beautiful blossoms. Iris has heard of tulips before, but she doesn't know if she's ever seen any, so she imagines a spray of lacy wildflowers of the sort the Master has spent the last few weeks painting. But van den Meer talks as if his gentlemen friends have a firm acquaintance with the tulip—brought in from Vienna, was it, or faraway Constantinople?—and, to be sure, they nod at his words. This is a commodity about which all bears can agree to admire.

Yet when van den Meer strikes a little brass bell that stands on a table, Iris wonders if some of the men have been play-acting their knowledge of tulips, for their jaws drop open when a girl comes into the room balancing a small bucket of blooming flowers on a silver tray.

Iris's jaw drops too. She can't help it.

The flowers are bright and intensely colored, a maroon-red shade striped with white. Richer than cloth, as rich as light. There are six blossoms of varying heights, on slender green stalks with ample, recumbent leaves. Only one blossom stands to each plant.

But the girl who carries them is equally striking. So blonde as to be nearly white, hair gleaming like new butter or goat's cheese. It *is* the child who talked to Ruth through the window. The one who asked if Ruth was a changeling, the one that Caspar said was considered a changeling herself. She looks like a human child. Only perfect. A perfect specimen.

What had she said to Ruth? "Thing, *get away from here.*"

"Ah, my Clara," says van den Meer, with the unbearable smile of a father's pride upon his face. "Look how she shows off the latest strain of blossom . . ."

Clara finds the tray heavy, and her father helps her to settle it upon the table in the center of the room. The investors—for such they are, Iris is learning—lean forward and speak in hushed tones about the blooms. There's no exotic scent, apparently, to attract admirers. It's the colors of the flowers, and how statuesque they are. Each man present wants to own a share of the next shipment from some port Iris hasn't heard mentioned before.

"Your appetites," says van den Meer proudly, "are just like the appetites of your fellow citizens, your friends and neighbors, from the jolliest merchants to the most dour men of faith. We're guaranteed a healthy return on our investment if we pool our resources and underwrite the cost of a shipment of tulip bulbs from the East. And as for our painter friend, Master Schoonmaker here, now that we have seen what he can do with ordinary materials" —van den Meer indicates the Master's painting in the edge of the room, eclipsed just now by the tulips, whose blossoms are standing goblets of bloody and pearly light—"our friend can take a subject more worthy of his talents and create for us a painting that we can mount at some formal occasion. We can stir up interest in this new tulip variety to our financial reward. We will have an advantage over other tulip mer-chants, by having a superior product, and by encouraging talk about it."

Clara's eyes twitch, just once, toward Iris. Clara doesn't come over, though, which allows Iris to observe her from a distance. Clara isn't quite the child she appeared through the window. She seems youthful because of the juvenile gown, the timid manner. But she must be close to Iris's age, nearer a young woman than a babbling child. Iris notices Clara's clean hands, her soft pink fingers, her neat nails. Like a very young girl, Clara puts a thumb in her mouth. Van den Meer gently reaches out and pulls the thumb away. He never pauses in his remarks.

Is this all that business is? A few remarks about cost, some calculations, a worry about rival shipments, a quick agreement in principle? Before another quarter hour has passed, van den Meer is ushering his investor friends out of the salon and toward a dining chamber somewhere below. When the room is nearly empty, he turns to the Master and says, "So, are you agreeable?"

The Master is turning the color of the tulips. He doesn't speak.

"Of course," says van den Meer, "there isn't any room for you to live here. Nor would my wife allow it. And I can't send my daughter out to your studio. She doesn't leave the house at all. But you can ship your materials into this salon, and do with the beauty of Clara and the tulips what you've managed with lesser materials. You've convinced us of your invaluable talent. And you'll be well paid."

Deliberately the Master says, "I had thought, that is, I had *hoped* to be commissioned for a portrait of the company of civic guards to which you belong."

"One thing leads to another; nothing happens all at once," says van den Meer. "I can't be absent from my guests for long. Are we agreed, or shall I send out for Bollongier? He's within a brisk walk of this room."

"We haven't even talked about the size of a payment," says the Master.

"It's only money," says van den Meer, "and aren't you an artist in need of money? If not, there are others in the Guild of Saint Luke who are eager for the work. Will you take on the assignment or no?"

The Master, struggling for time to think, says, "But why did you ask me to bring Iris here? What has she meant in this negotiation? I'd thought that your friends might judge my skill by comparing the model and what I've done with her. I'd hoped that if they approved of my work—"

"Oh, your girl," says van den Meer, "well, the girl. It's not a serious matter. But my wife is concerned for our daughter's education. My little Clara is so cloistered, she needs a companion, and it might occupy her mind and her time to learn English. She's already more than capable at French, and she has a small grasp of Latin as well. We only wish for her the best. Look—you want to see beauty," says van den Meer, a proud father, "look at her. Have you laid eyes upon a more pleasing figure? She'll grow to be a fine woman." His appreciation of his daughter makes Iris's eyes sting.

"Iris has a mother and a sister," says the Master. "They eat like horses."

"Bring them too," says van den Meer casually. "You forget that I can pay for what I want. We must keep the wife happy, isn't that so? Isn't that always the way?"

The Master strides out of the room without answering. Caspar shrugs in Iris's direction and then follows his mentor. The door to the street slams shut behind them. The slamming is the Master's loud opinion about van den Meer's suggestion.

Iris isn't sure what's expected of her. She's alone in the room with Clara and her father. Clara looks down at the tiled floor. Her face is shuttered and boxed; she pinches her lower lip with hidden teeth. She doesn't bother to look at Iris again. "Papa," she says, "may I go now?"

"I've bought you a new friend," says van den Meer. "But first she's needed in the dining hall to help the guests. Come, you, what's your name?" Iris holds out the pastry to him and remembers that she should curtsey, but she doesn't trust her knees.

2

THE IMP-RIDDLED HOUSE

The Small Room of Outside

Much to fear, in this rigid house, but much to admire too. And Iris loves to look. What's best about van den Meer's house is its skins and glazes, and how each rare thing accepts daylight or candlelight or shrugs itself against it. Iris wonders: Has looking at the Master's paintings developed in her this taste for surfaces and textures?

Look at the bowl on the polished table. A bowl from the Orient, van den Meer has told her. But it's not just one thing, a bowl. Look at all the effects that make it up: Deepest in, a lace of purple-gray hairline fractures. Covered by an eggshell wash, through which blue painted lines form blowsy chrysanthemum blossoms. The flowers are suspended in some thin distance of—for lack of a better word—shine. Inside the curve of the bowl, a reflection: a distorted Iris, too blurred to be perceived as ugly.

If she peers harder, will she catch something magical at her shoulder? Something intense and potent coming from behind, stealing up through the highly polished gloom of wealthy rooms?

It was Margarethe who had said it: "The devil himself may send out a whiskery hound to sniff us out, but we've no choice! Come, girls, come." Margarethe had announced their torturer—as they fled England—she had called it to them, she had worried it into being—

But no. Look. *Look.*

She pays attention. The varieties of Turkey carpet, on tables and walls. The crisp edges and rectangles of white linen. The ringed muscles of candlesticks, their glossy, bulbous reflections. The fur, the inlaid wood, the mementos from faraway places: Venice, Constantinople, Arabia, Cathay.

Schoonmaker's rooms had been sloppy and energetic. These van den Meer rooms are *composed*. The orderliness of them—their spanking cleanliness, for one thing—is a matter not just of pride but of mental clarity and rightness. A chair out of place?—no one in the house can think straight. Flowers left to stand in a vase until there's a reek of ditch water?—you'd think the bellicose Spaniards were banging at the city gates again.

Some hours after the party Caspar had arrived at the van den Meer's for Iris; he ushered her back to the studio to collect her things. There she found Margarethe arguing with the Master, and Ruth weeping. Schoonmaker didn't want them to go, but he couldn't or wouldn't pay for them to stay. "You have your boy, use him as you were wont to do," said Margarethe tauntingly, as if trading on a secret meaning that Iris couldn't be privy to. "And why not? You asked us for three things, and those we gave you: domestic help, a delivery of meadow flowers every day, and a face to paint. We're grateful to you for your hospitality, but we aren't beholden to you."

"When that peculiar van den Meer girl has tired of her new playmate, or learned whatever English she can pick up, you and your daughters will be out on the street," says the Master darkly.

"Watch," said Margarethe. She wore that expression common to cats making the acquaintance of baby birds. "Watch and see if that happens, Luykas Schoonmaker."

Iris and Ruth both turned to see if the Master would answer to this informality of a Christian name. How had their mother the right? Even Caspar seemed surprised.

But Luykas Schoonmaker pointed at the Fisher girls and said, "Ruth won't know enough to appreciate how she is being treated, but Iris will. She'll be slighted there. She won't make good on the talent for drawing that she possesses."

"And how do you know she possesses any such talent, and what good is it to her if she does?" cawed Margarethe. "She isn't a lady of leisure, to paint scenes of sunny gardens as the mood strikes her! Have you ever seen her as much as pick up a charcoal?"

"She's looked at drawings, even at some cost to her," said the Master. "Her hand clenches an imaginary stub of charcoal while I work my own charcoal across a page. There's

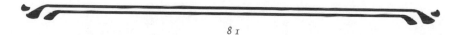

nothing in her at all but possibility; but that is rare enough."

"You're as trapped in your conceits as you are in your over-labored drawings," said Margarethe. "You make the world to seem a story, as if anything could happen. Like most men, you are blind to our fate."

"Don't go, Margarethe," said the Master.

"Pay us a salary to stay and we'll stay," said Margarethe, her chin high.

The Master looked at her as if she were offering to sleep with him for a fee. It was a look of disgust, but love and need crowded in too. Margarethe met his eyes just as intently, and continued, "Girls, bring your aprons from the hook, and your shoes from the doorsill. If I understand correctly, Luykas, what with your new commission, you'll be a regular visitor to the van den Meer household. We'll enjoy your friendship there, should we want it."

So, with Caspar to chaperone them, they had crossed the streets of Haarlem at dusk. Their settling in at the van den Meer household was less noisy but no less swift. And Iris had slept that night at the hearthstones, uneasily, feeling the building lifting above her in capable bones of brick. She remembered the face at an upstairs window, disappearing. This is a house of magic, she thought as she drifted to sleep, and she thinks the same on waking up there for the first time.

The family is small. Cornelius van den Meer is a warm but distant fatherhead, and he leaves to his wife, Henrika, the business of managing the household. From a public house beyond the Stathuis, van den Meer and his partners conduct a business of investments and merchant marinery. When he returns, reeking of pipe smoke, blusteringly good-natured because of ale and the flattering company of his peers, he sleeps. Iris peeks at him, sitting in the sunny garden, his head back against the wall and his mouth open. He's older than his wife. His beard is as much silver as brown, and his temples and thinning pate have gone entirely gray. His wife won't let him sit on the bench in the front of the house. In full view of the pious on their way to services, or the hungry buying their evening meal? She thinks it looks common, and says so.

Henrika believes in good manners. Her cheekbones are high and knobby, her wrists thin, her scent flowery and bewitching. But mostly it's her coloring that Iris admires, coppery pink blushes and white flushes playing under flawless skin. When Henrika comes to the door of a room, it's on silent feet, as if to make a floorboard creak would be to command more attention than she deserves.

Yet this is just a little drama, a masquerade, for though Henrika's step is silent, it is nonetheless heavy. Margarethe, in the privacy of the hearth, is quick to point out to Iris that Henrika's portrait, not her husband's, takes pride of place in the reception room. The lady in yellow and black silk, a bumblebee humming to herself. The queen of the family hive. And doesn't she know it! Henrika is happy to tell the provenance of each piece of furniture, each item of decoration. The house, whole and entire, was part of Henrika's dowry. "If the marriage should dissolve, she has the right to appeal to the law to reclaim all her assets," says Margarethe incredulously. "The wealth of this marriage rests on what she inherited from her father. Her husband brought to the holy union only business sense and good humor."

Iris, yawning, says, "What you learn in three or four days! How can you know about this? She's far too private to be confiding in you."

"Schoonmaker has lived in Haarlem all his life; he knows everything, though he pretends to be bored about it," says Margarethe. "He tells me that Henrika holds the purse strings." She twists her lower lip, an expression of reluctant approval at Henrika's power. "Do you see how Cornelius and Henrika disagree about their daughter, Clara? The hen-pecked man must leap to respond to every complaint that Henrika makes."

"Oh, Clara," says Iris. "Clara," she says again, biting her lip, for it's Iris who has the main worry now. It's Iris's job to befriend the distant, suspicious child, to gain her trust, to teach her English, to vary her days. And she hasn't made such a good start of it.

If Clara is indeed a changeling, there's no word spoken about it by her parents. She's considered a stroppy child—sullen, secre-tive, and ordinary. Her carrying the tulips into the parlor to show the visiting bear-investors must have been taxing on her, for she doesn't show up to meet the new household members. In fact, Iris sees very few signs of Clara's existence in the house at first, though she hears some: a soft footfall, the sound of a dropped or a thrown plate crashing on the floor, a cry of alarm such as a small child might utter when in the throes of a bad dream. Still the obscure child even when Iris is living under the same roof.

After several days of Clara simply refusing to appear at all, Henrika brings Iris to the door of Clara's room and calls in to her daughter, "Please, my dear, I want you to meet your new friend."

"No." The sound comes out like a little smothered yelp, as if even in the middle of the day Clara is huddled beneath bedclothes. She won't come out of her room.

The next day, Iris says loudly, "I am very lonely." She draws a deep breath in the gloom of the upstairs hall, and she leans her breast against Clara's door. She tries to make her voice wedge itself through a crack between the planks. "You were kind to my sister once. You let her take your little toy. So I want to talk to you."

"Go away."

Henrika's smile at Iris is brief but forgiving. "She's an unusual child, and I'm patient with her strange ways," she confides. "You have to be patient too."

"But how can I teach her English if I can't even see her?"

"She comes around. Go and help your mother, then. If I can coax her out with the promise of something special, I'll come and find you."

"What does she want more than anything?"

Henrika purses her lips. "She wants to be alone and to play by herself."

Well, thinks Iris, I'm not going to be the most welcome thing ever to enter her life, then. But there's not much that Iris can do about it, so she wanders downstairs. Margarethe says, "If you can't pry Clara out of her room, then take Ruth out for some exercise. Your sister the ox is banging into things again, which means she's not stretching her limbs as she ought."

They wander up and down the streets. Haarlem is becoming an easy place in which to feel at home. In the street next to Saint Bavo's, women hustle baskets of cloth on their backs. Men trundle wheelbarrows with kegs of ale. The window shutters, which drop down during the day, serve as ledges for the display of wares. Iris and Ruth inspect the goods, a pastime that costs nothing and annoys the shop-keepers. But if the Dutch find Ruth as grotesque as the English did, they keep it to themselves. Only a few children run after her and taunt her.

There is always Saint Bavo's to slip into if the hubbub of the streets gets too frantic for Ruth. Iris doesn't have strong feelings about churches one way or the other, but she remembers what the Master has told her about Saint Bavo's. Built as a Catholic cathedral, it's now in the hands of the Protestants. In foul weather it serves as a kind of indoor pub-lic park, where men and women and dogs go to shake off the wet. People stroll for exercise, conversation, and to view the decorations set against whitewashed walls. Iris listens to everything—she imagines bringing Clara here one day and saying all this in English to her. Look! The colored-glass win-dow on the church's west wall, and how one panel of it was removed because it celebrated too gloriously some Catholic bishop of long ago. The slabs in the floor to remember the dead. The lozenges, mounted on pillars, to remember the dead. The dead, the dead, always with us!

There's no memorial to her father, of course, not here or anywhere; there weren't even prayers mumbled in his memory—

To notice something else quickly—she can't help but notice, having listened to the Master all these weeks—there's very little in the way of religious painting. Not a crucifixion in sight. Not a Virgin as far as you can see. Not even in the most shadowy corners. No wonder the Master feels so useless. For a moment Iris imagines how he must suffer, for she's feeling useless too, wandering about a church instead of performing the task for which she and her mother and sister are being given food and lodging.

Ruth knows nothing of the gospel story, so far as Iris can tell. Her attention, such as it is, is caught by things seen, rather than by things heard. "Look!" says Iris suddenly. "The Queen of the Hairy-Chinned Gypsies!" It's that palsied old woman with the sticks, the spider woman poking along in the shadow of the apse. But when they draw closer, she's gone. Slipped out a side door? Or scurried in spider form up a pillar of Saint Bavo's, where she crouches, drinking in the news of people's murmured secrets?

Iris isn't accustomed to befriending children her own age. Having Ruth in the family has always meant that other children kept their distance. But maybe Iris can entice Clara with the appeal of the supernatural—especially if Clara is a supernatural child, a replacement creature left behind by thwarties when they stole the real Clara-baby away.

The next day, Iris pitches her voice to carry up the stairs, and she calls out, "Ruth, do you remember yesterday when we saw the Queen of the Hairy-Chinned Gypsies? And how she changed herself into a spider and fled from us?"

It takes only a minute to work. Clara appears at the head of the stairs.

Iris glances into the upper hall, which in its walnut paneling seems, even at noon, nearly dusky. She's amazed and a little frightened. Clara is almost like a ghost, a lambent thing with one hand out against the wall, a shimmeringness in the gloom, like a candle in a midnight forest. She is stunning to look at, with her immaculate skin and her dried-wheat hair. She comes forward, her eyes are hooded and sulky, and her lower lip protrudes in a way that can only mean trouble.

"Come down, some milk and bread, and a little honeyed fruit. It's time to meet this Iris," says Henrika calmly through the open door of her private office. At her table, in grey mid-morning light, she hunches working over a ledger book, an inky quill in one hand, rapid counting on the fingertips of the other.

"Ruth, the old Queen had legs like a spider's, but they were as huge as the hoop of a wagon wheel, weren't they?" says Iris.

Clara ventures down the stairs, close to the wall, but even behaving skittishly, she moves with poise.

"Have your breakfast, we're going out when you're dressed," Iris says to Clara with a nonchalant bossiness she doesn't quite feel. Clara slips into a chair and grabs some bread. Her father smiles and nods at her.

"Oh, Iris, but you won't go *out*," calls Henrika from her worktable. Her fingers are stained with ink, and she curses in a manner acceptable for well-bred goodwives.

"I want to take her to Saint Bavo's," says Iris. "We might be able to find the Queen of the Hairy-Chinned Gypsies, or the dwarf with the arms of an ape."

"Clara doesn't go out," says Henrika. "Well, in the walled garden, for some air, of course." Now she appears at the doorway, fixing Iris with a stern look. "She hasn't been away from home for three years. Not since a housemaid once shared some gossip: A changeling child had been born to a glassblower's daughter. Clara so pestered me to go look at it! I was worn down at last and, covering her with hood and cloak, I agreed to take her there and back again."

"A changeling?" says Iris. How can Henrika say such a thing so openly?

"By the time we got there, the thing had died, and crows had borne its body away."

"Oh," says Iris. Maybe Henrika doesn't know the gossip about her daughter Clara. "What did the crows do with the changeling's body?"

"Dropped it in the Haarlemsmeer, where all children without souls swim until the Judgment Day."

"But I hear they would like to drain the Haarlemsmeer," says Margarethe, bringing cheese from the kitchen and placing it where Clara can reach it. "What will happen to all the drowned soulless babies then?"

"I suspect they will be channeled out to sea," says Henrika calmly. "I don't really know. I have my mind on my figures."

"We could go look for a changeling, I suppose," says Iris craftily, peering at Clara to see if any interest is piqued. Clara looks curious but wary.

But Henrika holds out her quill like a finger, wagging it at Iris. "This is entirely forbidden. You may go out into the garden, or into any room of the house if you knock at the door first. But you may not bring Clara out the front door or out the side gate. Nor may you climb like an urchin over any wall or drop out of any window. You may not slither up the chimney nor burrow through the cellars. Do you understand me?"

"We are prisoners?" says Iris.

"Clara isn't fit for the world. She trembles so and breaks into chills. Visit the garden and the sheds beyond. Clara knows where she's permitted to go."

Up until now van den Meer has been bathing his face in the steam from his boerenkoffie, which combines the smells of the warmed beer, sugar, and nutmeg with the mattressy odor of his beard. But he tilts his chin parallel to the table and says, as if the next installment in an ongoing argument, "Do you remember hearing that in Delft the clergy banned gingerbread men at the feast of Sinter Klaas? And the children rebeled. They ran shrieking through the streets and wouldn't do their tasks. *Children will rebel eventually, my dear.*"

Henrika settles her hands at her side and lowers her eyes. In an apologetic tone, addressing the tabletop, she replies, "I am speaking to Iris. I am not speaking to you."

Van den Meer nods affably and says no more. But Iris sees the truth in Margarethe's observation: Although Henrika wears a guise of pretty deference, she acquiesces to no one, least of all her husband.

When Clara, who has appeared to pay little attention to this, finishes nibbling, Iris says, "I'll get my sister and we'll go outside into the garden. We'll wait for you there. Come out when you have dressed."

Iris finds Ruth. Iris hates using her sister like this, but huge Ruth may be a more likely attraction than Iris. After all, it was Margarethe's tussle with Ruth that caused Clara to lean out the window and scrutinize the ox girl. Perhaps, being disappointed in never seeing a changeling baby, Clara had seen the howling older Fisher girl as the next best thing: a grotesque.

The back of the house opens out onto a sizable lot, bricked and gated and those iron gates locked. To one side, a kitchen yard for washing and food preparation, for the growth of herbs and vegetables. To the other side, opening off the salon, a small garden, Italianate in design, with pebbled paths and orderly plantings, and pilasters at regular intervals surmounted by granite balls. Behind both kitchen yard and formal garden stands a huge shed, and beyond that is a farmyard, where the chickens and a cow are kept, and maybe other animals as well. The shed door, opening off the kitchen yard, has been locked so far.

Iris sinks onto the grass in the garden. Ivy crawls up two walls, making a green rustle when the wind pushes through. Ruth collapses next to her and moans in gentle hunger, for she adores gingerbread and the mention of it has likely made her mouth water. "No gingerbread," says Iris firmly.

When Clara emerges, she looks sly, but less truculent. Probably she's remembered that, after all, this is her home. It's *her* world. She pads across the grass to where the Fisher sisters are waiting. A cat, nearly lemon-colored, follows.

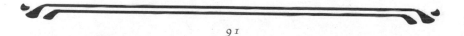

Iris decides that the problem of teaching English to Clara can wait. She lies with her head in the grass and doesn't look at Clara, but says, "Why did you want to see the changeling so much?"

"Tell me about the Queen of the Gypsies," says Clara. "Is she the Queen of Changelings too?"

"What is your interest in changelings?"

"Can't you tell? I am a changeling," says Clara.

"I've heard that said. But of course you're not," says Iris. "Changelings can't speak and run and think as people can."

"Maybe changelings in England can't," says Clara calmly. "Changelings here can."

Iris thinks of the face at the upmost window that first day—was it Clara in shadows, or Henrika in veils, or van den Meer himself, bearded and browed—or someone else?

Or something else?

"The devil himself will send out a whiskery hound to snuff us out!"—

Iris rushes on, to keep away from that notion. An imp here, knowing all things, lodged since before their arrival, awaiting them? "Did you ever see a changeling? I mean, other than yourself?" she says.

Clara shrugs. Her eyes slide over to Ruth and then slide away.

"Ruth is a big girl, a bit stupid, that's all," says Iris. "She's not a changeling."

"How do you know for sure?" says Clara. "Isn't she older than you?"

"Yes."

"Well, she would have been changed before you were born."

"Nonsense."

"Ask your mother."

"I won't. It's foolishness."

"Ask your father."

The wind blows the ivy for moments while Iris watches it. Eyes narrowed, Clara then says, "What?"

Iris doesn't answer.

Clara crawls a little closer. She studies Iris, as a small child will study a bug before smashing it with a stone. "Where is your father? Is he a changeling? Did he fly away?" There's no caress of tenderness in her words, but some unrefined brutality. But when Iris won't speak, Clara sighs, moves on, bored. "Well, then, tell me something else. Tell me about yourself. You aren't a changeling, just a child. I hardly ever meet children. Why are you called Iris?"

"It means a kind of flower," snaps Iris, angry at herself for the tears.

"Oh," says Clara in a superior voice. "Flowers. I know flowers. All we ever hear about is *tulip flowers*. We have a lot of plants growing under a glass roof behind the sheds, and somewhere to the south of town, a well-guarded plantation in the polderlands. Shall we look in the sheds?"

"Later," says Iris. "I've told you about my name. Now you tell me why you think you're a changeling."

"Because this is all the world I have. The greater world is poison to a changeling; I would die. So I am kept, for my own

health and good, merely here: in the pretty prison house, with this small room of outside adjacent to it." Suddenly Clara hoists her skirts to her knees and races back and forth across the sheltered space. She touches each of the three walls of the garden that cage them. "What is mine? These are mine: the song of birds, though you can't always see them. Pouncer the cat, when he wants to stay with me. Sometimes he doesn't. Look, the flat sky that sits on the garden walls like a leaden roof. Some snails. The same old bushes. Soon there will be enough dead leaves to have a fire, and then smoke will be a rope up into the sky. That's mine. It's all I have."

"There's a linden tree," says Iris.

"Where?"

"You can just catch sight of the crown of it. It must be growing on the other side of your garden wall."

"A bird in it. A green finch. That's mine. And that's all." Clara smacks her lips angrily. "At least it's not a crow."

"A green finch in a linden tree," says Iris. "Is it a magic finch?"

Clara looks suspiciously at Iris, as if afraid of being thought gullible. Clara's next question is partly taunting and partly hopeful. "Did you really meet a Queen of the Gypsies?"

Iris feels a bit guilty. Any old hobbled dame isn't an ancient angel; old women are just old women. Iris shrugs, noncommittal.

Clara responds with sass, as if to prove she doesn't care. "Let's go look at the tulips. We own many of them, to grow, to show, to sell. Since I'm not allowed to go outside of these walls, I can go to the shed and look, and the gardeners don't mind."

"My mother may mind."

Clara gives a shrug. "But my mother doesn't care, and it's her house, not your mother's. It doesn't matter if your mother minds. Come, Iris. Come, you too, Ruth." Ruth prefers to stay where she is.

The tulip shed is beyond the herb garden, reached through the kitchen door. Sided to shoulder height with rough-milled boards, it's open to the elements for a foot or two above. The boards of the roof aren't all fixed with nails. Some boards can be shifted so that in warm weather sun can come in, while the shed's walls protect the plants from the worst of the wind.

The plants are arranged in terra-cotta trays with porous bottoms. The trays stand on rough tables, and the soil of the nursery floor is dank. The plants appear in ranks, the bulbs apparently having been sunk at intervals of two or three weeks apart. Here are the newest trays of plantings, where nothing shows yet through the reddish-brown soil. Beyond, trays in which plants send up their shoots, trays where the plants grow taller, and then develop a head and some leaves. Finally, near where Iris and Clara stand, the flowers begin to show some color and to open up their petals.

Iris doesn't know how much Clara comprehends the world, but she does take part in her family's concern for the flowers. There are many different varieties of tulip, she tells Iris in a teacherly voice, and new fashions are being imported from the East on a monthly basis. The family's plantation beyond town is immense, but even within this small nursery there are eight varieties in full or near flower, not counting a few ranks that have passed their prime. Perhaps a hundred and twenty blossoms now? Some are all red and pink and orange, a study in burning colors; many are striped with red and white. Iris doesn't like the tulip's inelegant stem, which seems thick and lacking in grace, but the flowers have heavy heads, something like roses, and maybe those stems need to be strong as cane stalks.

A gardener comes through a door at the back and makes a remark that Iris can't hear, but she understands the tone. Gardeners don't want girls to be playing in the shed. Iris begins to back away, saying, "Come, come, Clara, let's go back to our small garden, where we can run without risk of damaging these things."

Clara doesn't speak at first. Iris doesn't know what is on her mind. Then Clara says, "Aren't these the finest of treasures? Each one springs up, and becomes more red than rubies, more fine than diamonds and more valuable, so we are told; and before you can run back here again to look, the petals have begun to drop and the leaves to yellow. Look, they sag, they fall. Are they the more wonderful because they live such a short time?"

"Like changeling babies?" says Iris, regretting the words almost the moment they're out of her mouth. More forcefully she says, "Let's talk about it away from here."

"Semper Augustus, Viceroy, the yellow-red of Leiden, I know these better than I know my Scripture verses," says Clara in a singsong manner. "The white crowns, the Admiral de Maans, the General Bols. The Pope's Head! They bloom and wither in a month's time. Here Papa tries to force the bulbs, for purposes of exciting investors, but out in the polder-fields, they grow only once a year, and bloom in the early spring, never to return."

Clara sighs. She stands, a young thing with a heavy adult thought in her mind, as Iris backs away. It's almost a dark thought, though Iris can't quite name it. A sudden slide of light comes through a shifting of clouds, slanting between two roof boards that have been pulled aside. Clara's hair blazes, white fire; suddenly Iris can't see her, just a glare of light, a child in an inside garden. For an instant Iris believes Clara really is a changeling.

Small Oils

Canvases, blocks of wood, varnished planks. Mounds of white powder, and blue, and red, and ochre. Stands of brushes in chipped clay pots. The smell, both intoxicating and vile, of oils and turps, and of minerals in their little heaps. Caspar, for the Master and for himself, sorts the ingredients, grinds, sifts, dampens, and seals them in small bowls with wax lids. Painting has come to the strict brick house on the western edge of the Grotemarkt.

Iris watches. It takes a long time for the Master to compose his painting. He moves Clara here, he moves her there. He sits her, he stands her. A hand on her waist, a hand at her bonnet strings, a hand on the table, a hand on her chin. Should she wear an apron and a cap, or her mother's rare jewels? This pose too dainty? This too coy, this too womanly? "No single position catches all of her grace," says the Master defensively when, after a week of hanging back, van den Meer looks in.

"This must be your masterpiece," says van den Meer. "But if you wait a year to decide on a stance for your model, the market for tulips may have softened and I won't have the money to pay you."

That day the Master decides.

It's a conventional pose, the Master tells Iris. Clara stands a few feet in from a window on the left. A spray of tulips lies cradled in her left hand, which falls in a soft curve onto a well-appointed tabletop. She holds a tulip bulb in her right hand and studies it as if entranced at the mystery that such imperial blooms can be generated from so humble a bulb. The sunlight, see, will sink at a noontime angle, and it will drop only on the edge of Clara's face, and on one tulip fallen out of the bouquet. The rest of Clara's form will be done in softer colors, set off by the shadow of the room, its costly dark-framed mirror, its chest of drawers, its tiles arranged around the corner of the mantelpiece.

But the color of the tulips? Van den Meer fusses about this. He wants the Master to use the *exact color and pattern* of the tulip that will be shipped in bulk the following month, and not available for growing and subsequent blossoming till the spring, if that. What color and pattern is that? "It's red," says van den Meer vaguely, "with a white stripe, a sort of pantaloon-ish look."

"Red," says the Master witheringly, "*red?* And how does the stripe go, exactly? I'll paint from nature or not at all."

Van den Meer scowls and scolds, while Iris huddles with her arms clapped around herself. She hears about how hard it is to fund such a commercial venture, and the financial risks that are run, especially by the weavers of Haarlem, who are very involved this year. The Master pays little mind. Calmly

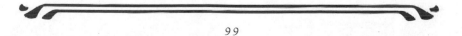

he continues to sketch the form of Clara in the elegant room, swiping the canvas with a rag reeking with linseed oil, correcting a mistake.

"Of course," says van den Meer, looking out the window and stroking his beard, almost as if talking to himself, "I could always, at this late date, decide to solicit the help of your rival, Bollongier."

"Damn you, damn damn damn," says the Master. "If I go back to painting my catalogue of God's errors, I paint you next, you brute. The worst flaw in God's plan: the henpecked husband. The unnatural in nature—"

At van den Meer's glance, the Master stops. He sighs. He agrees to paint whatever wretched variety of striped tulip van den Meer requires, as long as multiple plants are forced into bloom for the Master to examine during the preliminary studies and the final painting. Van den Meer accedes to this.

After a week, Clara refuses to sit for the sketches anymore. And Henrika seems ready to permit this drastic change of plans. But—maybe shamed by the Master's coarse remark about him—van den Meer puts his foot down and takes Henrika aside into her small office. There are loud words from both sides, and even with the door closed, everyone on the ground floor can hear about guilders and florins, risks and rewards.

Iris listens to all this. When Clara is pouting upstairs that evening, Iris murmurs to Henrika, "Why doesn't Clara want to sit for sketches?"

Henrika looks annoyed at this remark. Van den Meer

says, "Clara insists that the Master is rude and doesn't want to talk to her, only to look at her."

"It *is* tedious to sit so still," says Iris. "If you like, I can come in and engage her with tales told in English. She can listen while she poses."

Van den Meer says, "A charitable offer. So you're growing fond of our precious Clara?"

Iris wouldn't put it like that. She thinks: I am growing fond of these good meals. But the truth is that though Clara is willful and timid at once, grander-than-thou while still sucking her thumb, Iris feels at least a grudging regret for the girl. Never to go out beyond the house or garden walls!

Clara likes tales, so she agrees to return. Iris spins out fanciful episodes of her own design, peopled by talking animals, thwarties and household imps, fairies and saints, and the occasional magic comb, cooking pot, or horsehoe. Iris often weaves her tales around a poor benighted girl who is afraid to stray from home, but who is constantly tricked into leaving, or expelled, or jettisoned by force of earthquake, or blown out a window by a huge wind. Clara is made to smile, at least.

Henrika is quiet and pretends to be busy, but Iris notices that when Caspar or the Master are in the house, Henrika is never more than one room away from Clara. Henrika hovers like a bee over a flower, thinks Iris; then she remembers the painting of Henrika in her black-and-yellow bumblebee silks.

When he is not assisting the Master, Caspar does quick studies of his own. They are sketches in oils rather than completed paintings. Caspar has a gift for line but no strong eye

for color, so for the time being he roughs out domestic scenes on boards. Using reddish outlines, he lays in washes of ochre, highlighted with white when the underpainting is dry. He studies scenes of domestic labor with a certain mad joy.

Though Iris is bewitched by Caspar's small oils, she won't allow herself to be drawn—not after Ugly Girl with Wildflowers. Never again. But Ruth has no pride. Ruth doesn't compose her features to close him out.

A small cartoon of Ruth. The big girl is sitting almost elegantly, on a stool in the kitchen. She clenches the black kettle between her knees. She holds a spoon with two hands, in the true way Ruth does, stirring with the whole strength of her upper body. Her bowed hump of soft shoulders is rendered honestly but not with scorn.

Margarethe, looking over Iris's shoulder at this sketch, observes sharply, "You'd think the kettle is filled with limestone cement, the way Ruth seems to be applying such force to that spoon!"

"But that's how she looks," says Iris, marveling.

"I believe I was having her stir a respectable pottage," says Margarethe. "This painting implies an incompetence in the kitchen. Throw it out." But she's only teasing. Iris wonders: Is Margarethe pleased that Caspar had the charity to paint Ruth without correction of her features? Does Margarethe feel for her older daughter in some way that she rarely shows? Well, of course she must, or why endure such troubles of taking her children across the sea?

Ruth herself crows and claps to see Caspar's cartoons. She doesn't seem confused about the nature of the image on the board, and grins in her splay-toothed way at herself stirring dinner. She smiles at Caspar and lurches off to the kitchen to find him a strip of salted fish as a present, which he accepts with a bow.

Caspar's portrait of Margarethe is equally benign. Here she is in the herb garden, in the act of rising: one knee still to the ground, one foot planted in its muddy wooden shoe. She has a basket of simples across one forearm, articulated, Iris sees, by broken scratchy lines, parallel at one end for the stems, and fretted at the other to suggest all manner of seeds, leaves, and dried flowers. The delight, though, is in Margarethe's expression. It almost makes tears stand in Iris's eyes. Her mother as a laborer, at peace for once, for there's nothing lovely or unlovely about herbs, and they behave and they don't bother her.

Iris examines this study with delight. The well-regulated house looms up, brick and ivy and shutters and copings. Only on the third viewing does she notice that Caspar has painted a head of Henrika, looking down with a scowl out of an upper window. Henrika is never seen with any such scowl, and yet it is demonstrably she.

"Her head is too big for the window frame," says Iris helpfully.

"Yes," says Caspar.

She's embarrassed. She's tried to critique the sketch, and he's refused her stupid opinion. She rushes on, more generously. "Caspar, what you can do! A portrait of Mama and Henrika!"

"Not at all," he says, "I'm merely illustrating the old adage: Two dogs and one bone will rarely agree."

Iris bows to look again. Is this what she had seen on the day she'd arrived at this house? Had it been Henrika peering from the window that day?

Or is this clot of dark in Caspar's sketch, in a window even higher up, the last square of glass under the roof beam, actually a squinting, hunched creature of some sort? Is it just scrawled darkness, scribbled in, or can she make out tiny, leering features?

"Have you drawn an imp in this house?" says Iris, looking up.

"I didn't know you could see it too," he says, but then will say no more.

The
Masterpiece

The painting of Clara grows more and more like her—
thus more and more beautiful. Though Iris still has
never trespassed in the gallery of God's blunders, the Master's locked studio on the other side of town, she's sure that
no painting in the Master's house can be anywhere near as
compelling as this one. True, saints are inevitably good-
looking. All the Master's portraits of the holy populace have
been wreathed in light, their eyes crazy with vision. And the
Master's brutes must be as wretched as the saints are sacred.
The extreme edges of human possibility.

But Clara is merely splendid. Splendid as a human being.
Not only a heartbreaking concoction of blonds, cherry
blushes, and blue-ochre shadows, but a real girl, with an airy
hesitation that seems as much about her good looks as anything else. The tulips that languish in the bow of her left arm
look up toward her as a baby one day might.

Iris studies the painting in the late afternoon when the
Master has denounced the light for being fickle, as he does

daily, and stalked away. Caspar, who still makes his home with the Master but eats better in the van den Meer kitchen yard, brings Iris in to see. "He would have preferred a commission to do the civic guards. But he has always wanted to paint this legendary perfect child. Can you tell what he has done?" says Caspar. "Do you see how he's intensified the orange in this fold of carpet, so now the blues of her eyes blink three different ways at you instead of two?"

"I don't," says Iris. "But I see that it is more wonderful." And she thinks the Master has painted a kinder expression in Clara's eyes than is strictly warranted.

"Do you see the composition, a series of boxes, look, nine of them of different sizes—here, and here, and here—" Caspar points them out. "And broken in two places only, by this large curve that, since it is shadowed, only hints at a surprise, and then this tulip in full light, here? See how it seems about to fall off the floor?"

"I want to catch it," says Iris, laughing. "I want to save it."

"He teases, and pleases, and makes you stare, and slowly you come to realize that this isn't just any child, but a bloom as perfect as a tulip."

"She is looking at the bulb," says Iris. "She doesn't notice that the tulip is about to fall. Doesn't it make you uneasy?"

"She is noticing one thing and not noticing another, all happening at once," says Caspar. He chuckles; he's just realizing the cleverness of the Master's composition. "Look, and also this: It is about beginnings and endings, for here in the one hand is the hideous bulb, just as well lit as the tulip on the table. He has thought of how to catch us again and again!

There are so many things to see! And not only his brush techniques, which bewilder me and make me think I will never learn."

"You learn a lot and you see a lot," says Iris. "Remember that sketch you did of my mother in the herb garden, and Henrika in the house behind her. You caught as much there as the Master has here." She continues, "Only what you caught isn't as pretty to see."

Caspar slides her a sideways glance. "You're observant as a painter yourself, then, if you perceive that," he says in a confiding voice. Iris shivers with the compliment as if with a sudden chill.

Another thing that Iris notices about the Master's painting of Clara and the tulips is that its increasing perfection doesn't seem to make him elated but rather despondent. He won't talk to Iris about this—in fact, he has little use for her at all now that he has earned the commission. But he mutters to himself. Iris knows this. When she and Clara have tired of English, and fall into a sleepy state, Iris likes to hear the Master fret even as he adores his own work. Soon the day comes when he no longer needs Clara except once in a while, to assess skin tones relative to fabric or background. Still he mutters all the more.

His worry seems to revolve around how well the painting is going. He knows that it's sublime. He doesn't know if it will do the job that Cornelius van den Meer and cronies require of it— to work the viewing public into an even more hearty appetite for the very strain of tulip bulbs they are importing from Vienna and points east—but he no longer cares about that. He sings, not to Clara but to the painting of Clara, to the blue-brown shadows behind the open window, to the highlights in the silver salver on the mantel, to the folds in the apron, the bonnet, and the linen cloth on the table. He fusses over the glints in the diamond pendants, the mirrored gleams of the three ropes of pearl. He sings, and then he hisses in between his teeth as if in pain.

He touches the canvas with strokes more and more gentle and hesitant. "I am going to ruin you yet," he says once, and Iris, listening, thinks: Ruin who? Ruin you, exquisite painting? Ruin yourself, Master Luykas Schoonmaker? Ruin you, Clara van den Meer, real girl at the edge of childhood?

So he works more and more slowly, as if the tiniest touch of a brush might suddenly turn his masterpiece into a laughingstock. He stands back farther and farther from it, studying it for long stretches. He approaches the painting as a farmboy approaches a bull—gently, wishing it does not need to be done. He takes the troublesome jewels back to his studio, to do further studies, and get the rich highlights right.

Iris picks up another side to his unhappiness too. It seems that the more wonderful this painting becomes, the less chance there is of the Master's ever surpassing it. The more perfect every succulent detail, the more devastating. He weeps over his painting. He looks an old man, or, thinks Iris, like the old man he will soon become. Is that merely the contrast with Clara, so fresh, so young, so beautiful on the canvas? No. The painting itself is making him old, for he is struggling, as if he'll never have courage again to try to love the world in oil and varnish, canvas and light.

Rue, Sage, Thyme, and Temper

The day comes when the painting is done but for the caresses of varnish needed to protect against the ravages of centuries. All varnishes can't go on at once; some can be applied only after the painting has dried for months. It amazes Iris that the Master can think about the painting surviving for longer than his lifetime, but when she makes a joke about it he snaps at her. "And what makes you think beauty should go in and out of fashion like—like a rage of eating with forks, or an obsession with the music of the virginal—or a madness to adore tulips, for that matter? Will future generations look at this child and not be stunned by her perfection?"

"They'll be stunned by Schoonmaker's capturing of her perfection," intones Caspar, and this time it's not a poke but a compliment.

"And why not?" says the Master, unable to be humble now. He has no energy.

"I suspect," says Margarethe, passing through with a clutch of humble roots in her hands, "that they'll think you've flattered the child. They won't believe she looked so angelic." She says this with a measure of—what? Something that Iris can't name.

Henrika and Cornelius van den Meer plan a feast for their friends in Haarlem and Amsterdam, for those who have staked sums of capital on the tulip cargoes, and also for those whose tongues are waggish and whose wallets are heavy. It takes a number of days to arrange, to borrow benches from neighbors, to clean the strict house from front to back, from attic to cellars. Margarethe begins to sulk at Henrika and, from time to time, to disagree pointedly, even noisily, over methods of housewifery.

Iris helps, and turns out drawers and pokes in attic corners, looking for something magical here, a dragon's claw, the skeleton of a dead boggart, a fragment of the True Cross with which to work miracles. She finds nothing of the sort. She can't shuck off the feeling that the house is hiding something from her, though. The high, narrow place is haunted somehow, possessed by something fierce and potent, something gifted at disguise. She whirls about, trying to catch sight of it in the edges of the house's many looking glasses. Whatever it is—imp or else-thing—it's deft. It eludes her.

When the day of the party arrives at last, so too does autumn's first really biting cold weather. Late in the afternoon Iris and Ruth sweep fallen linden leaves off the paths in the garden. That is, Ruth pretends to sweep them first, and Iris follows up doing the actual job. The idea of a banquet makes the sisters giddy. Van den Meer has said they might sit in the kitchen and peer in from the doorway, as long as they make no noise, and remove themselves to their pallets in the cranny if Henrika tells them to go.

"It'll be night, and tapers will be lit, and there'll be music," says Iris, as much to herself as to Ruth. "And we'll look clean and smart, even though no one will see us." Margarethe has laundered their best aprons, and attempted some clumsy stitchwork upon the pockets. She pricked her finger and cursed and kept on, no matter how tired she became or how low the light guttered, and Iris and Ruth are thrilled with the idea of wearing clothes made pretty for a feast.

Clara, however, is cross. Van den Meer has told her that she may not sit in the kitchen with Iris and Ruth. Clara has to dress like an adult and dine with the rest of the guests. Clara applies to Henrika, expecting her to intervene as usual. But Henrika's face goes strangely aggrieved, and she won't even discuss the subject.

So Clara sulks in the kitchen while the Fisher sisters perform their chores.

"It isn't fair," says Clara. "I don't want to be snapped at and stared over like a new statue from France or a brass vase from Persia. I want to be in the kitchen with you."

"The perils of being the child of rich parents," says Margarethe smugly. "Suffer."

"What?" says Clara. Iris swivels her head at the edge in Clara's tone, but Margarethe is too busy to notice the danger.

"The changeling has to change herself again, this time into an adult," says Margarethe, as roughly as if Clara were her own daughter. "Live with what life brings you, young one, or you stay young and stupid forever—"

Clara starts up like a cat whose tail has been trod upon. It is one thing to play at being a changeling, thinks Iris, quite another to be teased about it! By an adult, no less.

Holding her fists an inch or two on either side of her ears, Clara begins to scream. Margarethe looks up guiltily. Clara yells that she won't dress to please her mother or her father, she won't speak nicely to the guests, and she won't come out of the kitchen. And besides that, she hopes the painting of Young Woman with Tulips will explode into flames. And she hates her mother and her father.

Iris and Ruth are frozen, not knowing what to do.

Margarethe takes to churning as a way of blocking out the noise. Iris is guilty: Too many stories about poor, timid girls who learn to have brave hearts? "Hush, Clara," says Iris, "you'll wake the imp!"

With her soft step, Henrika arrives. She insists that there's no more to discuss about it and that Clara is being wicked. Clara apparently intends to stay being wicked, for she won't stop screaming. Not until Ruth bursts into tears and sinks to her knees at Clara's hems, and wraps her awkward arms around the girl's hips. "Go away, you ugly ogre," says Clara—in passable English, Iris has to note. But Ruth has no faculty for shame and she doesn't budge, and eventually Clara collapses into her arms, mewing.

"No child of mine ever screamed like a hellcat," observes

Margarethe to the butter churn.

"That'll do, Clara," says Henrika, but it's clear she's speaking to Margarethe.

Clara sprints out to the walled garden, and Ruth lumbers after her. They leave the door open. Clara flings gravel at birds. Ruth runs her hands through the ivy. The air in the kitchen grows dank, though nothing has changed in the weather. The wind is still brisk, the sea air bracing. Beyond, rooks still caw and squabble over the tulip sheds. The light still seeps its thin yellow through the open door onto the gray flagstones.

Henrika turns her back to Margarethe. By habit Iris glances into the mirror, hoping to snatch a view of some peppery household spirit, but instead she sees the corner of Henrika's face. Henrika is vexed: both angry and anxious. The beautiful brow is furrowed, and Henrika pinches her lower lip between her teeth, thinking.

"A good dose of chamomile will settle her down," says Margarethe nonchalantly.

"Don't lecture me on the management of my own child," says Henrika in a cold voice, and she sweeps from the room.

"I was trying to *assist*," says Margarethe after her, with exaggerated politeness.

"Mama," says Iris, "you're not minding your tongue."

"Who are you to tell me to mind my tongue?" says Margarethe, languorously.

"What's gotten into you? You always say that we might be tossed out of here if we're not well behaved. There are others who can do the work we do!"

Margarethe puts aside the butter churn. She folds over a cloth to reveal a pair of dead hares roped at the ears. "There are few certainties in our lives, to be sure, but we won't be turned out for a moment's honest remark," says Margarethe.

"This isn't like you," says Iris. "You're the one who worries in August if the spring will come soon enough next March."

Margarethe beckons Iris near and whispers, "Haven't you noticed that queen-bee Henrika is with child?"

Though Iris thinks herself clever, she hasn't noticed this.

"Oh, it's early yet, but at the moment Henrika can't abide the look of food staring up from the kettle or spit. She can't afford to turn me out now. I'm too well trained in the ways of her household, and this feast is very important."

Iris doesn't answer. She doesn't like her mother to be fawning, but for her mother to be impertinent is equally upsetting. "She's our hostess and our protector," says Iris at last. "Can't you like her?"

"Like her? And what is there of her to like? That her father did handsomely in business? That she has pretensions toward a well-shaped mind? That she coddles her daughter and swaddles her into an unusual infancy? That she does the girl no good? The girl is rotten, or can't you see it?"

"So you notice Clara's unhappiness, at least," says Iris.

"Put it like this," says Margarethe. "If Ruth is trapped by her afflictions, to hobble and bawl through all her days, Clara is trapped as well. She's expected to be endlessly docile. Who knows why—because she's so attractive? We're all in our own prisons, I suppose, but Clara's is made worse for her by the fears and strengths of her mother. And maybe by her father's weakness."

"And what is the shape of your prison?" says Iris.

Margarethe rubs her nose and says, "There was always a window. You can endure any sort of prison if you can apprehend a window in the dark. Your father was that window for me. When he died, the window was shut. Oh, I know, you ache at the mention of Jack Fisher, but even so."

"You're going to go the rest of your life without another window somewhere in the dark?"

"You look for it," says Margarethe, suddenly impatient with such prattle. "I'm busy now. I have to skin this brace of hares."

Iris sits at her mother's side and watches. "Tell me what to do, I should know about this," she says.

"So you may find yourself at home in some burgher's kitchen when you are my age, preparing food for guests who won't see your face or ask your name," says Margarethe. "Why should I teach you a whit of it?"

"Because I'm ugly," says Iris, "and I have to know these things, so I can take care of myself someday."

Margarethe runs her hands over the hares as if she is trying to keep from tearing them apart with her fingers. She breathes heavily. Then she says, "Well, then, my dear, look carefully."

Mother and daughter labor over the carcass, removing unwanted extremities, bones, organs. Margarethe shows Iris how to peel back the skin of the skull, how to handle the flesh so it doesn't pull away from the bone too soon, how to rub scatterings of sage, thyme, and tarragon, to turn a dead animal into a sumptuous meal. After a while Henrika pads back into the kitchen. They all work side by side without speaking, selecting the most perfect fruits, withdrawing the bread from the side oven, hurrying with the newly purchased quails, for the hour is approaching when Young Woman with Tulips will be unveiled for the ravenous merchants.

Reception

The candles are lit, the tables spread with linen, and Henrika has seated herself at the virginal. "What a pretty picture," says Margarethe to van den Meer, but he doesn't hear the sourness in her voice, and he merely answers, "Oh, yes, isn't she?"

Two maidens from a household down the street have come to assist in the serving, so Margarethe can stand at the door and supervise both kitchen and dining salon at once. Caspar has been engaged to collect cloaks and staffs and hats. Iris and Ruth bring stools to the doorway and sit there, wondering about Clara, until at last there's a knock on the door and the first of the burghers arrives.

Almost at once a second guest knocks, and his wife behind him, so Caspar is kept busy, and Iris has to help. Henrika pauses at the virginal as if surprised by visitors. She plays the same melody each time until she is stopped by the new arrivals.

The Master appears. His new coat with its bit of braid can't disguise his fretfulness. He makes a round about the hall, greeting those he knows, mumbling shy hellos to strangers. Almost at once he escapes to the kitchen, where he shucks off the new coat and sits on the stool that Iris has vacated. He holds Ruth's hand for a bit.

"They're a worthy lot," says the Master to Margarethe, who, though in the midst of last-minute preparations, takes a moment to sneer.

"Stuffed pheasants and perfumed peacocks, full of airs. They're only merchants, not nobility," says she.

"They admire the talented and they count themselves as learned. Do you know that some of them have invested in the settlement of the New Netherlands across the tremendous Atlantic?"

"They have an uncommon passion for paintings, these Dutch," says Margarethe, as if in this instance she understands herself to be entirely and safely English.

"And why shouldn't they?" asks the Master. "The marvelous Reformation has torn away icon and ornament from the churches. What's left for the hungry eye to admire? My fellow Dutchmen make do with tedious scenes of the merry company. Scenes of meadow, woodland, the lot of the common husbandryman. Views of the city from this aspect or that. Or views of the comic lot of the desperately poor."

"If your painting is met with approval," says Margarethe, "just watch: You'll paint all of that. You'll spend your time gazing on the thick jowls and the double chins of everyone with guilders enough to pay you for their likeness."

"Don't remind me," says he. "My possible patrons are out there in the reception room right now."

"There's no shortage of subjects, Luykas, nor of coin to pay you for painting them."

"There's no shortage of painters in this part of Holland either."

She lays a pair of poached salmon on a salver and works them with her fingers to move the flesh back into correct form. "So you have a mixed mind? Like most of us. You want the work and the reputation, and you also want to despise your patrons for refusing to pay for religious subjects. This way you can be unhappy whatever happens next. Here, girl, this is ready; don't let the fish slide off onto the floor. Ruth, move your feet."

"You're a clever woman, Margarethe," says the Master. "If I'm honored and noticed tonight, as van den Meer suggests I will be, would you think of returning to my household and doing for me?"

"I think many things, silly and profound, each night as I put my head down between my daughters to take my rest."

"Well, add this proposal to your list."

Van den Meer is at the door. "Schoonmaker, we're going into the next room to show them your work," he says, "and you here gabbling in the vegetables like a soup boy? Get out here and prepare, at your advanced age, to make your career, and to make mine as well."

Van den Meer calls for Clara. When she doesn't come, he says to Margarethe, "Fetch her, please; she's upstairs and has to come down at once."

"I'm the princess of the pots and the hearth today, I'm not the nursery maid," says Margarethe. "Do it yourself."

"Though I'm distracted by the occasion," he replies formally, "I'm not insensible to insult, Margarethe Fisher."

Margarethe blushes; she's gone too far. She says in a low voice, "Iris, you do what's required now, in my stead."

Iris hurtles up the back stairs of the house. She goes to Clara's small chamber. The curtains of the bed nook are drawn. No candle is lit here, and shadows blunt the hard edges of the furniture.

"Clara?" says Iris. "Are you within?"

A rustle of bedclothes. Something is there.

"Clara?" Iris's voice is softer, frightened. "Come, open the curtains. Don't scare me so."

The twitch of the drape. The heave of labored breathing. Iris sweeps aside the cloth.

"Oh, come, what's the harm?" says Iris. She looks in and tries to smile.

The figure draws back, deeper into the shadows. "I hate them," says Clara.

"But why do you hate them? What have they done to you?"

"They walk about the world with such big steps," she says at last. Iris wonders if she means that they can stalk the world to their hearts' content without the supervision that every child chafes under, Clara more than most. But this is the way with grown people. It hardly seems a reason to hate them.

"If you go, and smile," says Iris, "and answer when you're spoken to, you can amuse them, and gratify your parents. Then when their attention is turned, for adults never think about one thing for long, you can walk away. They'll never notice."

"They already have me once," says the girl.

Iris says, "In the Master's painting. I know. I know. But you're beautiful enough to be seen in the flesh. Can't you be happy for that?"

"My father will sell his flowers," says Clara. "We'll become much wealthier than we are. I'm caught on that canvas to sell flowers."

"And so what does that matter?" says Iris. She has meant to be kind, but she's losing her patience. "When I was caught on a canvas by the Master, people laughed! There are worse things in the world than being a joy to behold and a use to your mother and your father."

"What would you know," says Clara, beginning to look wild, "your father is dead."

"None of that," says Iris, who is learning, "none of that!"

"Dead father, worms in his mouth, maggots in his eyes—"

"Come out of your bed," says Iris, "you little limb of Satan, come out; for if you don't, my mother and my sister and I will be thrown from your house for being unhelpful. And yes, my father is dead, and we can't afford to lose our position here. So if you won't descend the stairs for your own parents, for the sake of your future, then do it for me. Am I to be sent back to England, there to starve?"

It's a clumsy gambit, but it works. Clara throws her arms around Iris. "Don't go back to England," she says. "Learning English with you is the only joy I have." But the hug she gives Iris is hard and strong. The girl has arms like iron bars.

Iris goes on, trying not to flinch in Clara's embrace. "You would understand the joy of a full larder if you had ever had to live without one, and the joy of a living father if your father were dead. Let's not talk about this now. Come. Be brave like a girl in one of my stories."

So Iris pulls Clara down the back steps to the kitchen. Margarethe straightens Clara's clothes and pinches her cheeks. Van den Meer smiles vacantly, murmuring, "Follow me, duckling. We are just going in to view our future." Clara turns and looks one last time at Iris. Her eyes are nearly hollow. Her pretty upper lip twitches, twice.

Virginal

By the time the last guest has left, Clara is dead to the world, and Iris is barely awake herself. Ruth has crawled under the kitchen table and snores there in her ungainly way, her windmill fallen from her grasp. "It's the latest I've ever been up . . . the world is so still," says Iris, peering from the doorway. "Look, the stars almost clatter against each other, there are so many."

The Master calls for his coat. He's drunk and depressed over being so well celebrated. His apprentice, though, is giddy with relief. "Has it been a good evening, then, Caspar?" says Iris as Caspar supports the Master and slides an arm through his.

"The portrait of Clara excited everyone. It's the start of his career all over again," says Caspar. "If he doesn't choke in his sleep tonight, he's a made man. Your mother should consider his suggestion that she return to his household. He'll be able to afford it."

Iris doesn't know what she thinks. She's torn: the pleasure of being near the act of painting, or the benefit of a more assured schedule of meals in Henrika's well-run household? She answers Caspar merely with a happy shrug.

He leans down and puts his hand fondly on her brow. "You're a good child," he says. Then he and the Master depart, noisily, in streets that are slippery with a fine spray blown in from the midnight sea.

The door shuts, and Iris moves into the hall. Cornelius, Henrika, and Margarethe stand at various places in the room, their backs to each other: Henrika at the virginal, Cornelius before the painting, and Margarethe near the table littered with the pips and stems of the fruit and the rind of the cheese that finished the meal.

Though the adults are standing and facing in three directions, they're attending to each other too, in some way that Iris can't fathom—oh, she is sleepy! But she notices that Margarethe's hands at the table are dallying, not from exhaustion but from an effort to linger.

"We've had our triumph tonight, all of us," says van den Meer.

Henrika bows her head to the virginal. Margarethe nods her own head but doesn't answer.

"It's the beginning of our success, do you know what this means?" says van den Meer. "We were right to move slowly and to be sure that he was up to the job, that Schoonmaker. Our caution goaded him on. He surpassed every effort to date. He will not be known as the Master of the Dordrecht Altarpiece. He will be Schoonmaker, and Young Woman with Tulips will be admired and visited from afar. Soon we'll find the right venue in which to show it. People from as far away

as Florence and Rome will admire it, and admire our Clara—
and we will have no shortage of future investors either."

"I hate the thought of it being shown," says Henrika. Van
den Meer doesn't reply, and his wife continues in a quieter
tone. "She's never going to be more beautiful than she was
tonight."

At this van den Meer turns and drains a glass of port.
"What do you mean? Are you sad over the child's growing?"

She shakes her head. Van den Meer says, "There's the
new baby to make you happy, as Clara emerges into her adult
station. It's time for that."

"It's just that now," says Henrika, "Clara's beauty is
announced. The reputation of it will precede her, even in
this street."

"You couldn't wrap her in shawls forever," he says. "It's
been all these years till you would agree to another child, and
if you'd done it sooner, Henrika, you might have found a way
to release your loving claws off Clara before this. Let's hope
she can straighten out and thrive."

Henrika looks furiously sad. Van den Meer continues in a
kinder voice, "She'll be at home in any salon in the land;
she'll be welcome in France and England. She'll be a credit to
your family and to mine. She won't be able to help it."

Henrika turns her face. In the last of the candlelight, Iris
can see that tears are glistening. "Have we done well, husband?" she asks.

"Wife, we have triumphed, each one of us," says van
den Meer. "Nothing is lost tonight, and everything gained.
Schoonmaker walks away with appointments for five studio

visits from merchants wealthy enough to pay him hand-somely for his work. We've elevated our status here—"

"You've elevated your status," she says softly, reminding him that her bloodlines are too pure to be further purified.

He rolls over her remark, continuing, "—and we've im-pressed our colleagues with our ability to draw attention to our own stock of tulips. We've secured the rest of our invest-ment. We've introduced our daughter and launched her repu-tation as a figure of renown. We've worked hard for this, and there's nothing to be dismayed about. The conversation was brisk, the wine sweet, the food plentiful and delicious—"

"—Thank you," says Margarethe.

Van den Meer and his wife both look over at her. "You are indeed responsible," says Henrika, with no derision in her voice; she is too tired to squabble. "We're beholden to you for your skills."

"And to your daughter for befriending Clara and encour-aging her to come forward," says van den Meer.

"Then would this be the right time to approach you for a modest stipend?" says Margarethe.

"It's late, and I don't discuss such matters when I've been eating and drinking in such a full manner," says van den Meer.

"Besides," says Henrika, "this fine evening alone cost the household more than we could afford. And the new baby is on its way, and you know the fuss of that. Isn't it enough that you have a place to sleep and food to eat?"

"It is . . . gratifying," says Margarethe. "But my daughters are a little older than your Clara, and they don't have your

Clara's advantages. Put baldly, with their sorry looks, they are millstones around my neck. I have to think of them."

Iris shrinks back within the shadows. She doesn't like to hear such words.

"In any event," says van den Meer, "let's not mar this pleasant evening by such a discussion. Another time, Margarethe, tomorrow or the next day, find me in my hall and we'll consider the matter. I make no comment one way or another."

"But tonight I've received an offer of employment elsewhere," says Margarethe.

"Not from one of our guests!" says Henrika.

"Tomorrow is time enough, Henrika," says van den Meer.

"It's not to be endured," says Henrika. She sits up straight and holds her belly.

"It was from one of your guests," says Margarethe.

"Who?" says Henrika, in a passion.

"Henrika," says van den Meer warningly.

"It was from the Master. He believes that after tonight he'll be in a better position to afford to hire me as help. He's requested my return."

"Go then, go, if you must," says Henrika dismissively. "The ungratefulness!"

"We'll take this matter up in the morning," says van den Meer. "Margarethe, you're not doing the best for yourself."

"I don't ask to do the best for myself, only a little better than nothing," says Margarethe. "You've had a great success tonight, and you think you'll have more in the months to come. You'll be better prepared to reward a small staff. You've seen how I can serve, and serve I will."

"I protest this, Cornelius," says Henrika.

"You're too tired to protest, and you are with child," says her husband. "I will make the decision that needs to be made, and I will not make it tonight. How often have I to tell you this? Come, all, the lights are to be put out, the shutters barred and the food covered against the mice, and then to sleep. Our life begins again in the morning, as it always must."

"Who makes the decision that needs to be made?" asks Henrika as she blows the candle out. Iris sinks back in the darkness, ashamed of her mother's gall, but also proud of it.

Simples

"Clara's face is lengthening," says Margarethe. "If you still harbor some fancy that she is a changeling, Iris, notice that Clara is growing up. Changelings die young."

"*Some* changelings live to be old and broken," says Iris. "I saw an ancient madman with no teeth and cheeks as smooth as a melon. He laughed high and foolishly like any changeling."

"You beware your flighty mind!" says Margarethe. "It leads you astray into distracted moments, and then the devil will take you yet. Clara is no more a changeling than Ruth is."

Iris doesn't reply to this. She knows that though Ruth is huge, stupid, and inarticulate, she is herself and always has been. Iris can never know this of Clara, so the suspicion of a magical transformation will always linger, and can't be proven wrong.

The winter months grind along at their glacial rate. Margarethe and her daughters haven't returned to the Master's house on the poor side of town. Henrika's pregnancy is just too difficult. She doesn't carry herself easily. She complains of mysterious ailments, over which the midwives cluck their tongues with confusion. Is Henrika carrying twins perhaps? Has there been a change in her diet? Is the business worry suffered by Cornelius van den Meer proving to be conta-gious? Gossip has it that a fiscal crisis in the van den Meer household would be devastating. Much of Henrika's dowry has been advanced as collateral against business loans and would be lost.

Gossip also has it that there is a household demon living in the rafters of the attics, coming down only at dark, to gnaw at Henrika's innards and ruin her health.

Henrika takes to her bed more and more often. Van den Meer attends her with loving affection when his work allows. There *is* worry—it can't be kept hidden—about a missing ship that hasn't arrived in port with its expected cargo. Van den Meer and his colleagues disagree about whether to send out an investigator to trace the route and hunt for news. News, good or bad, will come eventually, but is it smarter to know of a disaster earlier, and thus prepare for it? The longer the wait, the stronger the storms of winter will become.

Margarethe is a boon to the household. True, Henrika complains about the English look of the food that Mar-garethe brings and sometimes even spoons into Henrika's mouth. Too salty, too savory, too foreign! "Always a remark," says Margarethe calmly. "Eat up, for your health." She knows that the queen bee of the household has little choice but to be grateful to the salaried chief of domestic affairs.

In the early part of winter Margarethe hangs the last of the herbs on strings about the kitchen and week by week, by

Henrika's special request, keeps a pot-au-feu on the hearth. The van den Meer household is much larger than any other Margarethe has lived in, and she takes to overseeing the cold room, the wine cellar, and whatever distant matters of barn-yard life that the hired men in the outbuildings will sullenly cede to her.

So, Margarethe being kept busy with household affairs, it's a time of liberation for the girls. Margarethe has no inter-est in sending the girls to school—well, Ruth can't learn, and Iris is needed to govern Ruth!—and van den Meer is accus-tomed to leaving the supervision of Clara to his wife. Every morning, once the fast has been broken, and ablutions com-pleted, and a few household tasks done, Iris and Ruth set out in their klompen to roam Haarlem and see what is to be seen.

Daily Iris and Ruth make their first stop at the Master's studio, where Caspar pauses in his task of gessoing panels and stretching canvases, grinding pigments and applying var-nishes. Daily he heats milk in a pan and adds to it flecks of bitter cocoa bean, drippings of honey, and small scoops of butter. Daily the Master roars at them for disturbing his peace and ruining his chance at a reputation. How is he to finish all the commissions he is getting, how, how, how?—but now the girls only giggle at him.

Ruth has little interest in painting. She'd rather sit in the kitchen and keep Caspar company. He sometimes carves faces out of potatoes to make her laugh. But Iris wanders into the studio and stands a safe distance away, since often her clothes are dripping with rain. She watches the inevitable brown beginnings of marks on canvas turn into the forms of human beings. She watches flesh tones consolidate. She watches heft emerge out of flatness. She hears the Master curse at his own mistakes with such language that Caspar rolls his eyes and sometimes puts his hands over Iris's ears.

The Master moans with grateful distress. Every little domestic animal wants to be memorialized in paint! The very Holy Family itself is being displaced by sinful self-regard: portraits of how wealthy everyone has become! "But I have to eat, I can't live by the word of God alone, no matter what Scripture says; I need bread too," he says. "Damn the human stomach, this fat betrayer of my ideals. Caspar! Another Portrait of Madame Unlucky-in-Looks, done up to appear as Madame Most-Marvelous-to-Behold. I'm no longer telling the truth with my art, I'm lying. But I have to. How else can I afford that sumptuous cocoa you girls drink every morning of my life? And are you going to leave me any at all, or will I sip this thinning fluid by accident and keel over to an insensible end?"

He works quickly, with mounting confidence. Caspar is learning faster too and becoming a genuine apprentice. When the Master takes off at great speed to the outhouse in the alley, Iris and Caspar relish a small privacy.

One day Caspar reaches out as if to stroke Iris's hair, and stops himself.

"Don't you want to pick up a chalk and try for yourself?" he says.

"Of course I do, but I'm never going to be an apprentice, so why fool myself?"

"When I am the Master, you can be my apprentice," says Caspar.

She laughs boldly at that. She hears the unfamiliar roll of her own chortling syllables—it stops her by its strangeness. And then she has to laugh all the more.

If Clara is growing older, then so too is Iris.

When the girls leave the studio, sometimes they wander through the Amsterdamse Poort to the meadow where Ruth gathered wildflowers. In the mornings the meadow is often still bleached with rimefrost, and Ruth seems puzzled that the flowers she was used to gathering are now no more than brittle brown stems. Still, the meadow is something of a haven for them. One day soon the cold may freeze all the canals over, and then, what a holiday! Better than kermis, Caspar promises, though they have no idea what kermis is. Carnival, he explains, before the hard season of Lent. Oh, Iris asks, is there a harder season than this?—but she can say such a thing now because she is not as unhappy as she once was.

With Henrika so often closed behind the bed drapes, Clara is listless and irksome. She's glad when the girls come home. Before the fire one day, munching small bits of ham flavored with clove, Iris tells Clara, "If you came with us, you wouldn't be so bored here."

"I can't go beyond the house, you know that," says Clara. "Mama won't allow it."

"She'd never know! She's not pacing the floorboards upstairs, peering out the windows!" says Iris. "She's flat on her back!"

"I understand," says Clara, "but all the same. It might get me."

"Who?" says Iris, thinking of the imp.

"Dark wings at the top." But Clara changes the subject herself now, adding briskly, "Before you were here, there was a woman from Flanders to teach me lace making. Before her, a woman from Paris who spoke to me in French. I had a man to teach me fingering on the keys of the virginal, and a man to train me in Scripture verses. Mama brings the world in to me. That's all I can know."

"It's not your mama who keeps you here, not really," says Iris. "I see it on your face. It's yourself."

"What do you say this for?" says Clara, lifting her chin with a pretense at bravery.

"You stand at the window and look up and down the street, but you can't bring yourself to step a foot away from the door," says Iris. She's taunting Clara, but she doesn't care this time. "You're a coward."

"I am not a coward."

"Then come do it right now."

"I won't."

Iris doesn't want to be mean, but she hates the sameness of everything. "I know what we can do," she says suddenly. "Ruth and I can put you in the wheelbarrow. We can wheel you out the back gate. We won't go into the marketplace, but away toward the banks of the canal. You can keep your eyes closed and not worry about a thing, and then you can open them up and you'll have been carried by magic across the prison walls of your world. It won't be *your* walking out. You won't even see. We'll be the ones who walk you out."

"It sounds foolish," says Clara.

"Let's try it. Why not?" says Iris.

"You won't dump me in the canal?"

"I promise," says Iris. "That is, I promise to try not to."

Clara gapes. But she has come to know how Iris teases, and suddenly she says, "All right. I'd like to see the canal. I can hardly even remember it."

The wheelbarrow is in a corner of the kitchen yard. At the bottom are some old brown sacks. Clara and Iris snap the clots of soil and the bug carcasses off them. Iris looks up, somewhat guiltily, to see if their venturing out will be observed. There is no dark clot at the top window —just the sky rushing over the steeply pitched roof, a giddy early winter blue with stripes of innocent thin cloud. Nothing untoward.

Clara sits in the barrow like a princess in a palanquin. "No," says Iris, "lie down, like you're dead."

"I don't want to be dead," says Clara.

"You won't really be," says Iris. "Pretend."

Clara begins to be reluctant, but she does as Iris tells her.

"I'm going to cover you with these sacks," says Iris. "Then even if your mother or anything should be looking out the window, she won't see you."

Clara sits up again. "Anything? What do you mean by that?"

But she allows herself to be urged back down. "It's all right," says Iris. "This'll be fun."

"Fun?" says Clara. Her voice is muffled.

"You know it will," says Iris bossily.

"Don't bump me," says Clara. "Don't put me in a place."

"We won't put you anywhere." Iris shows Ruth how to pick up one handle of the wheelbarrow. Ruth is strong and picks up both. Iris then goes around and says, "I might as well ride on top of you. Am I squashing you?"

"You're squashing me!"

"Forgive me, but I can't hear you," says Iris, "all those bags over your face—"

"You're *squashing* me!"

"Let's go, Ruth—"

They don't even get the wheelbarrow through the gate when Clara is sitting up, face red and purple. "Don't squash me! I'm not going!" She pushes Iris with a strength born of an outsized anger. Ruth stands and gapes, her arms dropped at her side.

"Iris," calls Margarethe from an upstairs window. "What are you doing?" Her voice is calm but low, insistent. "Come in at once and wait for me at the bottom of the stairs." It is not a voice to be disobeyed.

Expecting punishment, they leave the wheelbarrow halfway through the gate and trudge inside. Margarethe's unrushed tread is heard upstairs. The footsteps cross the hall—there's a moan, then a louder moaning—and now the sound of footsteps on the back stairs, and now Margarethe turns into the kitchen. "There you are," she says in an even voice. "Iris, I need you to run and fetch the midwife. I'm afraid that Henrika has taken a great pain, and at far too early a stage in the proceedings."

"But I don't know where the midwife lives!" says Iris.

"Use your brain and ask someone. I can't leave the struggling mother alone." Margarethe is standing with rare calm, not rushing back to attend to Henrika. "And I suppose you should run out to the Grotemarkt and ask who has seen Heer van den Meer."

But Iris is reaching out to touch Clara on the shoulder, for it has just dawned on them that Margarethe is carrying bedding in her arms. Dried blood, streaked brick brown, and raw blood, redder than any tulips that Cornelius van den Meer has brought to flower in his nurseries.

"Go, Iris, don't make me tell you again," says Margarethe, dumping the bedding in a corner and turning to head back up the stairs.

The house, with its bricked-in lives, seems suddenly hushed and severe as a chapel. Iris can feel the whole building crouching around and above her, almost breathing, waiting, poised, paused. What else is locked in here besides the van den Meer family? What thing has crept out of a watery mirror world, as strictly ruled as the original it reflects, to gnaw at Henrika so terribly that she bleeds redder than any paint?

Iris governs her wild thoughts, with effort, and then she turns and does as she is told.

3

THE GIRL OF ASHES

Flowers
for the Dead

Within the week Henrika worsens. Nothing helps, neither anything Margarethe can do with herbs, or the minister with psalms, or the surgeon with bleeding. By the Sabbath the only thing left to pray for is that cutting through the abdomen might save the baby inside. But this proves to be a false hope.

Mother and child are laid in a single casket, on a day after an ice storm. The sun glares off a world of glassy edges. The churchyard's features are mounded with snow. The teary men stand close to the grave that has proved hard to dig in such frozen soil. The predikant intones; in the wind his words are lost.

Clara has had to be threatened with a beating to make her join the mourners and come away from the house. At the churchyard she stands far back from the grave, with the other women. The goodwives—dry-eyed to the last of them—murmur that it's a decent enough crowd given the weather. Let's get the old grandmothers back to their hearths before their lungs give out! Iris doesn't recognize many of these people. But she sees the Queen of the Hairy-Chinned Gypsies, wrapped in dun-colored shawls, standing beyond the churchyard. Iris could swear the stick-limbed crone is watching, though the wrinkled lids are closed. Iris ducks her head, pretending to pray. When she looks again, the Queen is gone.

After the last somber *Amen*, Iris turns toward Clara. The girl's head is covered, her face wreathed in black fur, and the wind whips strands of her pale gold-white hair about her forehead. She is frightened to be out of the house, frightened by everything, but who wouldn't be in her situation?

A thick-set man approaches. He walks with gravity to Clara and lifts her chin in his hand. "What a legacy of beauty your mother leaves behind," he murmurs courteously. Clara's eyelids tighten and she pulls back; her hands swing behind her, grappling for Iris, who obliges by leaping forward and taking hold. But then Clara is called to her father's side, and she goes.

Iris meanders at the edge of the small crowd that ushers van den Meer back to his home. She ponders a new thought, powerful as a foreign country, powerful as magic itself—

It starts with this: *Henrika is dead.* Her hands are tucked into an ermine muff as if she can be protected from the cold down there in the black earth. Her blonde hair is clean, her eyes pressed closed, and an odor worse than rotting flowers has attended her removal to the bosom of the soil. Henrika was kind to Iris and Ruth, after a fashion. Henrika fought with Margarethe but didn't throw her out of the house. And *Henrika is dead . . .*

... and *Iris is alive*. That's how the thought goes, and it's a troublesome and guilty one, but Iris *feels* alive: She feels her skin tingle. As Margarethe smartens her daughter up to receive mourners at the door, Iris feels everything. How the hairs pull her scalp when Margarethe drags a brush across her head. Iris feels her wrists in the sleeves of her jerkin, feels her right wrist go back and forth within its cloth tunnel like a clapper in a bell! She feels her whole body within her clothes. It occurs to her that she can sense the cloth skin of her underskirt brush against the skin of her buttocks, and this makes her blush so mightily that Margarethe asks, "What nonsense are you hatching in your ugly head on this most terrible of days?"

She stands and doesn't answer.

All during the afternoon after the burial, neighbors come to call. Iris sits with her hands in her lap, as still as stone, and she can feel the blood climbing the column of her neck, in spirals. She can feel her breasts pooling in her shift. She can feel her nipples stiffen in the cold and relax in the warmth. She can feel her thoughts collect themselves. She tries to sense the household imp, that unseen menace, but it must be scared by the commotion of guests. It seems dissolved. The house is just a house, generating nothing more eerie than chill and dust. Even the mice who usually scrabble in the walls have gone silent, out of respect for the dead.

Distant family members arrive from their distance. Everything is strange and new. Everything feels richer, weirder. It's as if Iris was granted Henrika's life of feeling since Henrika clearly needed it no longer. Was I always here, thinks Iris, or

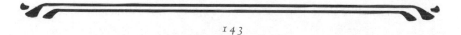

have I just been born? Why have I misplaced all my early memories, of childhood in the fens, of Papa? Why don't I attend?

But I must pay attention now, she thinks, because what other choice is there? Maybe when I die my soul will fly to meet God, but when that time comes I won't have the use of clever hands, nor the burden of an ugly face: hands and face will be planted like bulbs in the soil, while only the bloom of the spirit emerges elsewhere. So let my hands and my face make their way in this world, let my hungry eyes see, my tongue taste. It tastes the wet that seeps on either side of my nose. The world is salt. All the world is salt, and every field is sown in salt, and nothing can grow but I must feel everything, notice everything—

—why, why, she asks herself, but the urge to feel and notice is more urgent than the urge to answer questions. The commotion within her rises to a clamor, and she can barely keep herself on the bench at the side of the hall.

Notice, notice; let noticing take the place of screaming.

Notice Margarethe, doing the act of charity for bewildered van den Meer. Notice how she is modest in her helpfulness, her cap respectfully drawn forward to hide her face. Yet notice how she is here with a tray at van den Meer's left hand, urging him to take golden sherry she has trapped in small glasses like the ghosts of fish. Notice how van den Meer blinks up from the depths of his mourning and accepts Margarethe's consolation, though he doesn't seem to see her.

Notice Ruth, and how she's left out of this. How can Iris not have considered before that Ruth's being slow of tongue might not necessarily mean she is slow of feeling? Ruth on a low stool, even farther in the shadows, her roaming eye tracking up and down a bit of unadorned plastered wall. Notice Ruth, with her hands twisting on her knees, as if by dint of force she might fix her legs properly at last and make them work like legs. Ruth with her brown hair that no one has bothered to trim, and a pucker between the brows like a dimple in a potato. What does Ruth know of death, thinks Iris, and for that matter, what do I?

Notice Clara, the girl of the moment, caught in all this attention and hating it. The shock of grief can only partly obliterate Clara's lopsided temper. When she can escape from a bleary relative, she trails away. Iris sees Clara lower her glance and prepare to give a dozing great-aunt a kick in the ankle. But Clara feels Iris's eye upon her and keeps both feet on the floor.

Notice the Master and Caspar, and how bothered they both are, despite their masculine strength. The Master trembling with some kind of panic. Henrika's death brings up in him the need for verities, for the classic tales of the scriptures. Her death is the memento mori that time must also catch him at his crime: Painting interiors with beautiful merchants' daughters or wives, nothing worthy about them except exactitude—he's abandoned both sacred inspiration and cautionary fable. Look how he scratches his brow with a palsied hand not entirely wiped clean of paint! A few flecks of skin drift off. He isn't listening to that chattering neighbor. He's too deep within himself.

Notice Caspar.

Caspar, a blessing of a human being, with his expression as open as a convex mirror. How he follows the Master, see-

ing to his left elbow, muttering someone's name in his right ear, smoothing the way through the social currents for his teacher and his employer. Caspar the good apprentice, Caspar the reliable friend, and also

Caspar the handsome man.

Oh, Caspar, thinks Iris. Oh, *well*.

She watches him when she can bear to look at him again.

He is so—what is the word?—so right. So rightly formed. The good-sized shoulders, the capable chest. And then the tapering waist, the comfortable bottom, the well-turned calves, the thighs, the energetic feet. And the face, nested in all that glossy hair. The blunt who-cares nose, the wind-raw lips, eyebrows always askew, unmatched. A face with charity and mockery displayed in equal measure. Look at him, now tending to Clara, with all the affection of a courtier! What other man his age would care about the well-being of a girl? He is brushing her cheek with his hand, he is fiddling with her hair. Clara won't smile at him—how could she on this, the burial day of her mother?—but she does look at him and speak softly, and no one else, not even Iris, has gotten her to utter a word today.

Iris stands. She has to hold onto the edge of the chair. She must make Caspar speak to her or she'll die. They'll be opening up Henrika's grave and tossing Iris's own dead body right in with her unless she talks to Caspar at once, and makes Caspar look at her, and notice her somehow. If she isn't to be noticed she'll disappear from the room and perhaps never return. She'll evaporate like morning mist. She'll be as gone as the household imp seems to be.

She floats across the room. She is like a soulless spirit abroad from the depths of the Haarlemsmeer. "You have the power to charm our poor Clara," says Iris to Caspar.

He glances at her. "Charm isn't the word, I think," he says, but he winces at Iris, the most of a smile he can manage given the terms of the day. A smile nonetheless. So that's all right, then.

"Iris," says Margarethe. "You're needed in the kitchen now."

"I'm talking to Caspar," says Iris.

"Iris," says Margarethe, a tone that can't be ignored. So Iris turns away from Caspar, but not before catching his hand for a moment in her own. "Iris!" says Margarethe.

In the kitchen, a lot to be done. Iris isn't familiar with funeral customs of Haarlem, but today the abstemiousness of Calvinism, never fully embraced by the van den Meers, is being ignored entirely. There are bowls of oysters soaking in vinegar, and a brace of hares to unfasten from the spit, and a spill of produce from the cold cellar to be used in various ways. Margarethe, having made her silent procession about the salon, returns with rapid feet down the step to the kitchen, and there she sets a couple of hired girls and her own daughters to tasks. Caspar shows up in the doorway looking for a firkin of water. He's assigned to scrubbing potatoes before he knows what's happened.

"This is a sumptuous feast to prepare at the last minute," he says, observing Margarethe at the center of the whirlwind.

"People only die at the last minute," says Margarethe tartly, but Iris—clever Iris!—knows that her mother means more than this. And so does Caspar.

"These are potatoes that could have been scrubbed last night," says Caspar. "You aren't slack in the matter of household duties, Margarethe. Why this unseemly haste?"

"They are potatoes newly ordered in," says Margarethe, "this morning, if you must know. And likewise the bread that's about to burn if I do not—just this minute—Ruth, move your clumsy carcass from that stool, can't you see I need access to the oven—"

"What is this about?" says Caspar.

"At the last minute," says Margarethe, "van den Meer let it be known that he expected his colleagues to escort potential investors to his home to mourn the loss of his dear wife. Haven't you seen that the portrait of Young Woman with Tulips has been given pride of place in the hall?"

"He's removed the portrait of Henrika?" says Caspar.

"I had thought a painter would be more observant," says Margarethe wryly. "The beetroots, Iris, don't forget those."

With the house full of guests, Iris hasn't noticed the switch either. "But—surely they'll expect to see Henrika above the sideboard!" says Iris. "This is her house and that painting is the best token of her memory! It's not a time to trawl for investments!"

"You have no idea about this, and why should you, silly girl," says Margarethe, and relents a bit and adds, "as no more do I. But I should think that the best token of a parent's memory is her beautiful child. Besides, Cornelius tells me that there's even more money to be made in the tulip market this year, due to a strong season in the Exchange in Amsterdam. Cornelius and his partners must be protected against the potential loss of their shipment of bulbs. They hadn't yet been able to place the portrait in a venue that would guarantee discussion and snare investors. Timid Henrika had become uneasy about the painting of Young Girl with Tulips, and she had changed her mind about allowing its use for a commercial gain. So it's only sensible to take advantage of this sad but necessary gathering . . ."

"This is vile and corrupt," says Caspar.

"A father must take care of his daughter," says Margarethe. "You're a silly boy and don't know the ways of the world. Henrika would have expected no less of Cornelius."

"And a mother must take care of her own too, I suppose," says Caspar, but darkly, pitching a potato into the fireplace.

"Are you referring to me? I should say so. There is plague in Utrecht, I'm told," says Margarethe, "again. *Again*, mind you. This is a prosperous country and a fine time to be alive for all who will live to tell the tale, Caspar. I won't be thrown out on the street to watch my daughters starve, or waste away with the pox, or dribble their insides out with bloody flux. And who are you to talk? You take care of yourself, I've noticed, in any way that comes to hand, thanks to the Master."

"I am paid for services rendered," says Caspar sniffily. "I have a trade."

"Hah, is that what they call it, a trade," says Margarethe. "I believe that you are good at your 'trade.'"

"Mama," says Iris. She doesn't catch the drift of meaning, but she's offended at the tone.

"Let her accuse me of low morals," says Caspar bitterly.

"It's only from guilt that she finds the strength to make such claims of others."

"There's too much work to be done to waste time in talk. If you can't help, then be off," says Margarethe.

Iris glances. Caspar refuses to move. "I'm concerned for the well-being of your daughters, though not of you," he says. "I stay to assist them."

"Then let the girls sit on their stools and do their chores without the wagging of tongues," says Margarethe, but with a wave of her spoon she includes Caspar among the girls. Iris waits to see him leap up in anger, but he holds his tongue and merely works the harder.

All afternoon there is coming and going, and little chatting among the kitchen help except to learn what task is next. The lamps are lit as evening draws near, and platter after platter of delicacy goes out to the guests, and empty platters are returned.

Mid-evening, Clara stumbles into the kitchen and settles herself near the fire.

"If you're going to be in the way, you might as well help," says Margarethe.

"I'm tired," says Clara. "I've been standing at attention all day, silent unless spoken to by some hideous old man who wants to tell me I am more beautiful than the painting of me." She peers into the flames and scowls.

"Oh, I'll wager that makes the Master swell with pride," says Caspar, snickering.

"The Master left hours ago," says Clara. "Didn't you notice?"

"He must be offended that his painting is newly hung for such an occasion," says Caspar.

Clara says, "I don't know what you mean," but before Caspar can explain, Margarethe says, "Clara, stir the pot while you sit there, save me the extra steps."

"I don't know how," says Clara, "and I'm too tired."

"There is no lesson needed in the stirring of the pot," says Margarethe. "Pick up the spoon and stir it."

"I'm not a kitchen girl," says Clara. "I haven't stirred pots before."

"Do not anger me," says Margarethe. "I am working my fingers to the bone to help your poor bereaved father, and while you are in the kitchen you are in my domain. If I tell you to stir the pot, child, then stir the pot you will, if I have to beat you over the head to make it happen."

Caspar and Iris exchange glances. Clara sits up straight. "This is my home," she says. "I will not stir the pot for you or anyone else."

"Margarethe," says Caspar in a voice that betrays nothing of his earlier antagonism, "Margarethe, the girl's mother has been interred this morning. Charity, Margarethe."

"Charity works both ways," says Margarethe. She picks up a smoothed dowel she has been using to roll out pastry. "Clara? Will you stir the pot?"

"I will not," says Clara.

Plague and
Quarantine

The cold snap continues. The days are bleached into sameness by a cloud cover that never varies. Iris, when out on tasks for the household, watches the stolid Dutch at their business, maneuvering over the streets that freeze up into icy ruts every night. The Dutch are buttoned and swaddled against the winter, as stoic and skeptical as their cows. If they believe in imps and demons, within the household walls or outside the city proper, they betray no such faith.

Feeling both older and newer these days, Iris thinks of herself at last as both English and Dutch—English in her hope of catching a glimpse of the magical world living cheek by jowl with this one, Dutch in her impatience with Clara's fecklessness. Iris admits it: Clara is beginning to seem maudlin. At any rate, her crying morning, noon, and night doesn't make her father pay more attention to her, and it seems only to irritate Margarethe.

"On the streets of Amsterdam, Clara, the carcasses are laid out to be taken to the churchyard," says Margarethe one day.

"The plague comes and goes like a foul beast in the night, and Haarlem itself has known its ravages. Must I take you on a walking tour of the devil's handiwork in order to make you stop your sniffling? My own husband was dispatched with a blow to the skull, and even silly old Ruth didn't sob the way that you do. And Iris did as she was told, she dried her eyes and got on with it. Why can't you do the same?"

"Because I don't have a mother to tell me to do so," says Clara, wiping her eyes and her nose. "She isn't here to tell me to do as I'm told!"

"Well, I'm here," says Margarethe, "and I'll have to do."

Clara looks alarmed and angry at such a notion. But, so Iris observes, the anger at any rate has the effect of stilling Clara's tears.

Margarethe's remarks about the plague aren't idle. Those who work in the tulip sheds linger about the doorway to the kitchen, waiting for Margarethe to pass out cheese, bread, and pickled herrings. In return Margarethe collects news about the latest sufferers of the plague. "We shouldn't seem ungrateful for our room and board here," she says to her daughters. "Were we tossed onto the streets again, there to find lodging and food in some more despicable spot, we'd undoubtedly put ourselves in the path of contagion. God has seen fit to secure us here, and we must praise God for His providence."

"God took away Henrika and her baby so that we might be safe?" says Iris.

"Hush your voice," says Margarethe. "God might be listening to such doubt and punish us all."

"But I'm not clear on this point," says Iris. "God spoils other good lives to save our sorry ones?"

"I'll whip you into understanding if I must," says Margarethe.

Iris bows her head as if suddenly full of enlightenment. The prospect of Margarethe becoming pious alarms her.

The winter days crawl on. Comes the feast of Saint Nicolas. At Clara's instruction, the girls all set out their wooden shoes on the hearth. Margarethe sniffs. "You think that Sinter Klaas and his sooty helper, Zwarte Piet, will know that two ugly, hulking English girls live here? I wouldn't dream of treats if I were you."

"Mama in heaven will have told the good saint about Iris and Ruth," says Clara confidently.

"So we'll learn," says Margarethe.

And in the morning a small selection of sweets, nuts, and toys is found lodged in each wooden shoe. "But I received nothing more than you did," says Clara to Iris petulantly.

"Nor I more than you," says Iris. "Sinter Klaas has a fair hand."

"But I am the daughter of the household, and you are servants," says Clara.

"Oh," says Iris, brought up short. What to say? "Well, since we're all friends under this roof, whoever received a greater portion would have been bound by friendship to share it. So it's helpful that the favors are smartly divided already."

Clara looks disgruntled at this but holds her tongue.

* * *

Christmas arrives, and then Epiphany. "Now we get to select a king," says Clara. "Whoever discovers a bean baked into the morning cake." She's the lucky one, but her face falls when Ruth finds a bean in her portion too, and so does Iris.

"It is the feast of Driekoningen," observes Margarethe. "All three kings are honored here." Ruth sits up, proud to be a king. Iris and Clara fight over which one will have her face blackened as Melchior. But it scarcely matters, as Clara still won't leave the house, so Iris and Ruth trot off to join other children in the Grotemarkt at their strange songs about Herod and the Magi. Clara is a pouting Melchior from the front window.

The weeks of midwinter are endless. The mornings are locked in frost and fog, sometimes even curtained in snow. Too many days in a row the girls are kept inside. Though Clara teases and taunts the Fisher girls, she's pleased to have the company. But Iris and Ruth become impatient. When the weather lifts, they spend long days at the studio, leaving Clara behind.

Without Henrika's vigilance about education, Clara grows bored.

Margarethe scrupulously ignores her, and makes a practice of sending the girls out to do small tasks more and more often.

One day Iris is shucking her cloak in the hallway when she hears Margarethe remarking to Clara, "It isn't my job to keep you amused. And housework is not amusing, I'll grant you that, but it whiles the hours away. But you will set your-self above housework, won't you? And for the moment I let it go." Iris tiptoes forward and peers to see Margarethe push-ing a broom ostentatiously around Clara's feet and saying, "What delicate tender feet you have, too wonderful to stand upon to do some work and help us laboring folk."

The day arrives when Clara mutters to the pewter mug on the breakfast table, "I'll come with you tomorrow on your tasks if you like."

If there really had been a household imp—of any origin, Dutch or English—it must be long gone, for now is the time it should rattle its bones, chomp its teeth, flare its nostrils, scream with surprise. None of that. Iris notices nothing but cold, thick silence. She holds her breath. Ruth turns to look at Clara. Van den Meer pauses in his breakfast, holding a piece of bread aloft. His eyebrows lift.

"Come with us if you like. It makes no difference to me, none at all," says Margarethe. "It wasn't I who imposed this quarantine on you." But Iris senses a shudder of satisfaction running across her mother's shoulders.

The following morning, as soon as she can peel herself away from the warm hearth, Margarethe wraps herself in a cloak. Clara, nibbling her nails, stands ready. The last time she was away from the house was her mother's burial, when she was voiceless with grief. And before that it was years . . .

They set out toward the center of town, a quartet, Clara gripping Ruth's hand and looking this way and that. Margarethe's intentions are modest ones—a few onions here, a bit of lace there, a new candle mold from the smithy. "We traipse after you like ducklings," says Iris happily. "Even though Ruth has a hard time keeping up. Come on, Ruth, use your big, strong legs. Clara, look at that dog going after the goose!"

"No," says Clara, entranced, "the goose is going after the dog."

"A woman may walk abroad in Haarlem and conduct her business," says Margarethe with satisfaction. "In England a woman is rarely allowed such liberty. She is quarantined for fear of the society outside her door or her farmstead. Clara, don't fiddle with your collar." Margarethe has spoken loudly. Three dames of Haarlem turn and watch Clara attend. "That's an obedient child," says Margarethe.

Iris pulls back a step and thinks about this. Is Margarethe parading herself as Clara's mother-in-stead? Is she is making a show, all about town, of her care for the motherless child?

She studies Margarethe as they wait at the door of the tobacconist, where her mother wants to buy a pleasing blend for van den Meer's pipe. If Iris were to paint Margarethe, what would she notice?

There is the heavy brow, slightly protruding, like a lump of bread dough that has fallen forward from up top. Firmly marshaled eyebrows, knitted together in the act of watching the merchant cut the tobacco to the correct specifications. Margarethe's hand is soldered to her hip, a gesture of patience and intractability both. Her lips are pursed. The lower lip is nipped in, to be pinched by the upper teeth in moments of mild distress. And, Iris realizes, such moments are frequent. Margarethe lives a life of compromise. She takes nothing for granted and barters every sentence to her advantage.

How dear she is, even in her strictness, her chill.

There's another side of Margarethe to be seen later this day, for the route they take home from the shops brings them by an almshouse for old men. Maids and manservants are carrying several corpses out the door to await the gravedigger's cart. "Plague alarm," says the regent crossly when he sees Margarethe stop and stare. "Save yourself, and give the sufferers a chance to rest in peace from your scrutiny!"

"The dead are dead," says Margarethe bravely.

"Some here are corpses, some not yet," the regent replies. "We are carrying a few to the Leprozenhuis outside of town. You want to join them and the other lepers, jump in the cart."

"God save their souls, and yours," calls Margarethe, and she mutters a few lines of the first psalm that comes to mind, mutters them without conviction or accuracy.

"This is what stalks you," says Margarethe as the girls hurry after her. "This is the devil's work. There's nothing to anticipate but the broad scythe of the reaper that will cut you down. Only jump when it passes, and perhaps you may save yourself until the next sweep. If you don't jump, you don't save yourself."

Ruth jumps out of anxiety, as if she imagines the scythe to be passing exactly then.

"Changelings," says Clara ominously, about the invalids and the corpses.

"How high do you jump?" says Iris to her mother.

"Just you watch me," says Margarethe. "I've jumped from the fens of England to the threshold of the poorhouse of

Haarlem, and then jumped again. Just you watch me, and you'll learn what there is to learn. Give me room to cast my eel spear, and let follow what may."

Iris watches. Day after day she watches. She watches the ice form on the duck pond down the lane. She watches Margarethe sing as she prepares the hearty stew of root vegetables and prunes. She watches Clara alternately sulk and cozy up to Margarethe. She watches van den Meer's face grow longer as, with every passing week, the shipment of bulbs doesn't arrive.

Then she watches as Margarethe waits, and waits, and chooses the right moment to jump again.

The Nowhere Windmill

The three days before the beginning of Lent, Clara tells them, are called Vastenavond. It hardly seems right to feast like gluttons when Henrika is so newly buried. Besides, the practice of Lenten atonement has never been popular in the Fisher household before. But Margarethe throws herself into the preparations with energy, concocting a stew with mutton, citron, greens, and ginger. "We will take our religious obligations seriously," she says, ladling up to van den Meer and the three girls.

"I suppose we should," says van den Meer. He is brooding, perhaps out of mourning, or maybe—Iris hates to admit—out of fear of financial ruin. "This is a good hutsepot, Margarethe. As good as Henrika ever made."

"I don't think it's *that* good," says Clara stoutly, dropping her spoon.

"Now, if you're going to do things right," says van den Meer, "preparing for Lent, Margarethe, you might want to take yourself over to the House of Correction. Careful with a stuiver as you are, you'll appreciate that at kermis time, admission is free."

Margarethe stiffens. "I am correct enough," she says.

"Oh, I suppose!" He hasn't meant to be rude, Iris thinks. Has he? "There you can see the whores and the inmates learning their Bible lessons, being reshaped into Christian worthiness at the expense of the town. It's quite an amusement."

"I have far too much work in managing your household to amuse myself by visiting prisons," she says sharply. "Or alehouses, for that matter."

"You do good work," he says, chastised a bit. "You perform many kindnesses for me and my daughter."

"I should think so. And don't speak about whores in this house."

"It is my house, Margarethe," he reminds her.

"So it is," she gives back to him. "You inherited it from your wife, didn't you?"

"You're feisty for carnival time." His tone is black.

She relents. "I should have said, please don't speak about whores in front of my daughters."

"I won't," he says, still stung. "But who knows what others in the street say about this arrangement?"

Her anger is so intense that Iris imagines the roof might explode. Margarethe hurtles out the door. They watch her sliding on the ice in the streets, wind whipping her black cloaks into huge, crowlike wings. But as the girls continue munching the rest of their bread, Margarethe stalks back in. Her face is pink and even beautiful because of the intense cold. "Oh, come see," she cries, all fury forgotten. "The canals and the river have frozen over at last, and the whole town is out on the great ice road!"

It's the happiest day so far. Even Clara is caught up in the excitement, and van den Meer remembers there are shoes with runners, probably to be found somewhere in the sheds. After a time, two pair of skates are located. The leather is rotted from one skate, and of the second pair a runner snaps off. But Ruth's feet are far too big to squeeze into them anyway, so Iris and Clara each take a single skate, and the girls and Margarethe hurry out to the Spaarne.

The world is transformed. The skies are hugely gray as usual, and low, but this intensifies the feeling of magic and otherness. Some small boats sit frozen in the water, and children get running starts and glide up to the boats and crash into the sides. Dogs are yapping in every direction. The whole of Haarlem is out on the ice. Margarethe can't help but poke Iris and say, "Look, and see how it is: The rich have skates and warm cloaks, and there's a carriage converted to an ice boat! They can enjoy this oddness and take new pleasure in it. And the poor suffer even harder. Warmth is scarce, and food is absent. You can't live long on ice and snow."

"So are we rich or poor?" asks Iris.

"One skate to your name? You tell me," says Margarethe. "Balance very carefully, my dear. Very carefully indeed."

Enough of object lessons, when the carnival atmosphere spills over onto the city's icy ballroom floor! Iris hurries away,

letting Margarethe try to balance Ruth, for whom the ground itself is usually trouble enough, and ice is more treachery than treat. Iris links arms with timid Clara and off they go. Frost crinkles the moisture in their nostrils and the corners of their eyes.

"Look, a game," says Iris, "those boys and men, with sticks and a ball—"

"Kolf," says Clara.

Horses on the ice. Trees at the margins of the Spaarne, sticking up like spindly pillars. Toddlers on their bottoms, wailing. Granddames spinning about on skates as freely as any of the young men. There a predikant, looking sour, as if he's merely taking this route to reach his place of prayer the quickest way. Grizzled men from the fields punching holes in the ice and dropping in lines, hoping for fish. Goodwives at their gossip, toddlers in tow. A fat old man falls on his backside in front of them and farts explosively. Off to one side, someone has rigged up a boat with sails, and is trying to make it glide, but the wind isn't strong enough and there are too many giddy young maidens weighing it down. A teacher recites Bible verses to his students as they all lurch along, no skates at all, but smoothly enough on wooden shoes. As far as the eye can see along the curve of the river, tiny pegs of people, in black and gray and red. Someone has made the mistake of urging a cow onto the ice, and she collapses and sprawls there wailing. A pig has escaped and trots along with dispatch, minding its own business and occasionally hooting with pleasure or hunger.

Then, out from the shadow of a beech tree, wobbles the Queen of the Hairy-Chinned Gypsies. "Look!" says Iris, and

before Clara can protest, they are slithering up to her. "You never did turn Master Schoonmaker into a slug!" cries Iris gaily.

"Eh? What's that?" The old thing is deaf from a multitude of scarves, and cursing her canes. "Let him turn himself into a slug. Most folks do."

"You were going to magic him!"

"Why bother. It's your own job to change yourself. These days it's hard enough for a crooked old girl like me just to stay upright." But she peers a bit and grins, enjoying the fun as much as anyone. "I don't know you chicks, do I?"

"Where are the hairy-chinned gypsies today?"

"You're a giddy soul! Why, where they belong, of course, like all of us. Your pretty friend's a quiet one. Her tongue got frozen?"

"She's shy of society."

The crone makes a mocking face. "Then I'll push myself off and save you the bother. Beauty has consequence, but I'm ugly as sin, so I don't care. Good-bye!" With surprising speed she makes headway across the river. The two canes are leggy as usual, and the trailing ends of several scarves, brushing the ice, look like even more legs.

"A real queen should be glorious," says Clara, disappointed. "*She's* hardly a queen!"

"She's hardly alive," agrees Iris, which makes them both laugh. They fall against each other, turning themselves into a two-headed, wobble-legged Queen of the Hairy-Chinned Spiders. And now here is Caspar, speeding up to them, his face almost purple.

"Where's the Master, then? You've left him far behind?" cries Iris, delighted to see him.

"He has work to do; what does he care if the river is frozen or turned into honey or dried out from drought?" answers Caspar. "He's painting, cursing the cold, painting, munching on his bread, painting. You need to ask? Race you to the other side!"

"Wait! We only have two skates between us!" says Iris, but they are all off, laughing too hard to get up any momentum. Clara as jubilant as Iris, and both of them free of Margarethe and Ruth. Too ashamed to admit how wonderful it is not to have to bother with Ruth, for once, but today isn't a day for shame. There's enough of Lent ahead in life for that.

They tag each other and sprint along. Everything is changed. Ice has trapped every twig and reed, every broken hoop of bramble and each spike of fence. The crowds are mostly behind them now, but the friends can still hear the unanimous rush of "Ohh!" as the sun breaks through for a moment, diamonding the landscape.

Too much splendor. The sun burrows back beneath its blankets of cloud. It is early afternoon, but cold as dusk. "Shouldn't we turn back?" says Caspar. "We spend so much energy on the way out, we'll be tired returning."

"Just as far as the next bend," says Iris. "Who knows when we'll be able to ride the ice like this again?" It's nice to be out of the house too, and if Margarethe is being holy, Lent may be a more grim affair than usual.

They've passed beyond the place where the canal meets up with the Spaarne, and they're moving silently between open fields. Here and there a distant farmhouse, with the usual mess of old stork's nest on roof beams, and thin ropes

of smoke issuing from chimneys. Some cattle lowing, out of
sight. The birds are with them for a while, but then they disappear, as if they can feel a harder cold approaching, and are
making for home.

"This is the bend," says Caspar. "Come now, let's go back."

"No, that bend," says Iris.

"That bend is a different bend; it's just come up into view
as we passed this one," he says. "I can't stay out longer; the
Master will need me to stoke up the fire."

"He needs you to keep him warm? He needs you a lot,"
says Iris, affecting the ironic tone with which her mother dis-
cusses Caspar's apprenticeship. She has stung him; he whips
his head and scowls.

"He does indeed, and I'm taking advantage of him in skat-
ing so far with you," he says. "I'm going to turn around even
if you're not."

Iris hasn't meant to provoke a disagreement, but she's so
glad to be away from Ruth and Margarethe, she merely says,
"Well, go if you must; we're not bound by your obligations."

"Maybe we should turn back," says Clara. Out in the
world she's less certain of herself, and also less mean-spirited,
Iris has seen. For once, Iris can't help taking the one advantage she has over Clara—that is, the privilege of courage.

"I'm going to the next bend in the river," says Iris, "and
I'll find my own way back if I must." She doesn't say farewell
to Caspar, but pushes ahead. Proud as a hawk! Her left foot
launches and her right foot glides, and she's mastered the art
of balance. In a few minutes she hears Clara's voice calling
after her. She turns and waits.

They go to the next bend, and the next after it. "We'll be in Amsterdam before nightfall," says Iris approvingly.

"I have to stop and rest," says Clara, "and I need to lift my skirts and pee."

The landscape is so flat as to be almost vacant. It reminds Iris suddenly of the way she felt when she arrived in Haarlem—what, four, five months ago? As if there were nothing of the past, just a white sheet. In the distance, maybe because a wind is whipping up some blurring edge of snow, the fields merge with the sky. The only solid thing in the landscape besides themselves is a windmill in a nearby field, not all that far from the river's edge. "Come, we'll go there," says Iris, "and if we can open a door, you can squat down in some corner. It's too cold to do it outside."

Clara isn't up for arguing; she's shivering with the effort to hold her bladder. They climb the low bank of the river and slash-clump their way across the field without bothering to remove their skates. The windmill is an old one, abandoned. Only two of the four arms are left, and one of them hangs broken like the limp limb of a hanged man. Icicles make the other arm look as if draped with white fringe. "Icicles will slice you right in half," says Iris. "Mind them. Doesn't this whole place look like a big, ferocious creature, with a blunt head, or maybe headless, and those reaching arms?" A giant in the fields, growing larger as they near—no surprise that, but ominous in this white nothingness . . .

She tries the door. It's locked, but the wood has rotted and with a little protesting shriek, the weight of two healthy girls applied against it, the door springs open and they tum-

ble in. Clara makes for a corner and relieves herself. The piss steams on the dusty floor, pooling over ancient encrustations of bird shit.

Ancient, and not so ancient. A few flapping wings in the dark over their head. "Bats," says Iris. "Or maybe owls."

"Spirits," says Clara.

"Spirits, hah," says Iris. "Goblins maybe, but not spirits. Aren't all the local spirits trapped in the ice in Haarlemsmeer today? They can't get out."

"Spirits. I've been here before, I know. The crow at the top of the story."

"What crow, what story? You mean some tale I told, or the top story of your high house? You haven't been here before; you haven't been anywhere before. You don't go to the cathedral, you don't go to school. How could you be out here in the nowhere windmill?"

"I was," says Clara. "I remember now. I remember the shape."

"All windmills are the same shape."

"No, they're not. I remember these beams going up like an angle, see? And this machinery. These gears! I remember the noise they make. So loud! So loud that when the wind drives the arms, nobody outside can hear anyone inside."

"All windmills must have the same kind of machinery," says Iris patiently. "It's cold in here, shall we go now?"

"There's a trapdoor in the floor just below this beam," says Clara. "I remember."

"There's no trapdoor. The floor is stone." Iris kicks at the muck. "See?"

Clara is on her knees. "No. Look." She claws with her fingers, and old straw and debris comes up in moldy patches.
"I'm telling you what I know, and you're not listening. There's
a space down here. They put me there and they fed me. See the
hook?" She points at the beam above, from which a rusting
hook protrudes. "So I wouldn't get hurt, they put me in a basket and put the rope through that hook, and lowered me down
softly." She's cleared away enough rubbish to prove her point.
The floor is wooden, and there, there, is the edge of a trapdoor.

"Who put you down there?" says Iris. "When?"

"They did," says Clara.

"But who? Your father and mother?"

"No, no," says Clara angrily. "The others. The spirits.
The crow man, the others."

"I don't know what you're talking about."

"When I became a changeling," she says. "Don't you
know anything?"

"When did you become a changeling? What happened to
you?" says Iris. She peers at Clara's face in the gloom and
comes closer. The whole place suddenly smells strongly
of bird shit, new, powerful stuff. Iris is entranced by a sort of
terror, almost a pleasurable sensation—but she is scared of
Clara's monotonic recitation of these impossible facts. Iris
says, "Clara, what happened to you?"

"A long time ago." Clara looks in a strange, pointed way
at Iris, as if not sure that Iris isn't a spirit, hasn't squirreled
her away here to drop her in a trapdoor again. "A long time
ago happened to me, and I was a changeling. The crow man
changed me. That's all."

Her expression is familiar. She is badly scared, and something more. "Come," says Iris, "away from this place, whether you're having a bad dream or not, let's get out of this place." But Clara is slow to move, and Iris has to tug her. Once outside, they find the wind more bitter, the clouds lower, and the temperature dropping still further. "No talking, let's push on, and cocoa and butter at home to warm us up!" says Iris as gaily as she can. Caspar, damn him, has proven to be right. It's too far back. Iris even worries that they've turned in the wrong direction. But eventually the huddled spires of Haarlem appear, and what's left of the crowds still cavorting on the ice—mostly children and the poor. Everyone else has had enough.

They make the last few steps to the house in a stupor of exhaustion. Clara's face is changed now; it's vacant and far away. It doesn't have the piercing look that it had in the clammy husk of the windmill. She doesn't take any cocoa, she just climbs the stairs to bed, and though Iris would be glad to hear even the sound of weeping, there's only silence from above. Later, as she's falling asleep, Iris remembers when she saw that look on Clara's face before. It was the look that she had in her eyes when she stared out the window at Ruth and told her, "Get away from here." It was that look of being stabbed from inside.

Invitations

"It's the final day of kermis," says Margarethe, "and poor eating begins tomorrow. So today we feast."

Iris glances at Clara to see if she's pleased, but after the windmill afternoon Clara has seemed pleased by little. On a chest, she hunches in a slump-shouldered way, avoiding everyone's eyes. Iris feels sad for Clara, in a way she hasn't before, because Iris sees that Clara's fears are genuine, not theatrical, even though the reasons for the fears are more mysterious than ever. "Pancakes, Clara," says Iris brightly. Clara doesn't reply.

Margarethe sits over a three-legged pot, stirring batter that she will dribble into a flat pan with a long handle. Some apples are brought from the storehouse. Ruth is supposed to be peeling them, but she keeps forgetting and nibbling at them instead. Van den Meer is in the salon, recovering from a long day at the alehouse. He rests in the half-light, considering the portrait of his daughter with tulips.

"Iris, someone's at the door," says Margarethe, "and my hands are wet. See who it is." Iris admits one of van den

Meer's colleagues, who looks grim. Is it van Stolk or Handelaers or Maes? She can't keep all these brooding, scowl-faced
men straight. And this one more grim-looking than most.
Iris hurries to find more candles to brighten the room. She
fears the worst.

But by the time she's returned, the colleague has lifted
his eyebrows and brightened his eyes, and with his fist he is
buffeting van den Meer on the shoulder. The colleague has
only been pretending to gloom. The news is really fine: A
vessel, recently arrived from a port in France, has passed on
the gossip that the long-expected tulip-carrying ship isn't lost
at all. It has merely suffered a split mast, and has put in to
port in the south of France, where more misfortunes con-
spired to keep the ship unseaworthy for many weeks in a
row. Such crises are normal ones in the life of a sea captain,
and soon he is expected to announce departure, bound for
Holland. The tulip bulbs have been well stored; with luck
they'll suffer no hardship for their longer voyage. All is in
order, and since Lent has yet to begin—by a matter of
hours—celebration is allowed.

Iris brings the news into the kitchen, and Margarethe
takes stock of the situation at once. She removes her apron
and she hangs it on a peg in the larder. She pinches her
cheeks and fixes a few wisps of hair firmly beneath her bonnet. "Iris," she says, "see to the pancakes. Hold the dog away
from the sausage in that pot. Don't let Ruth sit near with her
backside to the fire for long or she'll get hives. Keep Clara
here for fifteen minutes and then send her in with three
glasses of gin. Afterward, put yourself and the girls to bed.

Do you understand me?"

"What are you doing?" says Iris.

"Jumping," says Margarethe.

Iris does as she's told. As she lies on her pallet, she hears the guest leave. For a long time she hears nothing more, only, once, the sound of a low giggle from the front room. At least she thinks it's a giggle. She can't remember having heard her mother giggle before.

In the morning, Margarethe is at her post preparing the modest Lenten breakfast. She's become engaged to van den Meer the night before, she tells them. "He'll have to be your stepfather," she says, "since I'm needed to be Clara's step-mother."

Ruth shrugs. It isn't clear if she understands the notion. But Iris does. She waits until Clara and Ruth have wandered off to their morning toilet. Iris faces her mother squarely across the kitchen floor. "You could have married the Master," she says to her mother.

"He hadn't the correct prospects," says Margarethe.

"He has talent," says Iris.

"Talent doesn't buy bread," says Margarethe.

"Of course it does!" says Iris. "Look! He lives and breathes and works! He eats!"

"Not another word from you," says Margarethe. "You're a foolish child, and you don't know what sacrifices I make to protect you and your sister. What if I should drop dead of the plague next week? Where would you turn? Answer me that, you smart child."

"I'd go directly to the one who cares for us," says Iris. "The Master, and for that matter, Caspar as well."

"The Master cares for his art, nothing more, and as for Caspar, his caring moves in another direction entirely," says Margarethe. "Do I have to spell out the nature of that particular sin? I can't; today is the beginning of Lent, and it doesn't suit my spiritual needs. You'll see it soon enough. The both of them are fools. They'd give you a home for one night as a Christian must, and feed you bread and porridge. Then before the week is out they'd ship you off to the poorhouse, or find an excuse to send you back to England. No, my girl, you know nothing of how we women are imprisoned in our lives, but there *are* ways to determine the sentence we must serve. You'll live to thank me."

"It's cold-blooded," says Iris.

"To be dead is more cold-blooded," says Margarethe. "Now, tell me when you're done venting your spleen. I have to work quickly to arrange the details, the better to secure his commitment to this notion. You'll have to do the scrubbing of the stoop this morning, and then polish the hasps and the handles on the front door. We must show right away that there is a new cleanliness pertinent to this change of situation. I'm not a simpleton, I know that small gestures carry big meanings. Neighbors on this street are ferocious ear-blowers, always whispering about me. I'll give them respectability. They can't bear that I'm here in this handsome house. They can't bear to see the sun shining in the water; they'd begrudge a hen her corn."

The wedding is more quickly arranged than Iris has thought possible. Caspar suspects that the period of mourning is coming to an end, and that neighbors' tongues might start wagging. Van den Meer is relying on local trade for the purchase of his tulip bulbs. He can't afford to scandalize his neighbors or those he meets at the Grotekerk of Saint Bavo's by living in flagrante delicto with an unattached housekeeper, even if she's a widow and a shrew and plain as a pumpkin besides.

In the weeks leading up to the wedding, Iris is kept at home more often than usual. So much to do! She has to manage kitchen chores so her mother can negotiate with the church authorities, with the suppliers of meats and wine, with van Antum the clothier for a new dress for the ceremony. Iris would rather throw down the cleaning cloths and run out into the street, heading in the direction of the Master's studio. She grows tired of Ruth's growled complaints, which she can seldom interpret, and of Clara's occasional mews for attention. "Why don't you go out with Margarethe if you're bored?" snaps Iris one day.

"I've seen the world again, and once is enough," says Clara. As if she knows this is silly, she stumbles on. "Besides, my skirt drags. It wants fixing, Iris."

"So your hem is ripped? Goodness, aren't you handy with a needle and thread? What did your mother teach you?"

"She taught me to turn for help when I needed it. She taught me that people would be kind and come to my aid."

"People admire you for your good looks, but sooner or later they'll know it if you've never met a needle and thread," says Iris. "Even a pretty flower has to learn to work, you know."

"You chatter and my hem stays torn," says Clara.

"I am only a little older than you are!" says Iris. "Why do you plague me?"

"You're my elder by experience," says Clara, a bit sadly. "I didn't ask for you to become my stepsister any more than you did, remember."

Iris realizes that she is being unkind. Sisters—be they stepsisters, half sisters, or full sisters—sisters must do for each other. Isn't this how her mother raised her? Ruth can never do for herself, so Iris must do for her; and now Iris must do for Clara as well.

But Iris won't mend the hem unless Clara promises to try threading the needle herself, and then practicing the stitch that Iris shows her. Clara protests, pouts, makes fun of Iris's bossiness, tries to stick her with a needle—but in the end learns how to mend a hem, and seems a bit happier for it.

The day before the wedding arrives, and Margarethe is having a final fitting of her marriage vestments. Iris begs to be allowed a few moments to herself, and Margarethe refuses. There's too much to do. But van den Meer has picked up from Margarethe that she hasn't invited Luykas Schoonmaker to the party. "Is it fear of what people will say?" he asks. "Because you were a housekeeper there before here? That can't be helped. That's filling the pothole after the calf has drowned. Everyone already knows about it. Schoonmaker is the painter of Young Woman with Tulips, and people will see that painting again. He should be here. Send Iris out to ask him to come."

"What about Caspar as well?" says Iris.

Van den Meer looks at her as if he has never seen her before. "Of course not," he says. "What use is that?"

"There is plague abroad," says Margarethe. "I hesitate to permit Iris—"

"*Margarethe*," says van den Meer. So she gives in, affecting wifely submission, as long as Iris promises not to go near the almshouse or the canal, or any other place where the plague is suspected of lingering.

Iris promises. She slips away without alerting Ruth of her intentions. At first Iris walks with dignity, head down, hands tucked into the waistband of her frock to keep them warm. But when she has turned a corner and is out of sight of the tall van den Meer house, she frees her hands to make running easier. It's heaven to thump her feet on the cobbles, to crack panes of ice that have formed in depressions in the road, to scatter the cold water collected below. It's heaven to know that it's still possible to run, though she doesn't know what she's running from, or why.

The Master hardly seems surprised to see her. "So the big day arrives tomorrow," he says. "I should've liked to attend."

"And you shall," says Iris. "I come to bid you welcome."

"And Caspar?" says the Master.

"He hasn't been invited. He is an apprentice, they say it isn't fitting," says Iris. "Where is he?"

"Out for supplies. Don't mind that, he'll be back. I know you love him best and you must put up with me, and pretend you really came to talk with me. It's sad for you." But the

Master is smiling as he says this, and Iris doesn't even bother to pretend to be shocked. She is growing up, she realizes.

Perhaps the Master knows what she's feeling, for he continues in a more serious tone. "Will you have some improvement in your lot by this handsome marriage your mother has arranged for herself?" he says. "I know she'll be more secure than ever I could make her, but how will it be for you? Will she let you go to study?"

"I don't know how to improve my lot, unless it's to take a heavy Spanish veil and hide my ugly face from the good citizens of Haarlem," says Iris.

"Self-mockery is an uglier thing than any human face, Iris. No one can pretend you are a pretty wench, but you are smart and you are kind. Don't betray those impulses in yourself. Don't belabor the lack of physical beauty, which in any case eventually flees those who have it, and makes them sad. I'm talking about how you'll spend your days now that your mother has married into a better situation. Will you be freed of being a housemaid? Will you be able to be a maiden of leisure?"

"I don't want to rest that much," says Iris. "It seems to me the Dutch aren't overly fond of resting, and in this I feel very Dutch."

"So I have seen. Now, sit down for a minute and listen to what I'm saying. I want to know if you would care to come and be an apprentice in this studio."

Iris has been examining the underdrawing on a gessoed surface. She feels the blood rush to her face, and her gaze falls to the floor for a moment. "You wouldn't do such an ungodly thing!" she says, hardly daring to hope.

"Many talented housewives of Haarlem put their nimble fingers to the creation of needlework or of etching on glass," says the Master. "It isn't such a bold step to move from needle to paintbrush."

"You have no idea of my abilities."

"I know that you can see. I know that you know how to look."

She wills herself then to turn and look at *him*. He has set down his brush on the edge of a board. A smear of earthy green is stroked along one cheek. He looks patient, tired, and charitable. He smiles at her.

"I've never drawn a line in my life," says Iris in a small voice.

"There was a moment in my life when the same was true of me," replies the Master.

"What would people say?"

"That along with your clever mother, you were rising in the world. Some would scoff and some would salute you. To consider what other people might say is hardly a good reason to take action or to defer it. You have your own life to live, Iris, and at its end, the only opinion that amounts to anything is that which God bestows."

"But a woman painting!"

"Haarlem has learned to tolerate Judith Leyster, who worked in the studio of Franz Hals until recently. Now she has her own apprentices. Maybe you'd rather go learn with her?" He isn't teasing; he's talking to her as a good friend.

"But"—(it is Lent, after all, and she can't help asking the question)—"do you really think that God smiles on a maiden who is bold enough to paint?"

"Can you deny it? If so, by whose authority?"

Iris begins to grin at the ridiculousness of it. "You're play-ing with me, Master! And not the first time. You borrowed my face to prove your worth to van den Meer, and you made a mockery of how I looked. Now you're mocking some secret desire I have."

"A painting is in the eye of a beholder," says the Master. "You could look at the painting of Iris with wildflowers, and you could ask yourself this: Did the Master see me with repugnance, or did he see me with my own beauty?"

But the idea of Iris having any beauty of her own is too much, and she falls to laughing, laughing until tears spring into her eyes, and she has to hide her face with her apron.

"There's no hurry," says the Master, turning back to his work. "I don't need an answer soon. But I've been waiting for you to ask me the question yourself, and you're being obtuse and slow about it.

"And," he adds, "I'm not being entirely selfless. You could be a big help to me. Especially if it turns out that, as I suspect, you have a small talent for this kind of work. The painting of Young Woman with Tulips has done for my rep-utation what my attempts at holy and unholy subjects haven't done. Haarlem now remembers that I exist, and my commissions have been mounting. I'll soon have more work than I can manage, unless I have an assistant to help me and to help Caspar."

At that, as if on cue, Caspar returns from his expedition, his arms full of lengths of cloth, vegetables, a jug of ale, and a freshly bled chicken for the pot. "Well, Iris! You got back safely from the frozen fields; did you skate as far as Muscovy?" He grins at her and shakes his hair out of his eyes. "I understand that by tomorrow you and I will have to be reintroduced. Iris van den Meer, I haven't had the pleasure!"

"How do you do," says Iris. "You'll need help plucking that chicken, good sir."

"If you can stay until it's stewed, you're welcome to nibble from its carcass. Come, let's leave the old man to his fussing," says Caspar, "and you can tell me all that is in your heart about this wedding tomorrow. I suspect your van den Meer is really going to hang out the broom. If he puts some money out for a party, he'll collect some more goodwill and some more investors. Come whisper some gossip to me."

The Master reassembles a dignified expression on his face, and Iris follows Caspar down the steps into the kitchen. Now that Margarethe is no longer in residence, the place is a mess—oyster shells on the floor, scraps of old squashes, a spill of dried beans in the corner, and mouse droppings everywhere. "The Master wants me to come apprentice," says Iris, "but I think he and you both need more help in the household department."

"He's told you about that, then?" says Caspar. "Oh, Iris, do come! Say you will. You can't lodge here, of course; it wouldn't be fitting. But you can come during the day, as often as you like, and begin to pick up a little of the work for him. We won't ask for you to bring the kitchen to rights—in fact, we won't allow it. You'll never be allowed to set foot inside the kitchen. That isn't the point. I could keep this place clean myself if it were important to do so."

"There's not a household in Haarlem that would approve of this proposal," says Iris.

"Approval is overrated," says Caspar, parroting his teacher. "Approval and disapproval alike satisfy those who deliver it more than those who receive it. I don't care for approval, and I don't mind doing without."

He throws the chicken down on the table and turns, with sudden elation, and grabs Iris's wrists in his hands. "Do say you'll come," he says. "It would be fun. You would be like a sister to me here. He can be old and miserable when work is going badly, or old and sententious when it's going well, but anyway he's always old, and older every minute. He needs you for help, but I need you for company. Try it anyway. Try it, Iris. Say you will."

She's caught, then, caught in his hands, like a bird who has alighted on a windowsill, looking for a crumb. Though he only holds her wrists, they seem—just now—to be the sole part of her that is truly alive. She is throbbing through her forearms, and her hands are numb. Her wrists ache with intensity. The skin on his palms is soft and warm, the warmest thing she has ever felt; his palms are small cushions, his fingers are fretted knobs of intention. If he snaps his hands, her wrists will both break and her life fly out of her heart through her unstopped veins.

"I can't," she says suddenly, "I can't possibly, I can't ever, no."

"Of course you can!" he says.

"I can't, I can't, don't you see?" she says, and she turns and flees. She leaves the studio behind, and runs on toward her small future and toward her mother's wedding. She can't spend years, months, weeks in there with Caspar; she can't spend a day, an hour. She can't bear another minute. He doesn't see how she burns for him. She runs to leave him behind. She doesn't turn back at the sound of his voice from the doorway. She listens instead to the thump of her wooden shoes on the cobbles, a loud punctuation, her only answer to the lovely, impossible suggestion: *No no, no no, no no.*

A Fair Light
on a Full Table

So the marriage. The predikant is a bit pompous and bothered by a cold. His noisy sneezes distract attention from the bride and the bridegroom. But then, thinks Iris, for that matter, even in her marriage finery, is Margarethe really much to look at herself? Her jaw is slightly receded and her upper teeth lean out in an overbite. Her skin is scrubbed, to be sure, but even if she never walks past a sunny doorway again in her life, she is still hopelessly brown as an egg. Hers is a hard face, even at a celebration, even in a moment of triumph.

As for van den Meer—or Papa Cornelius, as Iris is now expected to call him—he seems more depressed than anything. Perhaps Caspar is right, and van den Meer's marrying his housekeeper is a terrible mistake? Even though Margarethe's stock, two generations back, is solidly burgher, and the memory of her grandfather is still cherished in Haarlem? There stands van den Meer the entrepreneur at the door of his home, greeting the guests who have come to feast, and his chin is down upon his chest as if he hasn't slept well in days. Is he merely obliging propriety by this marriage? Or is there some genuine feeling for Margarethe? It's hard to tell.

As goes the wedding feast, so begin the weeks of their marriage: a celebration in the coldest of times, with spring only a dim hope.

Margarethe takes to her marriage bed without so much as a remark to her daughters. It leaves more room for Ruth and Iris by the hearth; they can keep warmer. But in more ways than this are they distanced from Margarethe. Their mother has decided that she can supervise the work of the household, and perform many tasks herself, but that a cook is needed to prepare the meals and to keep the kitchen in order. Before long she has hired a dull girl from Friesland whose only virtues, so far as Iris can make out, are a tireless application to any task assigned her, and a shyness that keeps her from objecting. Her name is Rebekka, and she doesn't wash enough. She smells of old potatoes.

Iris is assigned to be Rebekka's helpmeet from time to time, a situation she abhors. Rebekka is so listless of expression! Besides, she has no opinion about the imps and dragons and giants of the world. It's true, she's kind to Ruth, in an oblivious way, but she treats Clara and Iris as regrettable appliances in her arsenal of kitchen tools. She doesn't look at paintings or think about them. If she has memories of her home in Friesland, she doesn't bother to share them. "She's very private," says Iris.

"Admit it: She's as thick as a black pot," says Clara bitterly. "She's a fool, and she stinks."

"Stinging words! You're critical of everyone," observes Iris.

"Oh, not everyone," says Clara in an offhand manner. "Only everybody who's alive as well as most people who are dead. I feel quite neutral about anybody not yet born."

"I don't like this kind of talk. Ever since the day we went into the windmill, you've been cross. You're unpleasant to be with."

"You shouldn't have brought me there. It was too far to skate," says Clara.

"I didn't know you were going to be moody and queer about it. Where's Mama?"

"You mean Margarethe?"

"You know who I mean. Mama."

"She and Rebekka have gone to the market for fish and onions. She's not my mama." Clara plants her hands on her hips.

"She's near enough to it, and none other qualifies better," says Iris. "Don't you be sharp to her or you'll find she knows how to be sharp to you."

"You're in love with Caspar," says Clara idly. She takes an apple and inspects it for the brown softness. "You think I'm an idiot because I'm younger than you are. But I'm not as stupid as Ruth. I can tell."

"You have a lot more nonsense in your head than I realized!" says Iris. "Changelings and spirits and theories about romance!" Her heart stomps in her chest. It makes her jump to her feet like a grown woman, brushing her apron down with her hands as if she can't abide the waste of time in idle gossip. "Have you really nothing better to do?"

"I have nothing better to do," says Clara. Her voice begins to rise. "When have I had anything to do? I am too pretty to do anything but be looked at! Mama kept me from dirt and grime; Mama kept from the common people on the street, though we are hardy merchant stock, not royalty of any sort. Now Margarethe protects me from the plague. I would *relish* the plague for a change of routine!"

"Hush, that's a filthy sin!" says Iris. "And the corpses we've seen on the street, do they enjoy their change of routine? Clara! If you're so starved for activity, shovel the ashes from the hearth."

"I'm fanned and petted like a flower, I'm going to be planted in some rich man's garden so he can admire me!" shouts Clara. "Papa cherishes me for stupid reasons! Everything done in this household leans on me! Why do you think my father even married your mother? Just so there'd be no blemish on my reputation by his having an old, widowed harpy in the house!"

"You are evil," gasps Iris. "Can you say such things!"

"I can say a lot," says Clara.

"So it seems," says Margarethe at the doorway. Rebekka lurks behind her.

Clara has been sitting on a stool. At Margarethe's words she stands up slowly and faces her. Clara holds her hands at her side in a formal gesture. She doesn't apologize. She doesn't blink.

"I don't know whether to be offended or amused," says Margarethe. "Rebekka, set the fish in a basin of water for the time being, and then see to the floors and the bedding upstairs. You aren't beating the bedding well enough; the bedbugs thrive." Rebekka, who seems uninterested in the tension in the kitchen, does as she is told with the fish and then disappears up the back staircase. All the while Clara stands at attention, and Iris, with a sinking dread, discovers she feels responsible for the impasse between her mother and her new stepsister.

"Iris," says Margarethe, "go see to Ruth. She needs help washing again, I think; she's suffering the women's ailment and she's worried about it."

"Mama," says Iris in a careful voice, "don't take Clara's words seriously. She's still suffering herself, and learning how to be a daughter in a new family."

"I know Clara well," says Margarethe. "I know her type and I know how she deviates from her type. You have nothing to fear from me, Iris, and nor does Clara." She smiles in a clenched way. "All that stands in the way of harmony at home is an insufficient attention to the Fourth Commandment."

"But I honor my father and my mother," says Clara. "I honor my mother's memory and what she gave to me. And you're not my mother."

"The commandment requires that you yield to me as you did to her," says Margarethe. "I can't lay a claim to your heart, Clara, and I don't want to. But your behavior must reflect your understanding of my place in this house. I won't tolerate your abuse. Is that understood?"

"I understand," says Clara, "that you will not tolerate it."

"And you'll govern your behavior consequent to your understanding?"

"I understand," says the girl, "that you won't tolerate abuse. My behavior is a changing thing from hour to hour and day to day. We'll have to see, won't we? For there are things that I won't tolerate either." She begins to move away from the chair.

Margarethe neither strikes Clara for her insolence nor consoles her with an embrace. She merely says in an even tone, "Rebekka is feeling poorly today, and I've just learned we're to have guests at dinner. Your father has invited Master Schoonmaker and his apprentice. We'll need to make the room ready for guests. I will require your help."

"Require what you like," says Clara, and leaves the room.

Margarethe breathes a bit heavily, but only for a moment. Then, ignoring Iris, she begins to arrange the implements for an afternoon of cooking.

"Mama," says Iris, "you must see how unhappy Clara still is, what with her mother's death."

"I see how distraught you were with your father's death, you good daughter," says Margarethe. "You're my standard by which to judge Clara's behavior, Iris."

"I'm older," says Iris.

"Hardly," says Margarethe. "And you had no one to learn from. Was Ruth going to set you an example?"

"Well," says Iris, surprising herself somewhat, "in fact, Ruth did. Ruth was very brave when Papa died. And we all left—like that—like dark birds flying at night—"

"Ruth doesn't know how to be brave or cowardly any more than a loaf of bread does," says Margarethe sharply. "Didn't I tell you to go see to her? Let me be."

In the shed, under a table of potting implements, Ruth is lying with her hands between her legs. "Oh, come," says Iris, "it isn't that terrible, Ruth! Come with me and I'll help you wash, and bind you with a clean garment." And to herself she thinks, is there no end to what we must endure, even we whose lives are fairly safe?

When she's finished assisting her sister, she sneaks up the back stairs to find Clara and to console her. The girl is sitting in a straight-backed chair, looking out the window at the street below. "She may be my father's wife," says Clara with a cold clarity in her voice, "but she is *not* the mistress of this family. Not the family that I belong to. I am sorry that Papa has not made this clear to her. It is a mistake."

"You aren't old enough to be the mistress of your father's house!" says Iris bluntly. "And think of all the work that would fall on your shoulders if you were!"

"I'm beginning to think I would appreciate the responsibility of a good day's work," says Clara. "What else do I have? I don't want to go outside again, ever. But I don't want to die of boredom either."

"Beware what you request of life," says Iris. "If what you want is to work, then come downstairs and help me to arrange the table for guests."

"Do it yourself," says Clara. "I'm busy sulking."

"A pretty sulk you manage," says Iris, somewhat meanly. She leaves the girl alone. Iris thinks: Is it my lot in life to arrange peace among all parties? And why should that be?

The commotion in the kitchen is mercifully distracting. There are bread loaves to remove from the oven, and fruit to select, and cheese to liberate from its rind, and the glasses to collect from the cupboard. It isn't until there is a knock on the door that she realizes that she's been avoiding the most obvious fact: Caspar is coming to dine as well as the Master.

"I can't get the door, my hair is slipping from its bonnet," she says.

"Go, and forget your hair; who cares about *your* hair?" says Margarethe.

"Rebekka, you go," says Iris, but Rebekka is sitting before the fire with more than her usual listlessness, and she pays no attention to Iris.

"Do as you're told," says Margarethe to her daughter, sharply, when the knock is repeated.

So Iris does, and she escorts Caspar and the Master into the main room, where van den Meer sits inhaling his unlit tobacco in the well of his pipe. "Citron, mace, and rosemary, to the best of my knowledge," van den Meer says to the Master. "I don't hold that it cures you of worms, but it does delight the nostrils. Have some."

"I've come to work," says the Master, "if you remember. An hour of sketching while your family eats."

Caspar says in an aside to Iris, "You're about to disappear into the kitchen, but don't. You don't need to now. This is your home, you live here. Can't you sit and talk with me a while?"

"Our cook is feeling poorly," says Iris, watching the floor as if it were an icy pond about to crack beneath her feet. "I have to help Mama with her preparations. Time enough to talk when the work is done."

"Then I *will* indulge in some tobacco, sir," says Caspar to van den Meer.

"I didn't offer it to you, boy," says the host, and Iris

notices Caspar's face falling as she leaves the room to go back to her work at her mother's side.

"Are they here as guests of Papa Cornelius or as artists?" says Iris.

"The Master has asked for a favor," says Margarethe. "He's at work on a commission for a family in Amsterdam, I understand, to paint them in a grouping at home. He wants to show them some cartoons of a family at table, and he has come to study us and draw us while we eat our meal. It's my belief that Schoonmaker should be required to buy the supplies for this meal if he's to benefit from watching us eat it. Papa Cornelius disagrees. Papa Cornelius will be ruined if he doesn't watch every penny." Margarethe deposits the gleaming fish on a varnished plank and indicates that Iris should carry it in to the table. "Now," her mother continues, "we must play the role of the merry family, to honor the request Papa Cornelius makes. Clara," she calls, "Ruth, come to the table, that we may utter our grace and prove our worthiness to God to receive these blessings."

Ruth joins the others at the table. Clara won't.

"Iris," says Margarethe in a somewhat public voice, "please go tell your new stepsister that she is to come to the table at once."

"Mama," says Iris when she has returned, "she says she isn't hungry and she'll not come."

"Iris," says Margarethe, smiling as she serves the guests, "please be so good as to tell your new stepsister that if she does not come at once, she won't eat tonight and she won't eat tomorrow either."

"Margarethe," says van den Meer, "must you?" But Margarethe shoots him a look.

"I will behave as I see fit. You've asked me to do so, and you've entrusted me with the authority," says Margarethe. "Iris, do as I say."

Iris returns with a sullen and flushed Clara.

"Sit at my left, where I can reach you if I need to correct you," says Margarethe.

"My place is by my father," says Clara.

"Your place is where I say it is," says Margarethe.

"Let the girl put her bottom where she wants," says the Master, quaffing a glass of porter, but Margarethe gives him a look edged in ice, and he falls silent.

"Papa," says Clara. "Papa."

Cornelius van den Meer raises his eyes to the ceiling. He studies the candelabra as he says, "My business empire requires me to deal with squabbling investors, rats and squirrels who gnaw on flower bulbs, the fickleness of the buying public, the threat of accelerated hostilities with Spain. The squabbles around a dining table aren't my concern, and thanks be to God for that. I married a wife to manage the affairs within these walls, and, Clara, you will obey her or— you will obey her; that's all I have to say."

Clara sits down at the seat to the left of Margarethe. Her sweet face looks blank and tight. Margarethe rises and moves around the table, cursing mildly that Rebekka seems too under the weather to perform her duties. With ill-disguised pride Margarethe serves onto the best Ming china. She carries portions of food to the guests and then to her husband. Then she puts two full plates down before Ruth and Iris.

"But I don't want to eat this," says the Master, taking one bite and standing up again. "I'm here merely to sketch with a red chalk. Pass this on."

"I haven't a plate yet," says Clara. "I'll take it."

"You'll sit where you're ordered, and eat when I give you permission," says Margarethe. She turns the sweetest smile to the Master. "Leave your plate where it is. Surely you see how the candlelight falls nicely on it; you'll be able to draw it more faithfully in that fair light."

"It needs less to be rendered than to be eaten," says the Master with forced joviality. "Pass it to Clara, that's fine with me."

"Here, is there not enough?—I needn't eat," says Caspar, lifting his plate and holding it out.

"Are you all determined to undermine me?" says Margarethe. She stands and pounds the table with the bowl of a silver ladle. "I am the mother here! Are none of you willing to acknowledge my position?"

In the silence Iris sees even Papa Cornelius looks faintly alarmed, an alarm that he manages to cloak when his eyes briefly meet Iris's.

"We do what you say," says van den Meer in a small but steady voice, "or we do not eat at this table."

"Well, apparently I'm not eating at this table anyway, so what means that to me?" says Clara.

"I won't draw here if my presence causes anyone to go hungry," begins the Master.

It's unclear what will happen next; the room is struck silent. Iris glances from one person to another, and Ruth hides her face in her apron. Clara sits up straight, and she is suddenly no longer a child but a stripling adult, with that creature's feisty disregard for authority. Her lower lip stops trembling and her eyebrows draw closer together. She seems about to rise from the table and fling something at Margarethe.

But before she can, a sound from the kitchen causes all heads to turn. Margarethe won't move, and Iris is too much intrigued by the dynamics of the argument to budge from her bench. So it's Ruth who makes her cautious trundling step to the doorway of the kitchen to see what has caused the ruckus.

Pausing, Ruth turns back to the table. A white panic has come up in her face. She trembles and, to everyone's astonishment, makes a face that they can all read. She grasps her own neck and bulges her eyes out. The gargle of her uneducated throat completes the message. Rebekka is sick, sick or bludgeoned, or fainted, or dead.

Wind and Tide

"The imp again!" says Iris—she can't help herself. But in the commotion no one hears her, and she bites back the urge to repeat it, in case a stoat-toothed devilkin is crouching beneath the hutch or worming through the embers, listening. The fury in Margarethe's face is interior storm, and over the roof and against the windows, the wind has come up. The house is besieged.

Margarethe rocks Ruth aside and takes a closer look at Rebekka. "Go for the doctor, Caspar," she barks. "And you girls, back, out of here. All of you."

Caspar is at the door, winding his cloak up against his chin, when there is a sharp rap. He starts, and so do Iris and Ruth, who stand with him in the shadows of the hallway, gossiping and worrying about Rebekka. Caspar moves to open the door slowly, to peer around it and see who might be approaching at this hour. But the wind strikes a blow as he unlatches the hasp, and the door is thrown to with a crash.

"High wind, it's all," gasps Caspar to Ruth, who cowers against the wall as if more spirits are abroad in the dark and galloping their spectral steeds in the noisy air. Branches crack, and out in the nursery it sounds as if a table suddenly turns on its face, or is that more mischief afoot?—and there, at the door, a stocky man in a heavy green cape, one hand raised to pound again.

"Do you bring this wind with you, sir?" cries Caspar in what even Iris can see is a voice of false courage. But it's a kindly gesture meant to console Ruth, whose eyes are by now leaking down along her chin, which she holds in her clenched fists.

"Don't make small words with me," growls the stranger. His voice is rough and cracked, as if he's been shouting himself hoarse in the wind. "Let the scoundrel van den Meer come to hear the news himself, I want to see his face."

"This is not the hour," says Caspar, drawing himself up, offended at the stranger's tone. "He is taken up with a household crisis."

"Get the man or I'll push you over and call him myself," says the stranger. Without thinking, Iris puts her hand on Caspar's shoulder, a quiet apology for the man's rudeness, and she feels the apprentice shudder.

That she can make a young man tremble!

But the young man—her young man—Caspar—is no match for the visitor, who uses his broad chest to heave Caspar to the side as a bull will tumble a pesky hound. "Van den Meer," caws the visitor, "there's news from the dunes, and on the street; come and hear it from me before you hear it elsewhere!"

It's Clara who appears first—not to meet a stranger—she has been hurrying up the stairs away from the kitchen. At the sound of the stranger's voice she pauses at the doorway.

The man looks at her with interest. Suddenly Iris recognizes him: the kind stranger at the churchyard who chucked Clara's chin in his hand.

He drops his head and calls again, "Van den Meer!"

Clara doesn't mount the steps into the hall. She turns and goes back into the kitchen, and out the back door into the wind and the night, heading for the nursery, probably.

Van den Meer drops a bloody rag in the doorway of the kitchen. "Haven't you gone for the doctor yet, are you mad?" he yells at Caspar. "What are you waiting for, you simpleton?"

Ruth flinches, as always, when such a word is used.

Iris says, in a voice she hasn't previously used to Papa Cornelius, "He is answering the knock on your door. Don't criticize him for showing courtesy—"

"Iris," groans Caspar, "please!" With that, he throws himself into the dark and disappears from view.

"What fresh discontent is this, then, Nicolaes van Stolk?" says van den Meer.

"Collect your cloak and draw on stout shoes, if you would watch your fortune grow or collapse before your eyes," says van Stolk sourly, "for at the same time that a storm wind crosses the sea, tossing whales before it and scattering shoals of herring like flecks of sand from the dunes—indeed, tossing the very dunes themselves in the air, and shaping again that insubstantial margin that keeps Noah's flood from punishing the speculators—"

"God has promised not to punish us again with the flood—remember your Scriptures," says van den Meer harshly. "Pity when He was about the business of drowning useless species, He didn't include the flowery-tongued gossip among them. Tell me what you have to say, you who love the darkest news. Then take your leave."

"You aren't listening to me," says van Stolk. "The seas are high and the winds are of gale strength, and most of Haarlem is out on the sands to watch for whales—"

"What do I care about whales," says van den Meer heavily. "I have a housegirl with a bloody stomach, and it may be the plague—"

"The plague," says Iris, "no!—"

"—your fellow citizens watch," says van Stolk, "and they see at last the ship bearing your cargo, making small progress in the storm. *The ship*, van den Meer. Half of them have invested in your stock as primary investors, or else they have sold their shares for an impressive gain to more grasping souls. Many of your friends and neighbors are among them, who have more to lose by a sunken cargo even than you do. You who gorge on the fat of someone else's fortune. The least you can do, profiteer, is to join the anxious and keep watch over your wares in the water, and see how the hand of God treats one who prospers on the greed of others . . ."

"Stop your preaching," says van den Meer. "I'll come, because I must, but if you stand near me and prattle, I'll drown you myself in the first helpful wave."

The Master appears at the door from the kitchen to see what the fuss is. "Surely," he says, "you aren't going to leave when your kitchen girl is heaving blood—"

"She's a new girl," says van den Meer, "and as Margarethe married me to get a household to manage, this is part of the task. I will not," he says, and repeats in a stronger voice, "I will not be lectured by two guests, one at either side of my own hall!"

Van den Meer and van Stolk stumble out into the stormy evening, where, despite the clouds and the rising winds, a little late light is still dragging across the sky. The Master returns to the kitchen, where Margarethe can be heard heating a cauldron of water and calling for the slicing of lemons. Caspar is long gone, and Clara too. But Clara won't have ventured far. There is no place very far she can go.

Iris and Ruth look at each other. Ruth doesn't like it when two kitchen cats claw at each other. She likes it less when her family squabbles. She sits on her haunches, her petticoats and skirts every which way, her face mucky with fretting. Iris catches her breath, one hand out to steady herself against the dark oak chest. "Ruth," says Iris, "you mustn't fuss yourself. Everything will turn out all right. The weather is the hand of God, and so is the course of sickness—"

"Are you gaggling in there like goose sisters, when I need your help?" calls Margarethe, so the girls go in to help their mother.

Rebekka is laid on a cloth near the warmth of the fire. Iris can't help herself: She studies the scene for color. The bright red of the newest coughed blood, the brick brown of older, dryer spatterings, the goldfish scales of the copper kettle, the brown shadows in which the Master works at assembling a poultice of garlic and lemons. The smell is ferocious, and even the cat looks offended and keeps his distance. "Is it the plague, as Papa Cornelius says?" asks Iris.

"I'm no student of the physic. I'm merely trying to help the woman breathe," says Margarethe. "Lord preserve us, the plague at last in our own house, to bring us down just when we have survived our trials. I should cart this girl out into the storm and let God take her there, if take her He will!" But she makes no move to follow her own advice, and Iris is sent to hunt for extra blankets in the cupboard upstairs, as Rebekka seems unaccountably chilled, even near the fireplace.

The kitchen is too frightening for Ruth, and Clara is still missing, so after a while Iris settles Ruth in Clara's bed and stays by Ruth's side until she drifts into a fitful sleep. Iris naps too. It's late in the evening when the doctor is located at last—on the dunes, with other witnesses of the disaster that is inevitable . . . that might be averted . . . Just wait . . .

The doctor's arrival wakes Iris. Though she crouches in the stairwell to overhear, she can't make out his hushed report to Margarethe. But after the doctor leaves, Iris ventures into the kitchen, rubbing her eyes, pretending to be just awakened.

"Papa Cornelius still frets at the shore, where the storm takes on a greater fury, so the doctor says," says Margarethe. "I didn't know how the citizens of this town have taken to these investments. Tulips, yes, the mad passion for strong flowers; but the passion to invest, and to make money on speculation? If this cargo is lost, my girl, we are in another stew; so if the plague takes hold in this household, we might find ourselves well out of this sorry dilemma."

"Mama," says Iris. She yawns. "These are adult things, and I am a child."

"You're less a child than your older sister, and I need some comfort tonight," says Margarethe. "The Master has gone back to his studio, since there's nothing else he could do. Prepare me some weak tea, while I keep at this messy work, and Rebekka more or less dies in my lap."

"Clara went out to the nursery—has she come back in?" says Iris.

"That's her business, or so I am told," says Margarethe.

"Mama," says Iris. "Please. She is only a child—"

"Find her and mind her yourself," says Margarethe, "after I have my bowl of tea, to soothe me and keep me alert. Papa Cornelius will not be lectured by his guests, and I will not be lectured by my daughter. I don't care if Clara catches the plague herself—"

"Mama!" says Iris.

"If there's a fortune to inherit, should the cargo go through," says Margarethe, "you'd benefit more if Clara had gone to her grave."

"Oh, you aren't thinking rightly!" says Iris. She has no shame but she worries, for her mother has a wild look in her eye. "You rest, Mama, and let me sponge down poor Rebekka. This isn't like you, you mustn't say such a thing."

"You find Clara, then, and you do the deed of charity," says Margarethe, "but not until after my tea." She closes her eyes for a moment and says in a whisper, "Of course I don't mean such dreadful things, Iris. Of course I don't."

Iris makes the tea as quickly as possible and flees the kitchen sickroom.

The shed is dark and cold, yet even as it creaks beneath

the lashings of wind and rain, there is a smell of spring, of soil and the wet wooden handles of tools.

Clara is lying beneath a table of tulip bulbs near to flowering. Her eyes are rolled up in her head, and for an instant Iris believes that Clara has succumbed to the plague too. But it's merely a dreary half sleep, from which Clara starts as she realizes that Iris is approaching. "Who's there?" cries Clara.

"It's only me," says Iris. "Why are you out here when commotion plagues your family so inside?"

Clara allows herself to be embraced, and she weeps in Iris's arms. She doesn't answer the question. She merely says, in a dull voice, as if to herself and without expectation of an answer from her stepsister, "Oh, whatever is to become of me?"

The Girl
of Ashes

The death of Rebekka is a study in contrasts with the death, just six weeks earlier, of Henrika. Rebekka is bundled up and carted away within the hour, and if there's a service for the poor thing, or if anyone makes any attempt to inform whatever scrag ends of family she might have back in Friesland, Iris never learns about it. Rebekka leaves the household as quietly and anonymously as she has come. Perhaps the household imp is trapped in Rebekka's corpse and has been evacuated that way?

Perhaps. The storm has lifted, and, against all expectations, the ship bearing the precious cargo of tulip bulbs has straggled up the ice-choked but navigable Saarne to the tie-up. The ship didn't founder, there were no Leviathans washed up on the beach: The next day folks complain that they lost sleep over precious little in the way of disaster. But, Iris is realizing, this is their way of slighting their own anxiety. If the cargo had been ruined, a number of Haarlem investors would have suffered serious losses.

Van den Meer boasts of how he greeted the captain and escorted him to an inn for a hot rum and a bonus of a small sack of gold coins. A triumphant return! Van den Meer spends more time away from his home than he has before. He lingers at the public house where the college of tulip traders meets. He crows about lining up new investors for another shipment. He appears not to notice that Margarethe is being more strict and proprietary about the household— or, Iris wonders, is that part of what causes him to spend so many hours away?

As Margarethe spends less time in the kitchen, so she can be parading about the streets of Haarlem in new clothes, Clara takes up the slack by the hearth. She has put off the very young way of clothing herself that Henrika preferred. Clara dresses in plain garb, suitable for a maid. She has decided that she doesn't mind the chores, she tells Iris and Ruth. In fact, she'd rather learn small tricks of cooking instead of turns of Italian grammar or difficult passages in keyboard exercises. "It is a private place, the kitchen," she says simply, and by that Iris suspects she means, *Now that Margarethe is no longer here.*

Then the Easter season is upon them! At last! The brightening skies, the return of warm weather, the hilarity of children let out of doors, with less binding clothing, with longer legs than they possessed the season before. Iris wants to run with them, to ramble in the fields and meadows, but if Clara is growing into a young woman, so is Iris. The day comes when it's Iris's turn to seep and be sore as women do.

Ruth lies with her and puts her hands on her stomach for comfort, and Clara stands in the doorway looking queasy. "Could a worse trial be devised?" says Clara, treating Iris like a horrible specimen at a medical demonstration. "I hope such a trouble never comes to me."

"Go away," says Iris, who can't be kind while her lower regions clutch and ache.

Things settle down. Caspar arrives with word that the Master expects to see Iris in his studio, ready to learn to draw at the least, and to help out when the learning has made her ready. Iris won't even ask Margarethe for permission, for she knows what the answer would be. Besides, she's come to realize that what she feels for Caspar is love, pure and simple— well, now, isn't she old enough to know what love is?—and she won't be able to bear being so close to him every day without declaring herself. And she has no courage for that.

Ruth doesn't display much interest when she hears her sister and stepsister talking. Ruth has begun to pay more attention to the animals in the household—the cat, the chickens, the mice that can be rescued from the cat and kept in a small wire cage until they die. Is it merely that the family is getting older, and there are more diversions? Or does Ruth actually seem to be thriving, perhaps due to Margarethe's increased absences? Margarethe refuses to hire another girl from off the street to do housework, for fear the plague will come back and gain the foothold that it hasn't managed to get so far. So Clara does more of the housework, and Iris supervises and mopes and dreams of Caspar, and Ruth keeps to her small animals, and stands straighter and looks with a more secure gaze on the world than she's been known to do before.

It's Clara who, with a somewhat devious expression, finally says to Iris, "You alone are unhappy now. What are you waiting for?"

"I don't know what you mean," says Iris, folding some laundry that's been airing in the strengthening April light.

"There's no reason you shouldn't go to Master Schoonmaker's studio and learn a few things about drawing if you like."

"What? And leave you to manage the entire household by yourself?" says Iris. "I may not like supervising you in the housework, but I could hardly think of abandoning you here."

"Don't fret," says Clara. "It brings me nearer to my mother, to do the things that she did. I don't mind Margarethe out being the pride of Haarlem, making friends and spending money. The house is quieter when she's gone. I have something of what I want. So why shouldn't you? Don't you want to paint?"

"I do not know if it's proper for women to paint," says Iris.

"It may not be common," says Clara, "but surely it's neither impossible nor illegal. Wouldn't the Master tell you if it were? And why do you worry about propriety, anyway?"

Iris took a deep breath. "The Master already has a student, Caspar," she says.

"What does that matter? Besides, don't you care for him?" says Clara. Her frankness surprises Iris. "All the more reason to go spend time with him. A chance to get to know him better!"

"Don't be ridiculous," snaps Iris. "You don't want to be caged in the shell of some stupid marriage, Clara, but don't be caged by your own limited experience either. You must be able to see my plight. I'm not as pretty as you; I don't stimulate interest as you do."

"Caspar is very friendly to you," says Clara in an even voice, taking no offense. "You aren't a dull person, Iris, and for all your plainness you're interesting to look at. Why lock yourself in your own cage when someone is handing you a key? Why not learn a skill while spending time with people you care about? Just say what Margarethe would say: Give me room to cast my eel spear, and let everything else follow as it may."

Iris isn't fond of this sentiment. She retorts, "I can't leave you to manage the kitchen by yourself, Clara."

"Ruth can lend a hand when I need help," says Clara. "If you don't ask your mother for permission, Iris, I'll do it for you."

Iris slowly puts her face in her hands. Is there sense in what Clara is suggesting?

"You ought at least to know," says Clara. "What if you're wrong and Caspar could find himself in love with you? What if you lost this chance to learn?"

There is a grunt. Iris looks up through wet eyes. Ruth has come to the doorway, and perhaps she's listened to the conversation. She is nodding at Iris and grinning in an encouraging way.

"Ruth will help me when I need help, won't you, Ruth?" says Clara.

Ruth nods, puts the cat on the floor, and rolls her sleeves as if to begin scrubbing a floor.

"All right, then," says Iris. "I'll see if I can summon the courage to ask Mama."

"You do that," says Clara. She puts down the small hearth broom and suddenly, with a chuckle, dips her hands in the ashes. She smudges her cheeks and her forehead. "I am no beauty anymore, I'm a simple kitchen girl, a cinder-lass, at home in my ashes and char."

"Don't do that," says Iris, "it makes me shudder. In England we had a child's game about flowers and ashes—Ring a round of rosies, a pocket full of posies; Ashes, ashes, ashes, and down we fall. It is a simple ditty for toddlers to play, to walk and tumble and shriek with, but someone told me once it's a game that derived from fear of the plague, and the ashes are those that we crumple into if the plague should overtake our lives. So don't be the girl of ashes, not even in play; you're too good."

Iris thinks about Clara's offer and amends her remark: "You are far too good."

Clara purses her lips. "No, you are good, but what a simpleton! You don't even see that I'm merely looking after myself, as usual." Iris doesn't know if this is strictly true. Clara has been sad, bitterly severed from the possibilities of her life, but is she incapable of kindness? That would make her a sort of beautiful monster.

Clara shrugs as if she can see these thoughts on Iris's face. She continues, "I don't care if you're happy or not, not really. But if you're gone from the house, I'm the more secure

in my kitchen. The more needed, the more private. Call me Cinderling," says Clara, standing up straighter behind her mask of ashes. "Call me Ashgirl, Cinderella, I don't care. I am safe in the kitchen."

Finery

"**S**o rude an onion as I can be made to look like a rose," says Margarethe with pleasure. "What do you think of me now?"

She parades up and down the black and white tiles in her new garb. Iris holds her hands together to keep from wringing them. Her mother looks less like a rose than like a heap of unsold flowers at the end of market day, thrown together with no regard for effect. Iris has always thought that Margarethe is possessed of a sober good taste. Now she realizes, with a start, it is poverty that kept Margarethe in appealing browns, blacks, and whites. Left to her own devices and granted a decent purse, Margarethe would rather look like a strumpet.

But Margarethe doesn't notice Iris's disapproval. And Ruth is clapping her hands in appreciation and chuckling at the transformation. Clara, who has come from the kitchen with a basket of turnips in her arms, says merely, "This fills me with a strange joy," and turns around again.

"I should imagine it did," says Margarethe, missing the irony in Clara's tone.

"The colors," says Iris, because she can't think of another remark.

"And the finishing touch—I daren't wear them through the streets," says Margarethe. She unfolds a length of cloth and takes out a pair of dainty white shoes, in leather pounded so smooth as to fit like a skin. The leather shines with an oil so it's like looking at shoes of porcelain or cloudy glass.

"Hardly useful in the streets of Haarlem," says Iris, despite herself. "No matter how well the Dutch clean up after themselves and their horses."

"To be worn when I go forth in a carriage, door to door. Do I hear some disapproval in your voice?" says Margarethe. "Why shouldn't I be well turned out?"

"Please," says Iris, "I don't mean to be rude. They are soft as gloves, aren't they? Where will you wear them?"

"These shoes will open doors for us, as yet still closed," says Margarethe.

"That would be a sight," says Iris. "You mean, they can kick doors open?"

"Oh, the comic airs of the young," says Margarethe, but without rancor. "Put these away in the wardrobe, and wrap them carefully again so as to protect against marks and dirt. You still don't know what your mother is capable of on your behalf."

"And on your own," says Iris in an even voice.

"In a family, the good of one member advances the good of all members."

"Well," says Iris, "then may I propose the good of this member by asking for your permission to take up a position—for a few weeks only perhaps—as an associate in the Master's studio? He thinks I can learn some rudiments of drawing, while I help him with the preparation of colors and varnishes and the stretching of canvases and linens—"

"I should think not," says Margarethe, admiring herself in the mirror at the end of the room. "He's been filling your head with notions, and I disapprove."

"It does a girl no harm to learn a skill—" begins Iris.

"I won't have you being an assistant to anyone," says Margarethe. "Not when we can afford for you to learn the things that wealthier girls learn. A little French perhaps, some Italian—you're just as bright as Clara, though you didn't start so young, and now there's time for you to advance. Clara can mind our Ruth."

"I want to go to the studio," says Iris, "not just to assist him, but for what I can learn there. I am being selfish, Mama. I want to learn something I care about. I don't want to prattle in French."

Clara calls from the kitchen, in a pleasant voice, a long declarative sentence—in French. Perhaps she knows what she is doing, for Margarethe blushes—unable to understand—and she stands there for a moment, at a loss. Finally, in reply, and equally loudly, "If Clara really is willing to do the household chores that you might have done together, perhaps I can spare you."

"*Merci*," says Clara, and they all understand that. And Iris sees that she is the beneficiary of Clara's desire to stay home, whether Clara means to be helpful or not.

* * *

The next day Iris wraps a cloak around herself and takes a basket of bread and a pot of conserves, and makes her way through wet, sun-scrubbed streets. Haarlem is seeing to itself with its usual pride. Doorsills are swept, brasses polished, windows washed, gardens tended, loaves of bread cooling on sills. Iris realizes that there's a purpose in her step, and it has something to do with her heart, but, as well, it has something to do with her hands—they're eager and ready to grapple with a little red chalk, to try a few early lines on paper.

The Master and Caspar are busy arranging paintings in a sloping pile, smaller paintings nearer the wall, larger ones propped carefully at an angle over them, each one a few inches out from the last so that there's a protective edge of air between them. Caspar's face brightens at the sight of Iris in the doorway, but the Master is frowning and seems hardly to notice.

"If it's bread as a present, put it in the kitchen," he says. "Caspar, let's get the Annunciation next, the one in golds."

"I've come to the studio, not the kitchen," says Iris.

"Then you and Caspar shift these larger paintings, and let me get back to the portrait of Burgher Stoutbelly before I fully wake up from last night's ale. It turns my stomach to think of the time I spend on glorifying insignificant people, and I can only bear to do it when I am partly asleep or partly drunk, and at the moment I'm both. And don't talk to me. I'm in no mood for silly gossip."

"One piece of gossip a day is enough, eh?" says Caspar, winking at Iris.

She realizes the wink, though directed at her and meant

to draw her in, is an observation about the Master. "What piece of gossip is this?" she says, dropping her cloak and her basket and following Caspar into a side room, where more paintings are slanting in the gloom.

"Gossip for painters and social climbers alike," says Caspar.

"Fortunately I'm neither one, so I can hear the news without overexciting my heart," says Iris, whose heart is well excited as it is, to be in a dark, narrow space with Caspar leaning conspiratorially to whisper to her.

"At a party last night the word was bruited about that Marie de Medici is to spend a fortnight in Haarlem. She is the widow of Henry IV, and she's the Dowager Queen of France. She recently set up a house in Amsterdam, where she shocks the local shopkeepers by going right in and arguing their prices down. She's an old bull."

"I suppose even the very royal must travel sometimes," says Iris. "This hardly seems worth a sour mood."

"She's reported to have two aims," says Caspar. "She's called for an exhibition of the finest of living Dutch painters so that she can choose someone to do what she deems her last portrait—she's sixty-five years of age and faces the grim specter of death. So the painters are in a stew to select their best two or three works and submit them to the Haarlem governors. Everyone hopes to get invited to exhibit and maybe even to meet the Queen. She's holding a similar exercise in Amsterdam, and perhaps again in Rotterdam or Utrecht, though Rotterdam doesn't boast the native ability in painting that Haarlem does."

"Thus— Annunciations?" guesses Iris.

"She's from Florence, which is quite Catholic," says Caspar, heaving at the edge of a huge panel and motioning Iris to do likewise. "She won't have the aversion to devotional subjects that we friendly Calvinists do. But is the Master ruining his chances of being included in the exhibit by submitting work that's so out of fashion? After all, he has to gain the approval of the Haarlem fathers first."

"Surely they have in mind the Queen's taste too," says Iris. "As hosts they'll hope to make her happy."

"To the contrary, as hosts the Haarlem patriarchs are proud of thriving mightily without much of a royal family," says Caspar. "We Dutch all merely nod to our Frederick Henry, Prince of Orange. Still, since the word is that the French she-elephant is coming, the Master is willing to gamble. Let the Haarlem judges decide. The best commission of his life may hinge on this."

"I didn't think the Master was a social climber," says Iris.

"The painters don't necessarily thrill and puff up at that aspect of it," says Caspar. "Anyway, word also has it that the Queen has a secondary aim. She will preside at a ball, or perhaps a series of them, to introduce one of her relatives or godchildren to Dutch society. He may even be looking for a bride among the assembled ranks of young women."

"Surely not!" says Iris. "Members of royal families don't select spouses from the crowds who assemble to gape at them!"

"I should have thought the same," says Caspar. "But those who pay attention to the fortunes of nations remind us that there isn't any eligible young woman in the House of Orange-Nassau. Suppose Holland is to have a long, fruitful existence as a republic? For a foreign nobleman on the rise, a bride from the class of men who govern Holland through these prosperous years might be a wise course of action."

"And what about this nobleman's affections?" says Iris. "Isn't he to have some say in a choice of bride?"

"You ask me how these things work?" says Caspar, winking at her again. "What do I know of young men and their affections?"

They don't speak for a while. They heave eight of the Master's Annunciations out of storage. Once the paintings are set up around the room, a family resemblance can be seen among them—not only in the subject matter, but also in the choice of colors that the Master favors. When he finally throws his brushes down in disgust, cursing at the likes of Burgher Stoutbelly, he turns to study the Annunciations.

"Tripe," he announces at the first two. "The colors thud. They are painted with dung and piss. Take them away."

"They are heavy to carry," says Caspar, still breathing heavily.

"They muddy the light and stink up the room. Take them away."

Iris and Caspar carry them back to the side room.

Of the other six the Master says, "In this one the Virgin appears already pregnant. Not appropriate for the Annunciation. Take it away."

"She isn't pregnant," says Caspar. "She's merely well fed. So is Marie de Medici, they say."

"Take it away, but watch the frame on the doorway. This is one of the larger ones."

"This is hard work," says Iris in a whisper. "Am I going to get to draw at all today?"

"Stop whispering! You annoy me and cloud my thoughts," shouts the Master. "As if I'm not annoyed enough by my own obvious lack of talent. If you can find a knife in there, come in and slice my eyes out, as I clearly don't use them much in the production of paintings anyway. What was I thinking of?"

There are, in the end, only two pieces deemed worth considering. Iris admits that they are fine paintings, and as much good could be said about one as about the other. "No decision needs to be made immediately," says the Master. "But if you had to choose one on my behalf, Caspar, Iris, because I had just tumbled into a ditch and brained myself, which one would you choose, and why?"

"I wouldn't send an Annunciation," says Caspar, which enrages the Master so much that Caspar is forced to go outside and occupy himself well beyond the reach of the Master's fists.

"Well, you tell me, then, Iris," says the Master.

"For one reason alone, I prefer the squarer panel to the higher one," says Iris, thinking hard, but requiring herself to be as truthful as she is kind. "In this the Virgin has darker hair, and more tightly curled, the way I imagine the hair of Florentine women might be. Perhaps it would make Marie de Medici think of herself—"

"—Idolatrous idea!" says the Master.

"Like the Virgin, the Dowager Queen of France is also named Marie, remember," says Iris.

"—but fascinating and pertinent, to be sure," he continued. "Well, we'll see how that thought sits with us for a while. I'm not sure—"

"I assume you don't want to think about one of your portraits of the maimed, the evil, the fallen?—"

He doesn't even answer that.

"Then there's another possibility," says Iris cautiously. "Your best painting is Young Woman with Tulips. Why aren't you thinking about that?"

"The subject is a coarse one, however beautiful the model," says the Master.

"The way you painted it is superior, and you know it," says Iris. "Even I, who know nothing about painting, can see it."

"It will offend the Dowager Queen to see such a splendid young woman in her prime, and celebrated for just that. It will make her realize how much time has passed in her life—"

"Doesn't she realize that already, and isn't that why she's commissioning a final portrait?"

The Master strokes his beard and idly fingers a few breakfast crumbs from it onto the floor. "Well, I'll take the advice and ponder it in good time. It would mean asking van den Meer to borrow it. On the other hand, think of the people who would see it! Always hunting for investors as he does, he may realize this is the most public reception the painting can ever have. And even if Marie de Medici didn't give me the commission, many wealthy guests would also see it there. Things to think about. Hmmmm."

He ponders for a while, curses, and then remembers Iris. "Now that irritating Caspar has removed himself for a few moments, tell me why you've come to call."

"You asked me to be your assistant, don't you remember?" says Iris.

At this the Master turns and looks at her as if for the first time that day. "There are *many* items of gossip today, then," he says tenderly. "This is as important an announcement as the prattle that a foreign queen comes to dance her ancient feet on our republican floors. First things to be done first! Why didn't you tell me when you arrived? And you've been doing nothing but carting paintings back and forth!"

"What is an assistant expected to do?" she asks eagerly.

"Cart paintings," he says. "Get Caspar from outside and take these paintings out of my sight before I succumb to the temptation to coat them with a muddy oil wash and erase all my hopes of immortality. Work comes first, and drawing later. But drawing will come, my Iris. Before you leave today, you will draw."

Spine and Chamber

And draw she does.

She assumes that skill will guide her fingertips, that shapely lines will uncoil out of the pencil the moment she starts. Surely talent is a thing curled deeply inside, just waiting to be exercised, and at the slightest invitation it will stretch, shake itself, make itself known?

Talent, it seems, is not so insistent.

She pecks at the paper with small lines. She smudges them and begins again. She holds back, waiting for the paper to instruct her. She beats it with her hand. It won't deliver up its expectations. Perhaps it has none. The Master has said, "Observe the simplest thing and render it." She hoped for an apple, a chestnut, an egg. Instead he found her a porcelain seashell from some Afric strand.

It is quirky, both glazed and porous, a surface complicated by reflections, depths, stains. The shell stands at an angle like a mace. She hates it. She can't figure out its humblest tip, much less how it crowds its space with spikes, ribs, volutes, a stem or spine that curls like paper, a circlet of tiny points more ornate than any tiara that the she-elephant, Marie de Medici, might wear at a ball.

The Master pays her no attention, but moves to the other side of the room, where he shingles a canvas with broad strokes of charcoal green. She weeps a little to see his vigor and her own fear. When she spies Caspar moving about the back room, hanging a pot over the coals to boil some water and bruise some roots into a soup, she wipes her cheeks with the back of her hand.

"Look," says Caspar, coming in after a while. "Look how prettily you've smudged your cheekbones with that red chalk. You have a fine bone here and here—"

He touches her face. She casts her eyes to the floor. The paper is a wilderness of indecisive strokes, looking nothing like a seashell. Looking only like failure.

"And they give your face color too," says Caspar, lifting her chin.

"I'm not here to paint myself," she says, more fiercely than she has meant to. "I am to sketch an irritating accident of nature. Look how it brandishes its tips at me! I want to kill it."

"It's not alive," says Caspar. "Draw it, and you make it live."

"Let her be," says the Master in a good-humored, abstracted tone.

"You have to look before you can lift a crayon," says Caspar. "Isn't he saying so to you?"

"She knows how to look," says the Master.

Caspar pays him no attention. He pulls up a three-legged stool and perches on it. His shoulder is a few inches below

Iris's, and it rolls in toward her. Any moment it might touch her. She's afraid that if it does, she might recoil, not out of horror but just physical shock, the way an invisible bright bug sometimes leaps out of bundles of clean, sunny laundry and crackles on the tips of her fingers. She wills herself to attend to his words and not to the achingly sweet turn of his shoulder, how it swells just so into the cords of his slender neck.

"It's a brutish thing to draw, to be sure," Caspar is saying. "Think what the shell is like."

"It's like nothing I ever saw before," says Iris.

"Is it like nothing in nature or in the house or barn of man?"

"It's not like a cat, a flower, a table, or a cloud," says Iris.

"Isn't it like a big flower blossom," says Caspar, "snapped off a thick stem and laid on its side?"

"I never saw blossom so huge and garish," says Iris, and then, with a sinking heart, remembers what her mother looked like in the new finery that morning.

"Isn't it like a wheelbarrow, then?" says Caspar. "It balances on one point at this end, and its bulk rests so, and if you could imagine two stems instead of one to be the rafters of the shaft . . ."

"I never saw a seashell with wheels attached, and this isn't one either," says Iris.

He tries again. "Don't look at it, then, for what it reminds you of. I take that idea back. Look at it for its own set of proportions. Here. Squeeze your eyes closed, or nearly closed. So you can merely make out a blur of seashell. Can you do that?"

She closes her eyes entirely and thinks of Caspar, more boy than blur, skin more porcelain than a seashell, hair more spiky, voice more soothing, rhapsodic . . .

"Attend," he says, a bit impatiently. She obeys.

"Don't think of particulars," he says. "Think of general shapes. If you can make two motions of your hand across the paper, and you need to spend those motions on the most significant lines of this blurred shape, what motions will they be?"

She shrugs, but is able first to ball her fist, then to sweep it out, to represent the bulk of the seashell chamber on one end and the tapering stem on the other.

"And there you have your first lesson," he says. "Now make those two marks, without fear of how they relate to each other or to the seashell before you. Just sweep those marks on the page as if you're drawing in the flour on the bread-baking table."

"Don't forget to tell her to breathe, and blink, and swallow from time to time," says the Master, somewhat jeeringly.

"You taught me all this," says Caspar to the Master, though his eyes don't leave Iris's hands or the paper. "You just didn't know you were teaching it."

"I should have taught you to drown yourself in the ditch," says the Master.

"Keep at your work and we'll keep at ours," says Caspar. Iris waits for an irate response, but the Master only chuckles and, she sees, behaves.

She has a sloppy knob and the tentative stroke of a spine on the page. "Not bad. They speak to each other. A natural gift for the appropriate weight in the mark," Caspar muses.

"Now it's simply a matter of looking at the details and seeing what you see."

"I don't know how to draw the other side of the seashell," she says.

"It can't be seen from where you sit," he says, "so never mind it."

"You can see it, though," she says, "you can tell me."

"Drawing is the only honesty," he ventures. "Don't interpret. Merely observe. Don't think about what you see. Merely see it."

She draws the spine, she draws the chamber. She curses the paper, the chalk, her fingers, herself, the seashell. She can't curse Caspar. But, momentarily, once in a while, she can forget him. Slowly the seashell comes forward. It is a joke of a seashell, an abomination of a seashell, a curse of a seashell. It is still a seashell.

She walks home in the dusk. Many more hours have passed than she intended to spend. The lights are up in the house at home. There is the sound of caterwauling from the kitchens. Not more mischief, not a return of—

She stops herself. She has tried to put aside her tendency to be fanciful. She tries to think in terms she is sure of.

Not more plague, thinks Iris, hurrying.

But it isn't the plague.

Collapses

"Don't carry on so, just tell me!" says Iris, throwing her cloak aside.

Papa Cornelius sits slumped on a bench. One shoulder lifts higher than the other; at first Iris thinks he is in tears. But his face is sallow and his eyes apparently drained of tears, and his expression seems blanker than anything else. "We are ruined," he says, "the curse of our greed has been our undoing."

"Don't sit there and moan," screams Margarethe. "There are avenues to explore, surely; there are gullible fools beyond the reach of the information you have! Go sell your shares while you can instead of shivering like a ninny!"

"I can't take advantage of my neighbors and fellow citizens like that—"

"Of course you can, what else had you meant to do?" says Margarethe. "Your scruples didn't keep you from importing a new stock of tulips to tease the marketplace with! Why this sudden attack of conscience now?"

"Any moment we can be struck down, by plague if not by

insolvency," says van den Meer. "I won't put my immortal soul in peril—"

"So you'll put the mortal bodies of your daughter and your new wife and your adopted family at risk instead? When we have nothing left to eat, we'll thank you for saving our *souls?*"

"Don't blaspheme, Margarethe," he says, "it doesn't beautify you to do so."

"What's happened?" says Iris. "For the love of God, tell me!"

"It is her greed," says van den Meer. He has had his ale. "She is the fisherman's wife: always wanting something more, and more than that besides, and then still more."

"Who taught me greed?" says Margarethe. "Who is my tempter and my tutor?"

"Stop," he roars, "I taught you nothing!"

"Well, I teach you courage in adversity, and you are to march out there—"

But he is not taking lessons from his wife. He is in no mood to march. He puts his head in his hands and mumbles some tale of investments. "I can't understand this," says Iris, turning to her mother, looking quickly at Ruth and Clara, who are huddled, arms locked around each other's waists, in the doorway to the front room. "Don't spare me! I'm not as young and ignorant as I once was."

"The spring is here, the notion of a visiting monarch has spread," says Margarethe, with a gleam in her eye that shows the courage that comes from desperation. "For the last several years the value of the newest variety of tulip has risen, and risen, and on the street and in the halls the same lots of bulbs were being sold again and again, for ever higher prices, wave after wave of profit. Everyone knows this; everyone has invested. I alone didn't see it, for what do I know of money beyond the single coin a sharp woman can hide in her shoe? But this is the game that Papa Cornelius has been playing with Henrika's dowry, investing in a stock that others can speculate upon."

"That's not the misfortune! That's merely commerce, supplying what's in demand!" says van den Meer.

Margarethe continues. "One man could pay a fortune for the future value of the bulb crop, and turn around and sell his share for two fortunes an hour later. Men were buying not to own the tulips but to sell them again to the most aggressive purchaser. And the value of the lot of tulips, over which we all worried these months, has risen eightfold since arriving in port! A man who never invested in them, never saw them, never sweated over their possible loss in the storms at sea, never trod the dunes watching and praying, could make eight times in an hour what *husband* made in six months! Why should we have been denied income like that? Is it our low birth that keeps us ineligible?"

"Born high or low, we are low now," he groans.

"So I told him to do the same as his neighbors," says Margarethe grimly, "not just to import the bulbs and sell them, but to hazard a guess that there would be buyers to spend even more on the lot than he could! So I told him to buy back his share and sell it again in a while, and build up our coffers, and make us worthy guests to the ball! So I told him to do better in my time than he had ever done in Henrika's, lowly though I am!"

"And what has happened to the tulips? Did they burn? Are they infested with worms?" says Iris, beginning to understand.

"The tulips are the same tulips as ever they were," says Margarethe, "not more beautiful or less beautiful. Simply less desirable. Who knows why. Just as he stood, having paid the highest amount yet offered, and as he began to negotiate to sell for an even higher amount, news about sickness on the far side of town began to filter in. One of the purchasers who has a farm out that way excused himself from the bidding and went to check on relatives. Another merchant stroked his chin and said he couldn't afford to bid. And suddenly the mood had changed, and one by one the burghers and merchants began to offer their own lots for sale. The bulbs had, in an instant, become less valuable, though they are still the same bulbs, still ready for planting, still offering the same amount of beauty. And of future value—vanished like smoke. The tulips don't offer the same amount of return, and, like a wind suddenly veering from the east when it has blown from the west, the appetite for investing in tulip bulbs has become, in an afternoon, a frantic desire to unload them, to sell them for whatever could be gotten. The prices dropped precipitously all day."

"They'll surely rise again tomorrow?" says Iris, though with doubt.

"I've already sold them for a thirtieth what I paid," says van den Meer. "I had to. Tomorrow they may be worth a ninetieth what I paid."

"So they're sold," says Iris. "What does that mean to us?"

"It means," says van den Meer coldly, "I owe in cash and financial instruments many, many times more than my holdings are worth. I am bankrupt and have no resources. It means we lurch into poverty."

"It means we must find ourselves a chance to be bold, to reclaim ourselves and our fortune," says Margarethe.

"We don't have a foothold," says van den Meer.

"We have an invitation to one of the balls," says Margarethe. She withdraws from her sleeve a fold of creamy paper. "Perhaps you sold with an uncharacteristic lack of shrewdness, Cornelius. But the safe arrival of your shipment last month must have reached the ear of the household of Marie de Medici. Grand ladies in the court of her son, they say, arrange tulips in their bosoms—the rarer the bloom, the more exquisite the woman. The old war horse may be estranged from her son, but she's not insensible to style; she's a queen mother. Your notoriety as a major importer has brought you to the attention of the Pruyns, or whoever is proposing the guest list. No one is going to retract this invitation. We are going to the great hall and we are going to meet the Dowager Queen of France and her godson. We'll simply apply our wiles to a different marketplace. Now, take your salty chin out of your hands and stop your sniveling. There's much to be done, and precious little time in which to do it! Give me room to cast my eel spear, and let follow what may."

4

THE GALLERY OF GOD'S MISTAKES

Campaigns

Papa Cornelius is a limp puppet of himself, a rag without a manipulating hand inside. He lies on a bench under a blanket. He shows no interest in going back to the tavern where the college that oversees the buying and selling of tulip futures had met, drunk, and prospered. Margarethe plies him with reliable tisanes. Her skill fails her. She calls in the doctor.

"A bad case of humors, nothing more," the fellow snaps after a perfunctory examination. "I abhor malingerers. They waste my time. This is a house that's had more than its share of bad luck this year. One would almost think it were possessed."

"And what are you suggesting?" says Margarethe frostily.

He shakes his head and changes the subject. "The ailment will last its own course. There's nothing to be done. At least it isn't the plague." Nor, the doctor reassures Margarethe, is it contagious.

As van den Meer sinks deeper into lassitude—at times he won't even open his eyes and answer questions that his wife puts to him—Margarethe grows more determined not to buckle under the pressure herself. "I will manage this house, and I will recover our fortunes," she says to Iris. "He blames me, but he's the one who dithered about. Had he repurchased the lot of tulips a week earlier, when I proposed, he would've sold them long before the crash. I take no responsibility for his cowardice. I take responsibility only for the future, not the past. The past can't hurt you the way the future can."

"Not if you have survived it so far," says Iris grimly.

Margarethe and Iris walk back from the well in the Grotemarkt with basins of water. "Be fair to me, and listen," says Margarethe. "The collapse of the tulip market seems to have happened in many places at once. If Papa Cornelius had been less steeped in ale, he might have picked up on the news—apparently the fall in tulip futures happened in Amsterdam a few days earlier."

How terrible these times, thinks Iris. She sees that many sober citizens are ruined. Some families disappear under cover of darkness, leaving their entire houses and much heavy furniture to be repossessed. Inevitably it's only a small amount of what the unlucky investors are deemed to owe. There are rumors of suicides. Shame! Scandal! So governors and regents meet to see if there's a way to enforce a schedule of payments, a way to stem the swamping tide. Margarethe reports what she hears on the street to Iris. Though Iris follows little of it, she listens as closely as she can.

When Iris has spent only a couple of weeks in the studio, Margarethe calls her into the small room once used by Henrika for household governance. A ledger is open. A candle gutters. Dead flies in wiry clumps dot the windowsill. "This is no time for genteel hobbies," her mother says. "Your step-father is ailing, your sister is a bother, and your weary mother is busy trying to clothe herself and her daughters suitably for the upcoming ball of Marie de Medici and her eligible godson. Your stepsister has taken refuge in the kitchen and refuses to answer the door when a knock is heard. Weak thing. I can do nothing with her. I need you—to speak to creditors when they come to the door, to be both fawning and sly. Are you up for the task?"

"No," says Iris bluntly. And she's not. She has been trying, with a pencil, to be honest and unashamed. Besides, her time with Caspar is becoming, at least temporarily, lovely. He is full of a very household sort of joy, like the kind that abounds from ripe grapes, from big-bellied lutes. In the morning, when she approaches the Master's studio, Caspar will hear her coming to the door and rush, eager as a puppy, and meet her several feet out of the building, as if he wants to say his first hellos beyond the hearing of the Master. Caspar is a simple sort—is it true to say that? Simple, yes, and also firm and solid. Simple doesn't mean shallow.

"I can't leave the studio," says Iris. "Mama, how can I? Now?"

"That I phrase it as a question is merely courtesy," says Margarethe. "If all should go well, you'll have time enough for drawing in days to come. You must obey me now. I have no time to argue."

"Everything is a campaign with you," says Iris bitterly. "Did you ever love anything without the need to subdue it?"

"Never," says Margarethe, with a measure of pride.

"I'll obey you, of course," says Iris, somewhat ashamed. "But I can't imagine, after only these few days, how I can live without the attempt to draw. And I haven't even lifted a paintbrush yet!"

"You must lift a washbrush first," says Margarethe. "I want the front room to shine bright as gold. I'm having an interview with the clothier this afternoon—van Antum, who made my marriage gown. We van den Meers must look proper, stuffed with hidden coin. We must have tulips, even in the house, as if they don't make us gag." Margarethe points at Henrika's tulip vase, a porcelain pillar that stands two feet high and tapers like a model of a church's steeple. "Every spout must hold a perfect blossom. We are proud, Iris, and pride will see us through this devil's maze. Do you understand?"

So Iris goes to work. She fills the tulip vase with orange-headed flowers. Then she pulls a brush across the floor instead of a charcoal stick across a curl of paper. She sweeps soapy water across the brick and watches how the gray lye dries in patterns. She admires the patterns before she rinses them away. It's the best she can hope for.

But all at once she can't remake the form of Caspar in her mind; she can't remember what he looks like. Strong tears fall like drops of brewed tea—she's surprised at the heat of them.

Clara sometimes refuses to mount the step from the kitchen. Iris has to change the buckets of water from time to time, and to find other supplies. When entering the kitchen,

Iris watches Clara turn a shoulder to her. "Surely you haven't forbidden yourself to look at me too?" says Iris crossly.

"I'm busy with the stew," says Clara, though there's nothing but water being brought ponderously to a boil.

"I'm working hard to help Mama restore our fortunes," says Iris.

"She's done enough to ruin them," says Clara. "Can you really think her capable of anything but ineptitude so colossal it borders on malice?" Clara stirs a big spoon in the air, miming a witch at work over a vicious brew.

Iris is aghast. "You think she was malicious in her advice to your father?"

"I think," says Clara, "her greed blinds her."

"She's become your mother," says Iris, "when you had none."

"Once I had a mother," says Clara. "Now I have no mother, not even a stepmother. I have a big embarrassing crow who speaks in English and Dutch, and who like a crow snatches up every shiny thing, one after the other, until the accumulation of glitter is fanciful at best and a wicked scandal at worst. To say nothing of ugly."

"Let's leave this topic. You're distraught, and I'm exhausted," says Iris. "The clothier will be here momentarily and I have to finish cleaning the room. Mama is trying to borrow dresses for us to go to the ball."

"I," says Clara, "am not going to any *ball*."

Though Iris doesn't really know her mother's plans, she says stolidly, "The invitation is addressed to the family van den Meer. If she says you go, you go."

"Nonsense!" says Clara. "Look at me! My hair is limp, my back is aching, my knees are raw. My hands are cracked and unlovely. I have a father to tend to and a kitchen to clean. It's all I want. Nothing of the outside, please. Especially not parading myself like a strumpet."

"You can't be that perverse," says Iris. "Even I am willing to shame myself, to mortify myself with finery and take myself off to some hideous event, if it might improve our lot here. I, the monstrously ugly among us—"

"Oh," says Clara, "mercy, there is nothing monstrously ugly about you. Ruth may be unpleasing, but you are merely plain. If anything, it's my beauty that's monstrous, for it sweeps away any other aspect of my character. And why are you so sure that Margarethe wants me to attend? Now listen, a knock on the door."

"Let him in while I finish the lace runner!" breathes Iris.

Clara brays in a half whisper, "I *will not*. I'm not going to the door, I'm not entering the hall, I'm displaying myself before no one, ever again, not even in the privacy of this very house."

Not *in the privacy of my own house*, Iris notes, but *this very house*.

As if Clara doesn't even live here anymore.

"You are so selfish!—to deny my request for help!" snaps Iris, and throws down her work to race to the door.

Van Antum the clothier comes in, a man Iris recognizes from the street. As planned, Margarethe is sitting in a shadowy back room, keeping him waiting. "Please, settle yourself in comfort," says Iris. "There's tobacco if you'd like to smoke, and I can bring you a glass of something to refresh you."

"I would like nothing at all," says van Antum. He is plump and fussy, and smells of limes and spilled beer.

Margarethe struts into the room. She has borrowed a set of clothes from Henrika's wardrobe. She's stouter than Henrika every was, and Iris's careful eye catches the skirt fabric straining at the seams around the midriff. But Margarethe has developed a coquettish flutter that leads eyes away from such details. "How very good of you to come," says Margarethe in an affected air, almost as if she has a duke instead of a merchant in her parlor. "I shouldn't entertain you alone, for it isn't proper, but my husband is"—she pauses, beautifully, theatrically—"indisposed. Iris, before you leave to see to your sister, will you please—?"

She makes a motion with her hand. Iris obliges, though it makes her feel foolish. She turns about like a child being inspected for cleanliness. Then she curtseys at the paunchy old fellow and makes her way out of the room with as much dignity as she can muster.

"A standard size for a young woman. Perhaps a bit more like a beanpole than some," Margarethe is saying. "And her sister the opposite, a veritable ox. A lovely ox, but an ox just the same. Can you help us?" The voice goes up teasingly at the end, almost in a French manner. Iris has to grip the edge of the wall as she turns the corner to keep from crying out in disgust. Profanity that she has heard bantered by the Master and Caspar rises to her lips; it's an effort not to blurt it out. "I'm sure you can see your way to outfitting two belles. The reward," her mother is saying, "could, in time, be considerable."

What reward is that? There isn't enough coin in the household to cover the bottom of a pot.

"Clara?" calls Margarethe. "Can you come for a moment to the door?"

At first Iris thinks that Margarethe means to have van Antum take the measure, mentally, of Clara's lovely form— to prepare an outfit for the ball that Clara firmly is declining to attend. But when after Margarethe makes several requests Clara finally appears, sullen and covered in ashes, Iris puts her hand over her mouth, perceiving such a dreadful thought that she's ashamed of it.

"Isn't she truly a treasure?" Margarethe is saying.

Van Antum mouths his approval in wordless baby syllables. He folds his hands one over the other as if washing them.

"I'm sure I can do something that will flatter you, something to your satisfaction," he manages, at last, to say.

"Something grander than what I am wearing now," says Margarethe. "Something very grand is called for."

"Something very grand indeed," says the clothier, eyes clapped on Clara until she slips away into the shadows. His chin begins to tremble. "I think the very grandest I can muster."

The Gallery of God's Mistakes

Every day Margarethe comes back from the market with more stories about the Dowager Queen of France, Marie de Medici. It seems that most of Haarlem relieves its worry over financial panic through gossip about the great she-elephant. Iris is addicted to every scrap of opinion and news.

The Dowager Queen is ancient—perhaps as old as sixty-five. She is doughy, blowsy, and stupid, as well as highly strung and stylish. People whisper that her husband, Henry VI, had a different concubine reserved for every day of the year. "I'd have poisoned him for that," says Margarethe blandly. "But no wonder she dabbles in affairs of state."

The great Marie put in years of service as the regent during her son's childhood. Then, when little Louis XIII grew old enough to embrace his mother with a knife in his hand, Marie raised armies against him. Cardinal Richelieu—whom she considered no more than an elevated *domestique*—spoke out publicly against her. With frustrating regularity he was able to sidestep her assassination attempts. "How annoying for her," says Margarethe. Now Marie is in her dotage, safely exiled to the Spanish Netherlands, though reputed to be enjoying some sort of sweet reconciliation with her son.

As if courtly intrigues are as regular to Haarlem tongues as herrings, crones buzz that in her late years Marie de Medici has become tired of matters of government. She's begun to indulge in the affairs of courtiers, cousins, and syco-phants instead. Death is staring her in the face, and she intends to meddle with the world as much as possible before Death gets up its nerve to strangle her. Meddle in the world, and leave a record of her meddling. "Why do geese walk barefoot? Because they do; that's why geese walk barefoot," say the crones of Haarlem sagely. Why does the Dowager Queen of France meddle in the affairs of her godson? Why, what else are godsons for? What else is the good of life?

The proud stoics of Holland find the stories of Marie's exploits silly and entrancing. Though she's laughed at as a fool, she's still a powerful fool and a captivating one. The Dutch can be sullenly tolerant of their own House of Orange in the Hague—but royalty of a different stripe, be it Stuarts or Bourbons or Hapsburgs, carries a different pres-tige. Hasn't Rubens already memorialized Marie de Medici in the Palace of Luxembourg as a figure of history, someone grand as Charlemagne or Joan of Arc? And still the Queen Mother persists on the stage of the world, shrieking, con-niving, orchestrating her entertainments, fussing with the available material. "She's no different from your Schoonmaker," says Margarethe at one point to Iris, whose eyes open wide at tales of such intrigues. "She paints with real lives instead of with brushes and livid colors. We won't live to see her like again."

"Tell about the Prince," says Iris. "The one she is hoping to marry off."

"He is a distant cousin, or the son of such," says Margarethe vaguely. "That's right, a godson. I can't learn much about him, as he isn't a part of the regular court and little is known of him. He's called Philippe de Marsillac. Maybe he's one of the last links that the Dowager Queen has with her son, as Philippe is said to move freely back and forth between the court of Louis XIII and the court in exile of the Dowager Queen. Perhaps she means to marry her godson off to someone demonstrably not in any royal family of Europe as a way to break any possible use of him as an agent against her. Who can know how the crowned heads run their households? But her aim is clear. She's no more and no less than a marriage broker to this youth, the same as any conniving aunt or gassy old dame at a hearthside."

"She sounds heartless," says Iris. "Heartless and monstrous."

"I like her zeal," says Margarethe blandly. "Why shouldn't she arrange the world to suit herself? Wouldn't we all, if we could?"

"What wouldn't you do to comfort yourself?" says Iris.

"Precious little," says Margarethe, lifting her chin.

So I fear, says Iris, but to herself.

* * *

Her fears are borne out one afternoon when Margarethe takes herself off to the Master's studio. She insists that Iris join her; perhaps Margarethe wants to make sure that no impropriety is reported by canny-eyed neighbors. She intends to approach the Master for a loan. "That painting of Young Woman with Tulips restored his fortunes," she reasons to Iris as they hurry along. "Cornelius and Henrika revived Schoonmaker's career for him. He owes them something. He owes me."

"I owe you nothing," says the Master when asked. "Besides, it would make no difference if I did. You aren't the only ones struggling at the moment."

"*You* invested in tulip futures?" cries Margarethe.

"Oh, not I," he answers. "When do I have time to leave my studio? Though other painters did, and suffered for it. Caspar, my spy in all things, tells me that Franz Hals has lost a fortune, and the young Rembrandt in Amsterdam about whom everyone keeps chattering is also in a bad situation." He chuckles meanly. "I'd have lost the money if I could have managed to concentrate on doing so. As it is, since all my patrons are hugely in debt, I'll be lucky to be paid for existing commissions, let alone secure new ones any time soon. So it's all the more important for me to exhibit for the grand Marie."

"But I had wanted to borrow some money," says Margarethe again, hardly believing.

"I don't have the world spinning on my thumb. Wanting will get you nowhere."

He's looking for a study as he talks, shifting aside old paintings. The place has been a mess since Margarethe left for the van den Meers. By habit Iris goes to help him, and even Margarethe lends a hand, as if her kindliness will cause him to remember some hidden stash of florins. "You don't know how we are poised to suffer," she says.

"Suffering can make you strong," says the Master. "Look what it's done for me."

"Can't you sell something here you haven't yet sold?" Margarethe purses her lips at three Flights into Egypt, where holy mother Mary is variously demure, brave, and sleepy, but always a model of the perfect human form. Margarethe staring at Mary is like a stork scowling at a swan, thinks Iris.

"You know the market for religious painting is soft," says the Master.

"Can you sell Ugly Girl with Wildflowers and give us half the fee?"

"I painted over that," says the Master, "since it made Iris distressed."

"What about those others?" Margarethe has never showed interest in the Master's catalogue of misfits, but she's desperate. "Moods are grim now! Maybe you'll have a rush of offers—"

"You want to see those?" The Master's eyebrows lift. "Judge for yourself whether they'll stir the prospective buyers? I'll show you if you like. But you, Iris? After all this time?"

"I saw the plague take our Rebekka," says Iris, "more horrible than that can hardly be imagined."

But Iris wants to see if he has painted the imp of the van den Meers' household. She's not sure she believes in such a thing now, but she'd recognize it if she saw it. Wouldn't she?

With a stout key the Master unlocks the door to the gallery of God's mistakes. It's another high room, originally maybe a storage shed for farm implements. One wall is stone, and three have been daubed with mud plaster and white-washed. The Master pulls the tattered end of a curtain cover-ing a high window. Light rushes into the mildewy space. From paintings high up near the rafters, from paintings racked waist-height on lengths of raw-milled timber to pro-tect them from the damp floor, faces blink, or seem to. They come into the light again.

Reluctant, grimacing, pathetic, and beastly.

"Mercy!" says Margarethe, her hand on her heart.

Iris winds her fingers into her apron strings.

"I think of them as friends," says the Master, "for aren't we all this bruised?"

The dwarf that Iris had met, there he is, captured on canvas. The Master *had* painted him after all, or had he invented him?

"God created these errors," says the Master, as if reading her thoughts. "I merely took dictation." For all the bravado the dwarf had shown, he seems leery of being seen. He holds one splayed hand over his groin, though his other hand lifts aside the tunic to show a mysterious scar painted on his torso, a red bruise the shape of a ship's anchor.

"A dragon!" says Margarethe, looking further.

"A ewe with an extruded womb," says the Master. "Look more carefully. Was already dead when I saw her."

"Surely that's a dragon!"

"If you're sure," says the Master.

A child with the face of a parrot. Another dwarf, and a third—a whole family series of them. There's the Girl-Boy of Rotterdam, painted nude, all its disgusting punishments in view. A dog with a goiter that looks like a loaf of bread. A pair of siblings who sit so near that only one skin is needed to cover them both—an affliction of the sort Iris and Ruth had played at when they were being the Girl-Stag of the Meadow.

The joined siblings look at Iris and say, Sorry. The Girl-Boy looks at Iris and says, I don't know why I'm like this, but forgive me. The parrot-faced child is too young to speak, but squawks and bawls for pity.

"The Queen of the Hairy-Chinned Gypsies," says Iris, finding her.

"Old Dame Goos called herself that?" says the Master, amused. "To you? Sometimes she says she is so old, she is Bertha, the mother of Charlemagne. She is the Queen of Sheba. She even boasts, blasphemously, that she is God's own grandmother."

The Queen of the Hairy-Chinned Gypsies fixes an even gaze on Iris. Her look is neither remorseful nor angry. She's uglier than Ruth or Iris herself could ever be, shriveled and pocked, horny of hand, brown of tooth. She leans on her canes as if she's been walking the same road these thousand years. She says to Iris, And what will you make of yourself?

But before Iris can answer, Margarethe is interrupting her thoughts. Margarethe has had enough. She's backing away from the frog-footed, the beasties, and the damned. "You are a *fiend*, Luykas, to study these sinners so," she says. "Look at your work! In one room, holiness so perfectly portrayed that it borders on idolatry—in the next, venomous evil, incarnate and walking among us. You paint the beautiful and the ugly, but what of the in-between?"

She's looking for herself in a painting, as we all do, thinks Iris. Margarethe is trying to locate herself in the world. She has been badly scared.

"Young Girl with Tulips is in between," says the Master, "the here, the now. Clara, a real girl of Holland, rendered truthfully."

"What is the use of beauty? What is the consequence of this?" says Margarethe.

Iris thinks: For once Margarethe has forgotten her goal. She came to look at these paintings to remark on their interest to buyers. But she's gotten caught up in the ideas of them.

Margarethe steams on. "The beauty of flowers, the beauty of girls—even the beauty of painting, that's the subject of your work. What about the beauty of goodness? What about the splendid act? The question of Parcifal, the gesture of the Samaritan on the road? What about the widow who gives her only penny?"

The Master says, softly and in challenge, "And what would you know about that?"

In the courtroom of fiends, the gallery of God's mistakes, Margarethe squares her shoulders and answers him. "Only he with the hobbled foot fully knows the beauty of running. Only he with the severed ear can apprehend what the sweetest music must sound like. Our ailments complete us. That we in our sinful souls can even imagine charity—" She can't go on for a moment. "We may not always be able to practice charity, but that in this world we can even imagine it at all! *That* act of daring requires the greatest talent, greater than any you possess—"

The Master is humbled by shrill Margarethe. "As you like," he says. "So be it. We all do what we can. My job is to see, and testify."

The clamminess in the room becomes apparent. There is no imp here, however hard Iris looks.

"What can have brought you to such a perverse obsession as these!" says Margarethe.

"I look with regret, not prurience," the Master says hotly. "And I'm not the first to do so." He pokes about in a slope-shouldered wardrobe hunched in a corner, and he takes out a panel about two feet square. "This one is the starting point. It's not mine, I hasten to add. Strange panel of mysteries and miseries, isn't it? By one of the Flemish men. I bought it from the studio of Arentsz when I was an apprentice in Amsterdam. One of the Boschs, I think. A study, incomplete on the top left. Take it up in the light if you want to look at it."

"I don't think I do," says Margarethe. "Who could?"

"It's fabulous and unsettling. A portrait of a magic world. I avoid looking at it for years at a time, and then every now and then I scrutinize it as if I've never seen it before."

"It makes my eyes ache," says Margarethe.

But she and Iris drag it to a table and set it in the spring sunlight. "I'm not sure that these things are suitable for you to see," says Margarethe in a dull voice, but she's so curious about the busy painting that she forgets to nudge Iris away,

so they both examine the panel. If this is the magic world!—
or is it a dream, or a prophecy of some sort? The landscape is
pink and blue, and broken out with strange mountains
shaped like towers. But each part of the landscape is equally
near, and every part is home to creatures, birds, flowers, and
human beings, in ridiculous and shocking conjunction.

A naked woman with the head of a bird is trapped in a glass
bubble. Two men without clothes blow trumpets whose crowns
disappear into one another's smooth behinds. A girl looks out
over the lip of a huge sunflower, trapped there. A man shits gold
coins onto a hunk of bread that a woman is busy trying to cram
into her mouth. A baby with a bishop's miter pushes a man
backward into a well. Demons cavort carnally with men,
women, bear cubs, and plants. A sweet girl on her hands and
knees seems to have a vine growing out from between her legs,
and from the vine dangles a pear, an apple, and a violin.

"This is a painting by the devil himself," says Margarethe.

"Look, Mama," says Iris. "Up in this corner."

There's a dead man floating in a broad field of water. He's
naked, gray as the flesh of old fish. Above him a black bird
hovers on spread wings. The bird has pecked out the eyes of
the corpse. You can see both eyes in the bird's beak, one next
to the other, staring from the insignificant corner of the canvas right out at the viewer. Out of all the dozens of creatures
in situations of distress, or perhaps wild delight—it's hard to
tell—these are the only eyes that peer at the viewer.

"I can't look at this any longer, my own eyes ache," says
Margarethe. "They boil with small ghosts. What in the world
are we doing here, anyway?"

"You are coming to understand that I have no money to lend," says the Master. "And nothing from this gallery would interest the householder of Haarlem." He doesn't sound pleased to turn her down, nor does he sound sorry. "Put the painting back where you found it."

"I won't touch that vile thing," says Margarethe. "I'm a good Christian woman."

"Oh, I see," says the Master. "Well, leave it there; Caspar will replace it where it belongs when he returns."

"Caspar," says Margarethe. "I suppose you've given him all the money you might have given me."

"He's my apprentice, not my banker," says the Master. "Are you going to try to annoy me into loaning you money? There's none to loan. I have my own problems. Perhaps you should leave." He begins to wave them away, as if he's sorry he has let down his guard. "I'd thought you might learn some sympathy. But it's more of the same: The unfortunates of the world exist only to shore us up in our own high regard of ourselves."

"Sententious fool, let God's judgment be on you and me both, and see how we fare!" cries Margarethe. "Iris, come."

On the way home Margarethe rubs her eyes. "Damn! These eyes are bewitched. Caspar, and paintings like that in the house! They should be burned. Ruining a young man like that. Who probably deserves to be ruined. Oh, I see how Caspar has looked at you. Don't be fooled. His attentions are all to distract us from his real tastes. I'm no ninny in the world, you think I don't know?"

Even more than the Master's catalogue of God's errors,

the old, scratched painting of people in a magic world has alarmed Margarethe.

Iris says, "Mama, this is a hard time for you; I don't want to talk about Caspar. Let's just worry about the ball, if indeed we're going to go. Isn't there enough on our minds without berating other people?"

"Beauty has no use at all," says Margarethe, following her own thoughts. "It has no consequence. It lends nothing to the world. You're better off without any, my poor daughter."

Cinderella

Even safe in the cozy nook, Clara's becoming more and more inward. She twists her head away from the front rooms as a matter of course, ducks her eyes when Margarethe arrives at the door to complain, demand, or, once in a while, mutter appreciation. Iris watches, first with the eye of an artist and then with the grudging heart of a sister. Could a beauty like Clara nonetheless be one of God's mistakes?

"Clara," she says one day, "you're becoming a nun before my eyes."

Clara looks up from the churn. Her face is white and glazed with the effort, but she won't hand the job over to Iris to help. "You can call me Sister Cinderella," she says. "I'd be happy to take vows and live under a promise of silence, if I got permission for solitude."

"We haven't yet begun to starve, there's no need of that," says Iris with a proper horror.

"What choices have we, with Papa in his collapse and a madwoman at the helm of this household?" says Clara.

"Don't say such things," says Iris, and then, despite herself, is forced to clarify by adding, "I'm sure Papa Cornelius will recover."

"So you don't argue about your mother's madness," says Clara. Her acid tone contradicts the supplicating position of her shoulders and bowed head over the churn.

"Don't ask such betrayals of me," says Iris. "Please!"

"She is mad," says Clara. "Small steps to the madhouse still get us there at last."

"Madhouse or poorhouse, what is your choice?" says Iris, but she can't put her heart into the argument, and she doesn't know why she is defending her mother.

Clara just looks up. "I don't propose that anyone's path in this life is easy," she says. "Why do we argue, Iris? You and Ruth are all that's left to me of my old life, the life that seemed would be troubled only by an excess of happiness."

"Your father will recover," says Iris, a bit more kindly. She looks in the larder for flour so that she might prepare some dough for bread, but there's only the merest dusting of flour in the earthenware jug. She comes out to ask Clara where the day's flour has gone, has the bread dough been set to rise already, but she forgets her task when she sees Clara's shoulders shaking. "Oh, dear sister," says Iris, moving across the room to her, "your father will recover!"

"He hardly knows me!" says Clara. "His whole life is wiped away; it is as if his eyes have been bled of their memories, and they stare without seeing!"

"I know what that's like," says Iris. She struggles over what to say next. "Grieving and worry take many forms. It's simply a kind of sickness, but unlike the plague or the pox, it's not fatal. He'll recover. He will! You'll see! And you must do what you can to help him."

Clara blinks at her. In her life she hasn't often been asked to help. It's a proposition she doesn't seem to comprehend. She moves beyond it. Wipes her eyes. "He's there but gone. His body is warm and smells of him, but no more than a heap of garments retains the aroma and the heat of the body when you step from them to bathe. He hasn't given you much mind or much time, so how would you know, but I know: He isn't the man he was. He's hardly a man at all—just a collection of bodily habits, eating, breathing, relieving himself, muttering in his sleep. Don't you see how he's been reduced to nothing?"

"This is an indulgence, this pity and horror," says Iris coldly. "You do what needs to be done, and he'll return to you. He's a good man and he's broken by worry, but he's not dead, Clara. Not the way my father is dead."

Iris pauses, the thought of the floating dead man, his eyes in a bird's beak—

—and goes on. "Give him time to rest and all will be well."

Clara says, "You're older than I am, Iris, and you've seen sadness in your time, but you don't know everything about the world. Leave me to my grief."

"I'll find the biggest key I can and lock you in your cloister if you want," says Iris. "While you mope, at least the madwoman is at work, hard as ever, to fix the dilemma we are all in! If you were less critical you might be more help!"

Clara loses her patience at last, and calls out, "Ruth? Are you there, Ruth? Will you come and sing to me as you so prettily can? Ruth? There's an annoying gnat in the kitchen, saying things I can't understand. I need to be distracted. Ruth, come sing to me."

Ruth appears from some garden chore that has been given her, appropriate to her attention and her manual skills. She smiles at Iris and she sinks down on her knees before the butter churn. She hums a string of nonsense syllables, long ocean sounds unfettered by the pops and thuds with which real words start and close. Still, the unfocused noise is, in some vague way, musical, and Clara begins to thump the churn again, in time.

Iris tries to say, "And what of me, what about what I'm sacrificing, now that I'm ordered to abandon the studio?" But the start of her sentence is lost in Ruth's noises, and she can't finish it anyway, for her thought is just as self-pitying as any Clara has expressed, and Iris is ashamed.

Van Stolk and van Antum

"**T**ake them! Take the lot! Good riddance to them!"
Creditors come and cart away the entire stock of
tulip bulbs—sacks and sacks of bulbs, each bulb rustling as
if in its own paper parcel. Creditors also take those flowers
planted in sets of a dozen and twenty to the tub. Margarethe
complains of sores in her eyes—"Ever since seeing that
devil's painting of the magic world, all those immoral beasts
and flowers!"—and she paws at her eyes in frustration as if
to clear them of a film, a crust. Nonetheless, she oversees
the proceedings. She watches with a grim mouth, and she
orders Iris to make a record on paper of every exchange. The
language in which the commerce is carried out is salty or
apologetic, but Margarethe never lowers her chin or her
voice. Surely poor Papa Cornelius, slowly calcifying in his
stupor on the bed, can hear through the bed curtains how
Margarethe is dismantling his estate. Whether he understands what he's hearing is, of course, another matter. He
speaks little or not at all.

But one day he does emerge, half dressed and slovenly-looking, at the sound of the raspy voice of Nicolaes van Stolk. He's the man who approached Clara at her mother's burial, the barrel-chested citizen who had cried the bad news on the night that the storm had threatened the delivery of the tulip bulbs. Van Stolk has arrived with four sturdy lads to wander through van den Meer's house and look at the furnishings. It seems that van Stolk has paid off the brewers' loan to the van den Meers, and now the van den Meers are in debt to him. He intends to make a proposal to Margarethe about what he might take away in exchange for what is owed him.

"You would harvest the very bones out of our skin, would you?" hisses Margarethe.

"They would do me little good, for I couldn't resell them for a profit," says van Stolk jovially. "Good day, van den Meer. Hard moments come to us all." He doesn't look as if hard moments have come to him any time lately.

"You needn't bother with this tiresome visitor," says Margarethe to her husband, in what passes for charity, but is really an attempt to hurry up her negotiation without interference. "Go back to your couch and I'll have Ruth or Iris bring you something warm to drink." The girls try to urge van den Meer away.

"Why you wandering through my house?" says van den Meer to van Stolk.

"I fancy a few of the paintings," says van Stolk. "They aren't all of the highest caliber, and paintings have lost their value this season since the market is flooded with them. But

I'll offer you a fair price for a few lovely items, and deduct that from the amount that you owe me."

"Paintings," says Margarethe, interrupting what is bound to be her husband's objections, "they come and go, as quickly as the styles of clothes and the taste in predikants. We may as well make room for better-quality work, which we'll soon be able to afford. Why not relieve ourselves of a lesser grade of goods while we can—"

"Silence, you harpy," says her husband. "Get out of my house, van Stolk, before I force you out with my fists!"

"I will look at the painting of Young Woman with Tulips," says van Stolk calmly, ignoring him. "To my mind it's the only good piece here."

"You won't even look at it!" Van den Meer steps forward, and the step becomes a run. Even Margarethe shrinks from the expected crash of two full-grown male bodies. But the four youths lock their arms and hold van den Meer back, and van Stolk crosses the hall and flings the door open as if he owns the building.

"Here it is, a major work by a minor artist," he cries. "Splendid as I remembered it. The subject inspired the artist to heights of achievement he'll never again match. It's hard to distinguish which is more magnificent, the beauty of the girl or the sensitive skill of the rendering—but I suppose it doesn't matter. This is what art does, confuses the senses so to magnify the appreciation of the heart." He peers at it fondly, avariciously. "Those jewels the girl is wearing, aren't they Henrika's? They would fetch a pretty price."

"I believe she was buried in them," says Margarethe. "Don't think I haven't searched the drawers and cabinets. If you care to dig up her corpse, you're welcome to them, provided our accounts get the proper credit."

Van Stolk laughs, almost admirably. "You *are* a fiend. Now, young fellows, scramble up on this table and unhook the work from this wall."

"It's the most valuable piece in the house," says Margarethe shrilly, repeating for the fiftieth time the phrase with which she's ushered all recent visitors through the house.

"Since the house has been denuded of most of your husband's fine possessions, you're not saying much when you say that," says van Stolk.

"I won't have it!" roars van den Meer. Clara comes in from the kitchens at the noise. She claps her hands on her cheeks. Her first response is joy, to hear her father address a visitor, but when she sees who the visitor is, and how agitated her father has become, she flings herself at him.

"Let it go from this house, Papa," murmurs Clara. "Let him take it; he's only a scavenger. Besides, I hated it. It's a painting of vain hopes, and does me no justice."

"You're already changed from the girl in the painting," cries her father. "Look at you! A kitchen maid! Margarethe, what are you doing to my child?"

Margarethe, arguing with van Stolk about the cost of the painting, pays him no mind.

"Come away," says Clara, "come away, Papa; you're hardly dressed."

"My Clara," says her father, but when he reaches out his

hands, it's toward the smiling, beautiful child in the painting, not to the paler version of the same daughter who now holds her arms about him. "Clara, don't leave me as Henrika did!" He begins to sob.

"I already have a potential buyer for this piece," says van Stolk as he organizes the painting to be maneuvered out the door into the spring sunlight.

But van den Meer has rallied. He steps before the work and says, "I'll see about selling it to you in a few weeks' time, if I have to. You criticized me for engaging in speculation, and I see you are one of the first to profit in this decline. Don't think me fool enough not to notice. But the painting isn't mine to give you right now. If you take it from my house without my permission, the law will accuse you of theft. I'm informing you about this loudly and in the presence of witnesses."

"What are you speaking about?" says van Stolk.

"Luykas Schoonmaker the painter came to me last week and asked me for permission to borrow the painting to show in the exhibit for the visiting Queen."

"You never told me this!" says Margarethe.

"You were out on some scheme. He came to the door and Clara showed him into my bedchamber," says van den Meer. "It is my house, Margarethe, and my daughter, and my painting, and I agreed to the terms of the loan."

"What terms are those? What is he paying?" says Margarethe. "Iris, write this down."

"He is paying nothing. Those are the terms," says van den Meer. "Charity requires no less, and when we give up

charity, we give up our souls. Do you think I haven't learned anything in this hard year? There, I've said what I have to say. Remove the painting forcibly from these premises, van Stolk, and you violate the law. I'll have the schout and his deputies on you at once."

Van den Meer doesn't stop to see what happens, but turns and mounts the staircase. Clara follows, holding out a steadying hand. Van Stolk mutters to Margarethe, "I could ask for the very building if I chose. Don't provoke me, Dame van den Meer, for there isn't anything in your manner that calls forth a warm response, even in the most kindly breast in town, which mine demonstrably is not."

Van Stolk hasn't been gone an hour before another knock on the door summons Margarethe. It's the clothier again, Gerard van Antum, with some samples of lace and the first setting of undercoats and skirts to fit upon Margarethe's bony hips. Iris shows him into the street room. "I could care for some sherry," he admits, when he has been bustling about Margarethe with pins and scrutinizing glances, heaving for breath. His plumpness doesn't help him in his profession. He is like a huge ambulatory pincushion—overpadded.

"I believe we're just out of sherry," says Margarethe. She invents a fit of coughing to hide the next information, that there's nothing in the cupboard to substitute for sherry. Within a few days, at this rate, there will be no cupboard either.

"Give me a look at the pretty young thing, then," says Gerard van Antum.

"Not till I have a finished costume," says Margarethe.

"You forget," says the clothier, "I still have the pins in my hands."

"And when you loose them in me, you will have sacrificed your weapons, and it will be my turn," says Margarethe with a forced, gay laugh. "In lieu of sherry I will supply you with a cup of cocoa, and lace it with a flavoring capable of causing you to retch your liver up through your gullet."

He drops his hands; pins spill onto the floor.

"Learn from me, Iris, I'm a witty conversationalist, no?" says Margarethe. "I'm practicing for when I meet the Dowager Queen of France."

"The material you choose is very becoming," says van Antum in a humbled voice.

"I'm delighted you appreciate my taste," says Margarethe. Her eyes stare flintily out the window. "You catch the gossip that drops from every female tongue in the better streets of town. Why really is Marie de Medici displaying her godson here?"

"He's reputed to have an eye for the art of painting," says van Antum. "She relies on his taste in selecting her last portraitist. And there are other reasons."

"Pray tell."

But van Antum purses his mouth primly in Iris's direction. Margarethe sighs and tries another approach. "Clara?" she calls.

Ruth lumbers to the door of the kitchen. "I wanted Clara," says Margarethe.

"Ashgirl," says Ruth. Margarethe starts at the sound of comprehensible syllables from Ruth's mouth.

"Ashgirl?" she says. She's not so much questioning Ruth's

words as the fact that they can be uttered at all. Her voice goes up the register as if enraged. "*Ashgirl?*"

Clara appears then, pushing Ruth behind her into the kitchen to stem the tide of Margarethe's apparent disapproval. "What is it?" she says tiredly.

"Since when is Ruth able to call you Ashgirl?" says Margarethe.

"She's learned to sing some words," says Clara. "I hardly know how."

"You hardly know how, Ashgirl?" says Margarethe. "Charchild, Cinderfeet, you hardly know *how?*"

"We spend much time in the kitchen," says Clara, "singing and telling stories. She's growing older, too, and listens well."

The clothier doesn't care about the improvement in Ruth's speech. His hands have dropped to the hem of Margarethe's skirt, and he clutches it as if to keep himself from rocking on his knees straight onto the floor. He has seen Clara only once before, and that time she disappeared without a word. "Introduce me," he mutters to Margarethe, and then hits her lightly on the ankle to get her attention. "Introduce me, will you?"

"Oh, very well," says Margarethe. "Are we settled on the size of the ruff, then, and your finding a set of pearl drops to fix in my ears? I can't locate Henrika's diamond pendants. I'll dig up her coffin if I must—"

Van Antum is too transfixed to reply to this comic boast. "Hello," he murmurs, "hello hello."

"So we're agreed," Margarethe continues. "Yes, then, I will tell you: This is my stepdaughter, Clara van den Meer.

Don't mind her filth; she enjoys nothing more than to pretend to be a maid. We call her Cinderella as a game.

"Cinderella," says Margarethe, as if to prove such, "Cinderella, don't stand there looking sullen. Say hello to our own Gerard van Antum, and then, if you would be so kind, prepare for him a nice warm tankard of hot cocoa. Iris, go help her. Then, dear man, you can tell me more about Philippe de Marsillac and why he needs help procuring a bride."

The Night
Before the Ball

"It's to be the most stylish affair held in all of the Protestant Netherlands this year! And such sinful excess and expense!"

There are plenty of occasions for Haarlem folk to disapprove, Iris notices, but not many people who receive the precious invitations actually turn them down. "Better to observe firsthand—all the family will want to hear about the excesses" is the attitude most people take. And they keep the shoemakers busy with new footgear cut from the latest patterns imported from Paris.

For many it's a good time for a ball. Most of those who have suffered in the collapse of the tulip market have sold out and fled, or else, like Margarethe, they are trying gamely to proceed as if the best prospects lie ahead. And who's to say this isn't true? In the family of nations, the Netherlands is still a fledgling in the nest . . . Sprung out of a local gabble of small farmers and fishermen, a handful of provinces has become a nation of international merchants who share a growing sense of destiny. The brave market talk asserts just this.

"Those who have fallen will arise."

"Doesn't Holland get the freshest air off the ocean each day, and breathe the newest thoughts? Isn't the ocean itself our own high road to be galloped across in steeds of timber and sailcloth?"

Who cares that the crones and the predikants, using separate sets of words, murmur jeremiads that too much optimism is bad for the soul, and attracts perhaps more attention from God than, strictly speaking, is desirable?

But Marie de Medici is blowing into town like a galleon herself, with her godson, the profoundly handsome and well-positioned Philippe de Marsillac. He is said to have an eye for painting, and his godmother trusts his opinion. But how *can* it be that he isn't equipped to select a wife for himself? An eye for painting also suggests an eye for feminine beauty, surely? Or is he a slow-wit?

Nonetheless, he has been seen, and so has she; Haarlem isn't that large that a large person can easily hide herself or her nephew. And she is gross and unbecoming, and he her opposite in every way.

As the great day draws nearer, Iris and Ruth succumb to the various fittings that the clothier insists are necessary. Iris can see that van Antum is smitten with the splendor of Clara van den Meer, and that Margarethe limits his sight of Clara to a few moments at the end of each session. Even with her eyes continuing to ache and fail, Margarethe directs such occasions with finesse. She calls "Cinderella!" to the back of the house and then arrests Clara as she approaches, saying, "Don't move, I've dropped a pin and you'll step on it."

So Clara, backlit by the sunlight splashing in a kitchen doorway and reflecting off newly washed tiles, hovers like a Catholic angel, her blond hair escaping its cap in a nimbus, her very arches poised to avoid fallen pins, giving her a look of one who has just set down from heaven.

Margarethe plays Clara even more deviously when Nicolaes van Stolk comes to call. It's become clear that his interest in the painting of *Young Woman with Tulips* is simply a mask for his interest in the model. First Margarethe sends Ruth upstairs to sit with Papa Cornelius and make sure he doesn't get out of bed. Then Iris is called in for the sake of propriety. Margarethe closes the doors to the front room so Papa Cornelius can't hear. "Our Cinderling? The poor thing is down with a cold," says Margarethe to Nicolaes van Stolk. "Can't you hear her sneezing in the inglenook?"

"I can't," says van Stolk irritably.

"It's the strangest thing. As my eyes fail me, my hearing improves," says Margarethe. "I can even hear her wiping her eyes, for she'd like to come and present herself to you, but she's in far too miserable a state to do it, and she wouldn't care for you to see her so trembling and vulnerable."

Van Stolk coughs and adjusts himself in the chair. "I could tolerate it," he manages.

"Nonsense," says Margarethe. "I wouldn't hear of it. The theory of contagion has some validity, and I'd never forgive myself if you were to come down with a sniffle just before the ball."

"I don't have any intention of going to pay homage to the Dowager Queen of France!" says van Stolk, drawing himself upright.

"No, of course not," says Margarethe soothingly. "You haven't got an eligible daughter to parade before the desirable Philippe de Marsillac, nor have you a wife to prod you into going so that she can attend on your arm. You must be very lonely at times." She smiles, but, Iris notes, not with anything like her old ability to flirt. As her eyesight deteriorates, so does her status as a coquette—her attraction now exists solely in the girls she is raising. "More lager for the gentleman," says Margarethe to Iris, who comes forward and pours. "I could do with a bit of money to buy myself a new pair of shoes," Margarethe continues. "The wonderful white kid leather shoes I had made for me will be unsuitable, I'm afraid. With my faltering step, I tend to kick out at the floor and the edges of walls and furniture, and the marks on white leather will offend. But the shoemaker won't advance me any more credit. Might I trouble you for a small loan?"

"I would expect some collateral," says van Stolk.

"I hear our Cinderella pulling the shawl tightly about her breast," says Margarethe smoothly. "She is cold and needs warming. How very taxing for her. Even the kitchen with its ashy fires can't satisfy her. I would put her to bed in an instant if I thought she would hear of it. In bed she might be warmed."

Van Stolk collapses before Margarethe's campaigns and hands over some coin for a new pair of shoes. The shoemaker is summoned within the hour, and Margarethe demands a pair of dark, elegant shoes with the brightest, largest buckles a lady's foot could sensibly support. Or maybe shoe roses? "You or Ruth can take the white ones," says Margarethe.

But Ruth's big, splayed feet are far too big and Iris's feet too narrow. The beautiful white shoes, almost like dancing slippers, are cut too low. Even if Iris inserts a wedge of padding she can't keep the shoes from slipping off her feet and clapping their heels on the floor as she walks. "When my eyesight improves," says Margarethe, "I'll be able to maneuver in those slippers again. Put them aside, Iris, and let's think about the matter of your hair."

They consider her hair. It's limp and lackluster. Margarethe washes it in eggs and holds up strands in the light. "Is my eyesight still getting worse," she growls, "or is your hair an even less agreeable color than usual?"

"I can't change the color of my hair at will," says Iris.

"What good is it being a painter if you can't paint yourself?" says Margarethe.

Ruth is even more difficult to deal with. Her hair has all the energy and abundance that Iris's lacks; the problem is that exuberance is hard to rein in. Even strapped and capped, Ruth's hair seems to have miraculous powers of escape. The only solution is to cut a good deal of it off and hope that Ruth can keep her cap on. But what if the French style requires women to remove their caps at a ball? This is the kind of small detail that plagues Margarethe and that bores Iris. As for Ruth, she hustles back to the kitchen as quickly as she is allowed. Splendid clothes and new shoes and renovations to her scalp! Iris can see that the ball is going to terrify her sister. Will Clara be there to keep Ruth calm? Iris still isn't sure.

The house is half empty of furniture. All of Henrika's luxuries are gone, but some chairs and tables and wardrobes remain. Despite herself, Iris sees how the light falls differently in emptier rooms. It is spring light, there is a touch of green to it, brought in when the sun filters through the tender leaves of the linden trees. Iris never expected to live in such a beautiful building, so the thought of leaving it soon seems only a return to the normal hard way of life. But she knows it will be torment for Clara, who by now even avoids approaching a window or standing in an open doorway in case van Stolk is outside.

Iris is in the kitchen, trying to help Clara come up with a meal out of what little they have left in the larder, when Margarethe stumps through, to root in chests once again with the hope of finding silver spoons or missing jewelry that she might pawn. It's a fruitless task, but Margarethe is obsessed with the idea that Henrika's wealth was limitless. "We don't have much left to eat," says Clara to Margarethe. "We're down to almost nothing. We'll be petitioning the regents of the Holy Ghost orphanage before long."

"I'm told they won't take children over the age of seven anymore," says Margarethe. "But don't worry."

"Van Stolk is coming to claim possession of the house on the day after the ball!" says Clara. "What are we going to do?

Do you mean to say that Papa has been so ruined by this crisis that he qualifies for the old men's home, where he can sun himself in the courtyard with the other toothless indigents?"

"You fret for nothing," says Margarethe. "I've passed by the Oudemannenhuis many times. The regents run it well. Everyone is kept clean and quiet."

Clara says with scorn, "For the rest of us, then? Do your daughters and I qualify as spinsters, to be taken in at one of the hofjes?"

"Pity you never learned to be a seamstress," says Margarethe. "There's still time."

"And you, will you escape under cover of darkness and fly on your broomstick to thwart the happiness of some other household?"

Clara has spoken with zeal and contempt, but Iris starts and drops a kettle on the bricks. Margarethe peers as best she can from one to the other. "So Iris is peddling stories, is she?" says Margarethe coldly.

"I never—!" cries Iris.

"No, I'm sure you never have," says Margarethe. "Clara, the root-bound, sun-starved cutting just concocts a story like that on her own. Wonderful, Iris. Thank you. Now, shall we remember the central tasks of the day, and abandon interest in such gossip? We have to eat. *We* have been hungry before, *Cinderella*, though perhaps hunger is a novelty for you."

"Hunger makes us thin, but plague can make us bloat and buxom, for an hour before we die—" says Iris.

"Don't mock your blind old mother," says Margarethe, striking out with a walking stick. "I'll have food in your mouths before three days are out, mark my words. You take me for a fool like my gibbering husband, but I'm not to be discounted yet. Philippe de Marsillac will have you for a bride, Iris. Wait and see."

"You are *mad*," says Iris. "Your blindness is seeping from your eyes into your brain. You're forgetting what your daughters look like, and what the others look like next to us. We aren't worthy to stand behind a bank of flowers. We aren't acceptable for leading the ducks to the millpond. What can I offer to a prince that any other young woman of Haarlem cannot?"

"You have endurance," says Margarethe harshly. "You've inherited that from me."

"All of Holland has endurance, that's Holland's essential quality," cries Iris. "You're lying to yourself, because you can see no other way out!"

"I can see other ways out, and I can see more than you think," says Margarethe. "Perhaps the cloud of darkness in my eyes now has dimmed the sharp aspect of the world to me, but I see other things that I couldn't see before. I see how people worry and how their lives are bound and trapped along that thread." She reaches for a knife; perhaps she is going to try to harvest some of Ruth's incredible hair. Half blind as she is. "Don't I know it by knowing myself, with my own terror of poverty and hunger gnawing at me night and day? But I am cannier than the moon, my girls, because I am blinded now to appearances. This eligible young man has an eye for painting; it's why he is here. You are one of Haarlem's only young women to try your hand at it—"

"I have sketched once or twice! You are bewitched with worry yourself, and puff my abilities like a bubble of soap," says Iris. "And bubbles pop."

"We always have Cinderella to farm out to the highest bidder," says Margarethe.

There's nothing untoward in her remark. It's the right and duty of a mother to amplify the family fortunes. But Margarethe hasn't said this so bluntly before, and the room is still.

"I am not attending the ball," says Clara quietly.

"I should say not," says Margarethe. "We agree for once. But I'll tell you why. However pleasant you look, you aren't the intelligent girl that Iris is. And you have nothing in your face or manner of human kindness. But if you attended the ball, you might have a good chance at attracting the attention of Philippe de Marsillac. You'd put my own daughters in the shadows. If he found you worthy of pursuit, you'd allow it to happen, and turn from us all. You'd disappear into another life, and we'd be no better off than before—worse, in fact, for I have your father to feed now too until he comes to his senses."

"I wouldn't forsake my own father!" says Clara.

"No, perhaps not," agrees Margarethe cannily, "but you haven't offered to stand by your stepmother or stepsisters with the same passion. If your father dies, as well he might, of a broken spirit or a broken purse, your ties to your step-family are broken too. You don't have any feeling of obliga-tion toward us, and why should you?"

"But you'd marry me off to the clothier or to van Stolk?" says Clara.

"They're local men, and for the sake of his trade a man needs to be seen to be kind to his wife's kin," says Margarethe. "If you marry van Stolk, we all might stay in this house."

"I'd rather die," says Clara. "He is a rapacious bird, a crow."

"But what choice do you have? You won't even leave the house, so if Nicolaes van Stolk is going to possess it and move in, he will have to possess you too . . ."

"I'll take to the woods. I'll follow the bridlepath to Amsterdam or Leiden. I'll find my windmill and bury myself in the changeling's room. I'll drown myself in the Haarlemsmeer."

"Talk, talk. You who are timid at every threshold." Margarethe heaves herself away, and the knife that she carries seems to make several comments of its own by how it slices the air.

"Don't you want to go to the ball?" says Iris softly.

"This house is about to fall in upon itself with her maneuverings," says Clara. "In a week's time we will be ruined. She is living in her crazed mind. But I won't marry van Stolk, not after how he's treated my father. I would rather kill my father and myself both."

"You should come," says Iris. "Come to the ball!"

"Stop about that," says Clara. "I'm taking this firkin of hot water and honey upstairs to Papa. It soothes him to see me as the afternoon fades; otherwise he is agitated. Soon the day will be here when I can't do this."

Iris follows Clara up the back stairs and along the passage to the front room. Van den Meer has climbed out of the bed, but sits in a state of half dress, looking glassily about him. "Papa, adjust your clothes, you have female visitors," says Clara at the door, and van den Meer pulls his dressing gown closed.

"It is all a game of verkeer-spel, isn't it," he mumbles. "The game of turns. Anything can happen."

Clara gives him the concoction, which he sips without apparent relish. "All things change, Papa. You know that."

"So do you, my changeling."

"Change from what?" says Iris. She can't help herself. Clara seems older, through all this disaster; she should be able to answer now. "Who were you before you were a changeling?"

Clara sits down heavily on a stool and runs her hands on the painted tiles on the wall, as if their blue designs show pictures of her past rather than of Cain and Abel, Noah and the flood, Moses with the stone tablets.

"I was a foolish, ugly child," says Clara, "a bad child who didn't mind my mother. I strayed from her apron hem, and they found me and turned me into a good child. They made me fair and obedient, and gave me beauty and gifts of music and language."

"They did this in the windmill?" says Iris. "They put you in a hole in the windmill and taught you music?"

Clara shrugs and nods. A ghost of that old look, a thinner, transparent version of it, flutters on her face.

"Who did this to you?" says Iris. She can't help it. She turns to van den Meer and says, "Was it you?"

"It wasn't me." He isn't even offended at her accusation. "We never did learn who it was."

"It was the bird spirits who swarm on the banks of the Haarlemsmeer," says Clara.

Van den Meer bobs his chin agreeably and says, "It was probably rogues passing through from Antwerp. Or who knows, maybe the hairy-chinned gypsies."

"Papa!" says Clara sharply.

"Tell me," says Iris, putting her shoulder between Clara's face and her father's.

A decade-long habit of reticence slips off van den Meer as easily as his enthusiasm for business has. He tells Iris, while Clara draws in a series of small breaths, one two three, one two three.

"Henrika had gone to the market for lobsters and lemons. Clara was three or four, an eager, ambitious child, full of spunk in the legs and wind in the lungs. She was hard to manage, and Henrika lost sight of her in the crowds. I think it was the evening before a feast day. Clara was well known on the streets then, affable and easygoing, and we were frightened. We hoped some good soul would find her and bring her home to us."

"It was the spirits who found me!" whispered Clara. "The bird."

"But evening came and there was still no word. Henrika had me call in the civic guards and the schout—the sheriff— and his men also took up the hunt. Haarlem treasures its children. How much it treasured Clara van den Meer, daughter of Cornelius van den Meer and, more importantly, daughter of his wealthy and important wife, Henrika Vinckboons! Citizens and militia alike joined the search, but it was terrifying, for the more places we could think to look, the more distraught we were to find she wasn't there. We feared she had stumbled into a canal and drowned. Or worse."

"Nothing like that," says Clara. "Nothing at all. The long boat ride to the other world, where I would be changed. My little house under the floor. It was warm. There was a blanket. There were nice sweets and fruit, and the saw-voiced spirit sang to me when I cried." Clara rocks a bit, as if she has a baby in her arms.

"There was a note found stuck in our front shutters. They would return Clara if Henrika gave them many florins in a chest. It was half of the Vinckboons fortune. Quickly we had to arrange to sell off the outlying farms that brought in rent. Not much left except this house and what was in it. But Henrika, a natural mother, would hear of nothing else but to supply what was asked and get our Clara back."

"They had no use for florins," says Clara. "They wanted to change me into a good girl, that's all. They comforted me and kept me warm."

"For three days," says van den Meer, "I whipped the schout and his men into more and more furious searching, offering rewards nearly equal to the amount that Clara was being ransomed for. Some suspected it was a plot of the Spaniards, infiltrating Haarlem and demoralizing the town before an attack. Some guessed it was witches wanting the child's blood for their unholy sabbath."

"They were pretty," says Clara. "They were kind. The spirits of the water."

"And Henrika was mad with fear. So we paid the fee, leaving it at night in the middle of the forest as directed. We hid ourselves and watched it for many hours, till a note came to the house saying the money wouldn't be collected nor Clara returned until we'd given up our vigil. In the end, we were too distraught to do anything but stay at home and wait. And a note then was delivered to the alehouse where I had been accustomed to having my midday meal, saying that Clara was hidden in a windmill to the south of the town."

"When I was changed, they left me. They gave me the windmill toy to remember them by," says Clara. "The one Ruth took from me, and that she has chewed to pieces."

"Was Clara hurt?" says Iris. She drops to her knees and wraps her arms around Clara's shoulders from behind. "Did they hurt her?"

"In none of the worst ways that you can imagine," says van den Meer. "Didn't we make sure of that at once? It was money they were after, not evil deeds."

"I am a changeling," says Clara.

"So Henrika allowed her to say," says van den Meer, "and ever after has Clara been kept to the house, until in time she herself chose to stay within its walls. It's as good a story as any, the changeling story. Who knows, perhaps it's true. But the spirits who changed her had a big appetite for cash."

Clara makes a half turn on the stool. Her face is slack but open. The eyes have lost that pierced appearance. One hand claws at the thumb of the other for a moment, then falls as if utterly exhausted.

"And so until Henrika died, you rarely left the house again?" says Iris.

"My mother was affrighted for me, and I learned terror from her. But if I heard of other changelings, I wanted to meet them," says Clara. "But I never could meet any. People say a lot about changelings, but they are hard to find. When I first saw her, I had thought that Ruth was one—"

There's a thump at the door. Ruth has been standing there listening, and she has lost her balance.

The Changeling

The household is asleep except for Clara and Iris.

They sit in the flickering light of the embers, holding hands.

"Don't you see?" says Iris. "It's a way to avoid having to marry van Stolk, and it's a way to save your father. You may not be able to save this house, but you don't need this house. You are changed again, you're back to the person you were when you were three or four. You're strong and have brave muscles and ample breath. And a good heart, Clara, a good heart! You can manage the act of charity!"

"I don't understand what you're saying," says Clara. Her voice is small, but it isn't weak.

"Look at the picture I'm drawing for you," says Iris firmly. "I mean, close your eyes and look at it. Stare at it inside yourself so you can see it. I am painting it for you. There's little Clara in the dark. She isn't scared, she's not hurt, she's just having an adventure, and the bird spirits are being nice to her, but now the ceiling is opening up. The light is coming down. She is holding up her arms and being lifted high. It's her mother. It's Henrika. She's saying, Come now, Clara, come; it's time to grow up. And up you come. You aren't a changeling. You're still yourself. The dark hole is too small for you now. You can leave the little box, you can climb out. All the way out."

"But I am a changeling," says Clara.

"Look at what you can change to, then," says Iris carefully. She hardly knows if she is colluding with her mother—to save the family fortunes by marrying *one* of them off to the Prince, anyway, the most likely one—or if she's merely trying to bring poor forgotten Clara back into the world—any world but her sadness. She thinks she may never again be sure of why she does anything—but it seems the only thing to do. Iris pushes on. "Clara, no one disputes that you are the most splendid beauty of the town. A beautiful young woman, and brave. You *can* go outside. No one will take you or steal you or hide you away. Come to the ball, Clara; come to the feast. At least see what it is like."

"I'm not ready to be seen," says Clara.

"No," says Iris, "but, like me, you are ready to look. Look at yourself."

Clara closes her eyes for a moment and bows her head. In the moonlight her hair is the color of alabaster. When she lifts her gaze to Iris's again, she says in a sober voice, untroubled by notions, "The truth of what I've learned today isn't about changelings. It's that my family's financial worries are partly my fault. Maybe all my fault. If I hadn't wandered away from my mother, those rogues wouldn't have stolen me. My family lost half their wealth to preserve my life, and that set up the conditions for their zealous husbanding of their resources."

"You didn't make them wealthy, nor did you make them greedy," says Iris firmly.

"No," says Clara, "but I made them poor. Without intention and without guile, but nonetheless. So maybe it *is* time to do my part. I won't marry van Stolk, not for all the caskets of pearls you can import from the Indian Ocean. But if I can go in disguise, cloaked as a nun, as a crone, I will allow myself to meet this Prince. One step at a time. I'll climb out of the dark hole and go, at least, to look at him, as you say. And then we will see what we will see."

Iris clasps Clara's hands again, and then goes to find a quill, a pot of ink, a scrap of paper, and her cloak.

Small Magic

The next day, when so much needs to be done, Margarethe develops a redness along the rims of her eyes. She knows cures herself—the larder has been filled with small jugs and vials and pockets of herbs and powders since the first few weeks of Margarethe's arrival in the strict house—but she has no balm for sore eyes. She decides to hie herself along to a nursewife for some unguent. Not daring to try to step out on the streets alone, she takes Ruth for a strong arm to lean upon. When she leaves, barking instructions about Papa Cornelius's breakfast over her shoulder to Iris and Clara, the girls go into the kitchen. There, in a little heap under an upturned saucer, stands a red trace of hot ground pepper.

"Ruth brought Margarethe her morning cup," muses Clara. "And Margarethe demands that her eyes be wiped by a clean linen every morning, for the crust of night makes things even worse . . . You don't suppose . . . ?"

"Ruth is the foolish one," says Iris briskly, "haven't you noticed? Are you suggesting that Ruth irritated my mother's eyes with red pepper? Why would she do that? You can't possibly think her capable of such wickedness."

"No doubt Margarethe's tears will have healing properties eventually," says Clara. "That is, if Margarethe could ever bring herself to shed a tear over anything. But this is puzzling. Are you and Ruth scheming at something?"

"Mama is the capable herbalist," says Iris. "Though I suppose her daughters must have picked up something of the properties of plants along the way. But I can't worry about this. There is too much else to do, my dear." She grins at Clara with the force of her secret idea.

They put together a tray—a hard crust of bread softened by holding it over a steaming kettle, a cup of tea—and Clara brings it to her father in his room. While Iris is fiddling through the wardrobes to see if there is anything that might be smart enough to serve as a gown for Clara, she hears a voice in the kitchen. She calls, "Just a moment," and goes down to find Caspar lounging on a bench, his legs stretched out to the fire.

"You found my note in the door," she says.

"You must have been up very early to deliver that before we were awake."

"And you are good enough to answer my call for help, and here you are, making yourself comfortable."

"Why not?" he says. "I can sniff that the witch is out of the house."

"Oh, don't be cruel," says Iris. "She is my mother, after all."

"Don't mind me," he says. "I understand you're now destitute?"

"We haven't got a crumb to spare," says Iris, but looking at him makes her feel like laughing all over—as if she could laugh not just with her mouth but with her eyes, her heart, her very limbs.

"Your mother might have done better to marry the Master when he asked her," says Caspar. "*He* didn't lose a fortune in the great tulip crash."

"So he's told us, but he also says that his customers did, and that'll mean that fewer people can come along to have their portraits painted."

"It does mean that," admits Caspar. "It makes even more desirable the landing of the Dowager Queen's commission. But he still has a lot of commissions to fulfill, and while the food on the table is plain, it's plentiful."

"Well, Margarethe may have married the wrong man," says Iris, "but there's no changing that now. Margarethe will do what she will, and when."

"I hope you don't marry the wrong man," says Caspar.

"That's a pleasant assumption you make, that I will marry at all!" says Iris.

"I don't know whether it's pleasant or not," says Caspar. "Depends on your estimation of marriage, I guess. But I just hope, if you do wed, that you do so for reasons other than Margarethe's."

"Margarethe married to keep her daughters fed," says Iris. "Not that it's any of your concern, but why shouldn't she do that? Isn't that her responsibility as a mother?"

"I don't want to argue," says Caspar. He laughs and holds up his hands. "I was glad to find your note! I had to get out of the Master's studio today. He's making me mad. He's in a frenzy of worry about this ball. The trimming of the beard! The brushing of the coat! The polishing of the buckles! The steaming of the sash! You never saw such goings-on. I'm glad I'm too lowly a little worm to be involved."

"What is this now," says Iris, casting him an amused look, "I think I detect that you would like to go to the ball too."

"Anything else but that," he cries. "I'd stomp on the train of the Dowager Queen of France and pull it to the ground, causing Louis the Latest to collude with Spain and rise in arms against the Lowlands. I'd say the wrong things to the wrong people and offend everyone. I'd get thrown out on my backside and land in a mud puddle. This isn't something that I yearn to do."

"Good," says Iris, "for there's only one miracle to perform in any given day, and I have my work cut out for me. And you'll help me?"

He raises an eyebrow.

She sits on a stool and draws it close to him. She doesn't need to speak so low, as only Clara and Papa Cornelius are in the house, and upstairs. But she likes to speak low, as it requires her to lean nearer. And then she gets to smell the splendid smell of him, the slightly damp cottony resiny vegetable smell. She tells him of her plan.

"You're going to usher Clara into a ball where she has no introduction?" he says.

"We have invitations for four," says Iris, "but Papa Cornelius is far too ill to attend. I'll just tell the doorman than the fourth of our party is to follow."

"But without your mother's approval? That cunning har-ridan will rise up like an asp and strike Clara dead—"

"I don't think so," says Iris. "You haven't been around enough to know how severely Margarethe's sight has deterio-rated. I think it's possible she won't even recognize Clara if she's not expecting to see her there. Besides, if we can arrange a headdress with a veil in the Spanish style, there will be mystery. Clara can hide behind her veil, and none will identify her, nor see her beauty unless she chooses. She can dally on the margins and watch a little."

"I thought she didn't want to go to the ball. What's changed her mind?" says Caspar, leaning forward.

"Never mind about that." Iris is still amazed that her midnight conversation with Clara has had any effect. "Keep to the matters at hand."

"And you expect to find her a suitable gown—*today?*" says Caspar. "You're taking this miracle of transformation onto yourself?"

"I could use some help," says Iris.

"You could use some small magic," says Caspar, "but there is no such thing in the Netherlands."

"So I've heard tell," says Iris, sighing. "In England the small folk live under the soil and deep in the hedges, and they come out to assist the deserving, to cast spells and to reward the poor."

"Clara is beautiful," admits Caspar, "but deserving?"

With a firmness that hides her doubt, Iris says, "At least Clara has paid some attention to Ruth, and Clara has seen to her father's needs. She's been a friend to me, and she remembers her mother nightly in her prayers. Don't you think she deserves the hand of the spirit world?"

"Some small magic," says Caspar. "Didn't you tell me once you thought there was an imp in residence? Couldn't you ask it for help?"

"Nonsense—the nonsense of my silly youth," says Iris, blushing. "When I began to look at the world as it *is* . . . well, the unseen world of my fancy seems less beguiling, even less possible."

"As may be, but we're painters, Iris; we ought to be capable of small magic together."

"I should think so!" says Iris. "Didn't I make Ruth and myself into the Girl-Stag of the Meadow? I can do my own magic! And you as well. At least magic enough to find a gown, a set of shoes, an escort to the door? I can manage to groom Clara, to pinch her cheeks into redness; I can keep an eye on her once we are there. But how shall we get a gown for her?"

"I can paint a gown, but I can't sew one," says Caspar.

Iris thinks of the Master painting, with loving strokes, the gown worn by the Young Girl with Tulips. To paint such a gown again . . . To magic it up . . .

In a low voice she says, "I've been considering this for some time. Do you remember the jewels that Clara wore for Young Woman with Tulips?"

"I do. They were precious gems of Henrika's, diamonds from Antwerp, I think. And some strings of pearls, weren't there?"

"And didn't the Master bring them back to his studio so he could study them for highlights?"

Caspar cocks his head to one side, shrugs, then nods.

"I never listed them as among our assets to be sold. Margarethe has assumed that Henrika was buried in them. But I think they could still be at the Master's studio, slung under some heap of painting rags or some bedding that needs airing. The place is such a mess! If they're there, if you could find them, could you use them to barter for a suitable gown? At least as collateral on the loan of a gown?"

"You're bold!" says Caspar. "It's a good thing we didn't let you keep house when you came to draw, or you'd probably have unearthed them. Look, if the jewels are there, I'll find them. And then? There are ways to do such things. Leave it to me. The Master has access to a number of the wealthier homes in recent weeks. I know maids and stable boys the whole town through. But I need to look at Clara first."

"You know what she looks like," says Iris. "You know her coloring."

"I need to look with the eyes of a painter," he says. "I need to look at her to measure her form, so I can find a gown that will fit her as well as suit her."

Iris says, with a heaviness of heart that surprises her, "Well, I hope you're capable, for here she comes." Clara comes hurrying into the kitchen.

"Oh, the silly man is here," she says.

"Stand still and let me look at you," says Caspar.

"I don't like to be looked at by painters," says Clara.

"I'm looking at you to costume you in gold," he says. "Don't think I can't do it, Clara van den Meer."

Her mouth makes a clumsy pout, and her eyes flicker first to him and then to Iris, who shrugs. Clara raises her arms, and the form of her body stands out against the whitewashed walls of the fireplace nook.

She is so beautiful to look at. Iris finds herself holding her breath as Caspar walks just a little closer. His eyes judge proportions. He holds a hand up quickly to frame relative shapes. He memorizes her form. Caspar isn't indecent, and he doesn't approach Clara too closely. When he's done, he turns and says to them both, "I'll find you a gold gown by this evening. I'll take care of that part, you may rest assured. You spend your time worrying your other problems out."

They don't know what to say. He bounds to the door and says again, "I trust you won't marry the wrong man." But this time it isn't clear to which of them he is speaking.

Tulip and Turnips

Margarethe is back before the sun has reached its midpoint. Her eyes are puffy from the nursewife's rinsing baths. She's in a foul temper. She slams the door closed behind her when she comes in. Ruth hides from her mother beneath the stairs, in a nonsense space she has feathered with a spare blanket, old rags, and a few dollys.

"What I put up with," rails Margarethe, "what is asked of me! What have I done to deserve indignity after indignity?"

Iris and Clara exchange glances. Clara ducks her head over the pot, though there's little in it but water, a knob of butter, a last carrot, a handful of dusty old herbs—and the last of that red pepper.

Iris draws in her breath, tightens her apron strings, and goes hurrying out into the hall.

Margarethe is stalking back and forth on the black and white tiles, holding her hands out to keep from hitting the walls. "Here at least I might open my stride, and not fear the laughter and scorn of my neighbors!" she cries, bumping against a chest of drawers and striking it with the flat of her hand. "And is there an argument to be made, then, for the plague to attack the lowly, who don't deserve to live and thrive? If so, let me make it, and beg for the privilege of buboes and sores."

"What are you talking about?" says Iris.

"Oh, it's you, my younger daughter," says Margarethe, turning toward Iris and raising the back of her hand as if to smite her. "The one who schemes and connives behind my back!"

"I do no such thing!" cries Iris. "What are you about, flapping there like a crow?"

"Like a blind crow," admonishes Margarethe, "but not a deaf one. I hear what I hear, even being led through the streets of Haarlem like a pig to the slaughterhouse."

"What have you heard?" says Iris.

"That it was you who first suggested that Luykas Schoonmaker send the painting of Young Woman with Tulips to the exhibition hall at the Pruyn household," says Margarethe.

"Is that all? Of course I did. Why not? It's his best work," says Iris. "It's better than the fawning Madonnas and the bleary-eyed angels—"

"You will undermine every strategy I undertake on your behalf, will you," Margarethe roars. "Come near to me, girl, so I may strike you as pleases me!"

"You are not to strike me," says Iris. "This world is not yours to arrange as you please!"

"Is it not, is it not," says Margarethe, turning around and around in the middle of the hall, as if in her rage she can no longer tell where Iris's voice is coming from. "I'll say it is not.

Everything and everyone stands in my way, I who have nothing but the humblest intentions. Who is it who called me the fisherman's wife, greedy to be housewife, duchess, queen, empress, and god? A woman wants the smallest things in life—a man to take care of her daughters, food for their mouths, a little bit of security, no more than a shawl and a hunk of bread—and everything that she is seen to do is a scandal, a testament to avarice, an emblem of greed. And the world conspires against her to show her up, to bully her at every corner, to scratch at her with its clawed opinions, until the very breath that she draws is resented."

"You will want some tea," says Iris.

"I—will—want—something—more—than—tea," says Margarethe. She advances on Iris and makes to glare at her through her red-rimmed eyes. "I will have my way, though my own flesh and blood sees fit to conspire against me like a two-bit demon from an outlying village of hell. The imps that plague me, the little demons like squirrels that scamper in my path! Your brain should ache, you reprobate, you turncoat, for daring to meddle in things that are beyond you! Have you no idea what a burden a thankless daughter is?"

Iris draws herself back into the doorway. Despite her anger, regret makes her timid. "I didn't mean a thing by it —what is a girl's foolish opinion to a man like Master Schoonmaker?"

"You are the greatest fool in the land," says Margarethe. "I can no longer hope to marry myself to a stronger man than van den Meer—"

"—not least because you are still married to him," snaps Iris.

"—but you, more fool you, have no idea of your own value. You're to be presented to a minor nobleman, and yet at your own suggestion that painting of a rival beauty is to be hanging in the same house! Have you no sense?"

"You are clearly deranged," says Iris. "I am young and stupid—you have kept me such, barely teaching me my letters—and I am going to the ball to gawk at the highborn, nothing more—"

"No mother, however hard she tries, can convince her children of their own worth," says Margarethe. "Their children turn to evil sprites around their knees. I'm not going to stand for it. I'm going to go early to the Pruyns' house and argue that the painting be removed. Clara is the most splendid beauty the town has to offer, and any fool worth his salt would seek her out on the basis of that painting, even if just to see how far from truth the lecherous painter may have strayed. Anyone who sees Clara knows old Schoonmaker hasn't even been up to the task; she is more amazing than he could capture. You will thwart me at every step, but when it comes to a struggle between mother and daughter, my little one, remember"—she draws near to Iris and grins at her—"mothers have the advantage of knowing not only how and why they behave, but how and why daughters behave as they do. For mothers were all daughters once, but daughters take their time to learn to be mothers . . ."

Her hand sweeps out and knocks a bowl off the sideboard. Shards scatter. A moan from the space under the stairs: Ruth in distress. "Forgive us our trespasses," says Margarethe, "and get out of our way."

* * *

There is a bath, and a small amount of powder to apply, and bodices to lace, and skirts to step into, and bonnets to adjust. Clara helps Margarethe first, who calls in a hoarse voice for the hired carriage to approach the front of the house. She'll send it back for Iris and Ruth in an hour or two. She leaves, cursing and braying and twitching, without the aid of an assistant. "What I need to do I can see well enough for," she mutters. The whiff of approbation dissipates only slowly upon her departure.

"She is a witch," says Iris, but it isn't as if that is what she truly thinks—it's merely a notion to venture upon the air, and to consider how such a sentence sounds. Does speaking a dubious thing make it more true? How shallow the words are, really—*She is a witch*. One might as well say, *She is a mother*, thinks Iris; that about covers the same terrain, doesn't it?

It's late afternoon by the time Caspar returns. He carries a dark cloth over his arm, a long cape of some sort, but in the slanting light of the dining hall he opens it gently. Inside is laid a dress of such sumptuousness that Iris, Ruth, and Clara all gasp.

"It isn't a gown," says Iris, "it's a waterfall of golden coins!"

"Fool! I can't wear such a thing and hope to hide my face!" says Clara. "I want a cloak of invisibility, and you've brought me a fountain of light!"

"Mmmm," murmurs Ruth, and strokes the thing as if it is a huge sleeping cat.

Caspar's face is pinched with pleasure. "You don't expect me to be denied on such a matter," he says. "I haven't spent the day going hither and yon, striking my own bargains, paying such prices as needed to be paid, in order to procure this for you just to have you deem it too fantastic to wear! I'll warrant you can slip into it in a moment. Try it on, anyway, and see. Look, the ruff that I chose—it will show off your chin and your subtle cheek the way a gilded frame displays a masterpiece."

Iris sees his delight, sees how his eye fall on Clara. Iris becomes no more than the cast-off brown cloak that has slipped to the floor, a puddle of shadow, a shade. "Try it on," Iris mutters. She doesn't mean to speak so softly. She has to say it again, and raises her voice above a whisper. "Go on, Clara; at least give us that much new to consider."

"I'll step out of the room. You make the adjustments you need to," says Caspar. He's nearly cutting capers with satis-faction. "Now, for the first time, I wish I had pestered the Master to secure an invitation to the ball for me! I can't bear to think what the expressions will be. Maybe I'll dig up a dig-nified garb of my own and sidle in."

"Go on," says Iris, "play the role. You've gone this far, Clara. You owe him this at least."

He prances out. Clara rolls her eyes and says, "This is becoming a terrible mistake. I will not heap attention on myself. Even Caspar, who I thought would understand, will turn me into a plaything for the eyes."

"He's an artist, what do you expect?" says Iris crossly. "Go scrub your hands so you don't soil the thing when we get it over your head."

"You are vexed," says Clara.

"I am bewildered by what we're doing," says Iris.

"No," says Clara, "you're vexed. You don't like the way Caspar looks at me."

There's nothing for Iris to say. She goes and strokes Ruth's chin, and thinks back to the times when she had only had one sibling, and an ugly, silent one at that. For a moment she wishes that time could come again.

A look of love and devotion blooms in Ruth's eyes as Clara begins to transform herself from the maid of ashes to a golden lady. There, like a revelation, come Clara's pink cheeks, emerging from under soapy scrubbing. There are the lithesome limbs, the limbs of a young woman already, though they have so often seemed to be the hardy pegs of a girl. Clara's head turns, and though her eyes are doleful, the light in them is real and urgent. Of course Ruth has to smile. It's a sisterly smile. She does better at this than I do, thinks Iris, and out of guilt she hurries to Clara's side, to help her struggle into the remarkable gown.

"I won't wear a ruff," says Clara. "Cast it aside. I'll drape my head with lace in the Spanish way, and let them think me a spy from Castile or Aragon if they must. I can't put my head forward like a haunch of venison on a platter, to be admired and devoured. I'll hide myself in folds of closely worked lace."

Clara turns in the light from the window. The waist comes cinching in as if it has been sculpted exactly for her. The simple collar, designed with the expectation of a ruff to conceal it, falls open in a fashion just this side of censurable. The skirt is full and cascades to the floor in a sequence of stripes: gold, bronze, black, with a coppery red braid trained upon the seams of each panel.

"There isn't the draftsman in Holland who could capture you," murmurs Iris.

"Nobody will capture me," says Clara defiantly.

"I have caught you," says Iris suddenly, and taps where her heart stands pounding in her chest. "It's just that, looking at your loveliness, the tears in my eyes confuse my memory, and I won't be able to hold you. But for now I have caught you."

Her voice breaks.

"Don't be ashamed," says Clara. "And don't be alarmed. I won't take Caspar from you."

"Caspar isn't mine," says Iris boldly. "He is the Master's, as I understand it."

Clara raises an eyebrow. Iris doesn't explain what she has heard from Margarethe. Before Clara can ask, Ruth is suddenly on her knees before the chest, rummaging through folds of linen. She gives a grunt of satisfaction and withdraws from the chest the pair of white kid slippers that Margarethe has forsaken.

"They'll never fit me," says Clara. But she draws them on, and they fit like a dream.

She turns and drapes a black veil over her head. She tugs the folds to close upon her face. In the early evening spring light, the shoes glow, looking like glass, as if the pure white skin of her feet are shining through.

White shoes, golden gown, black lace veil, and the perfect features of Clara even more stunning behind the veil than revealed. Though by now Iris knows better than to say so, for the veil is the device that makes Clara capable of moving from the house and out to the Pruyn family home, in which the festivities will soon begin.

"You look serene, and distant, and mysterious," says Iris. "You make us look like a couple of turnips, but that is no different. We are turnips and you are a tulip."

"I'm not recognizable as Clara van den Meer?" she says.

"Those who've seen you most recently know you as Cinderella," says Iris. "But you're not Cinderella, and you aren't even Clara van den Meer. You are Clarissa de Beaumont, I say."

"De Beaumont is not a Spanish name. I am Clarissa Santiago. Clarissa Santiago of Aragon."

She stands, she spins. Clarissa Santiago in her dark veil. It's the first time Iris has ever seen her stepsister look, for just a moment, as if she doesn't mind being beautiful.

"May I see?" calls Caspar from the hall. "Are you decent?"

They don't answer him directly. Everything about this moment hovers, trembles, all their sweet, unreasonable hopes on view before anything has had the chance to go wrong. A stepsister spins on black and white tiles, in glass slippers and a gold gown, and two stepsisters watch with unrelieved admiration. The light pours in, strengthening in its golden hue as the sun sinks and the evening approaches. Clara is as otherworldly as the Donkeywoman, the Girl-Boy. Extreme beauty is an affliction . . .

5
THE BALL

The Medici Ball

The great evening arrives at last.

The girls at the door of the house, caught in a sweep of updraft that makes an airy rustle of silks. Ruth is panting with panic even before she has settled herself in the carriage, and she keeps ducking her face into her hands and sniffling. "Courage, and if not courage, then good manners, Ruth!" says Iris sharply. But she doesn't know the manners for riding in a carriage herself, let alone the directions. She's glad that the driver has already made several excursions to the opulent estate of the Pruyn family, where the ball is about to be under way.

The wind that strikes last autumn's leaves out of gutters and hedges is a warm one. The stars shimmer in their fastenings, and a moon releases a bruising pinkness upon the world. The houses seem to draw away from the carriage as it passes, as if huddling behind their shuttered windows. The streets of Haarlem are curiously empty. Citizens either have been invited to the ball and are on their way, or they haven't and so are keeping close to home out of disappointment or even shame.

Iris peers from behind the curtain. Now, how does Margarethe intend to pay for this carriage, these clothes? She's mortgaging their future, betting as outrageously as she had goaded Cornelius van den Meer to bet, only now on a different commodity.

Iris slumps against the backboard. Margarethe is mad to think that Iris might hope to attract the attention of a visiting French prince. Is this the maneuver of someone who's been driven to the abyss by worry? Or are there yet deeper currents of strategy at work in Margarethe? At any rate, a ball is something Iris can study, coolly, without fear of being noticed or hope of attaining advance.

Iris finds that she notices the way things look outside—the rooflines, the twitching limbs of trees—rather than noticing herself and her sister inside this carriage, on this evening of all strange evenings. She lectures herself to attend. How do you see that girl called Ruth, how do you see the girl called Iris? Look at them as if you are to draw these young girls. Not what you know of them, how you think they go, but how do they appear? Caspar has taught her the lesson of the Master: Don't approach something to draw as if you know what it is; approach it as if you've never experienced it before. Apprehend it by surprise. Startle it into liveliness.

Iris glances at Ruth and then, quickly, glances away. What has she seen? A solid face with a knotted expression. No, don't presume that it's an expression of stupidity. What if it's a look of earnest effort? The brow furrows. If her nose is a little weak, her jaw is strong. The passion in the eyes that still gleams with the last of her nervous tears is nonethe-

less passion. Among the stolid Dutch passion is often put down to too much ale. But there are the few who think it an essential element in a person's humors.

Ruth's skin is smooth, as if it's stretched to capacity to cover the area that her large bones require. She wears her clothes awkwardly, and her hair is, to put it mildly, seditious. Her hands clutch each other without comfort.

Still, her clothes are something of a success, a generous gown of blue folds, billowing to hide the softly bowed shape of her legs, and a blouse and waistcoat to match the skirt.

And Iris herself? Ah, the inner eye blinks, and the spirit trembles, at the dangerous cost of seeing one's self as one is.

She can only look for a minute, with her eyes closed, at Iris Fisher van den Meer. She sees herself as if in a memory, a distant and unchangeable figure.

The girl sat in a corner of the carriage. She wore a neatly pressed cap of bleached linen—white with a blue under-tone. From beneath the turned-up edges her hair showed in the briefest of scallops; three or four fringey loops of field-mouse brown laid against her cheek like the papery scales of a fish. Though her nose was long and unregener-ate, and her lips thin, pursed like a minister's mouth, her color was good. Her cheeks were flushed—well, wasn't she on her way to her first ball? Her eyes were cast down, perhaps even closed, and the lashes that sealed them were too thin to notice, and the brows that overarched them drove inward, a gesture of contemplation. So perhaps she was an intelligent thing, despite her lack of education.

She was thin and rangy rather than full; she resembled a boy more than a buxom Holland maiden. Yet her clothes weren't ill-suited: a gown of shimmering lavender intercut with a lace the color of whipped eggs. Her hands didn't fiddle with the pleats at the gathered waist of her gown. She seemed, if not at peace with herself, then at least interested in developing herself, whoever she might be.

Is this the main thing that painters of portraits care about? The person on the verge of becoming someone else? Changing isn't just the province of the young, Iris thinks, imagining Margarethe with her mad eye—Papa Cornelius in his stupor—even Caspar, glowing with more fervent beauty than either Ruth or she possesses.

Or Clara, Clara turned Cinderella turned Clarissa Santiago of Aragon, becoming someone new by turns, escaping away from something, or toward something else.

Before Iris turns away from herself, she has one last glimpse and thinks: Were I to paint myself, that would be what I would try to capture: a person intent on seeing, even if what is to be seen isn't yet fully comprehended.

The carriage makes its way out the city gate and into the countryside. The grand home of the Pruyns is said to be the only estate that rivals any of the civic buildings of Haarlem. As the carriage wheels along a broad avenue of elms and the buildings begin to come into view, Iris can only gasp. Not like any structure she has seen before, not the rough brick and timber buildings of the lowlands in England, with their heavy brows of thatch, nor like the more rectilinear Dutch homes of Haarlem streets. Not like the imp-empty house of the van den Meers, broad-shouldered and severe. There has been some struggle between the Pruyns, the Coeymans, and the Beverwijck families as to which family would host the Dowager Queen and her godson, but the Pruyns have won the honor because their estate is the most ample and bucolic.

And there it is, as the carriage pulls in a drive shaded by copper beeches on either side. The carriage passes ivied walls surmounted by stone urns, and enters a courtyard through an elegant gatehouse. "Venetian, and in limestone," murmurs Iris to Ruth, parroting what she's heard. But she likes the strong triangle of the gatehouse roof and the broad, flat stretch of facade.

They alight with as much grace as they can manage. "You know your instruction," says Iris firmly to the driver, who rolls his eyes but nods. He is returning to the van den Meer house in Haarlem for a third time, now to collect Clarissa of Aragon. In ordinary circumstances he might hardly be trusted, thinks Iris, so Margarethe must have dreamed up sufficient reward for him to accept the increase of his duties. He clicks the reins and hurries the carriage off—there is a line behind him—and Iris and Ruth turn to survey the Pruyn manor house from close up.

The stone is a golden pink, lit by several well-trimmed torches giving an even, ample light. Servants suited up in a French fashion stand in two ranks, one on either side of the door. Ruth stumbles on the steps and barks a wordless curse, but a servant reaches out and steadies her elbow. By the time Ruth lifts her head and smiles she has already had the strength to blink back the tears of shame.

Because the air is nice and the crowd already substantial, the double doors of the Pruyn manor are thrown open. The melodies from a small orchestra can't pretty the atmosphere as much as Iris might have expected, for the nervous chatter spilling from within drowns out much of the music.

Iris and Ruth pass into the hall, and see that women are handing in cloaks at a small room off the atrium. Arriving without cloaks, the girls stand on the side until some more confident-looking townsfolk have prepared themselves for entering the main ballroom. Iris is too shy to announce their names, so she just pokes Ruth in the ribs, and they sail along in the wake of a prominent landowner from the east edge of town. "Heer Ochtervelt and family," announces a manservant, and Iris and Ruth play the part of country cousins of the Ochtervelts, trailing like an afterthought down the three steps into the broad ballroom. The Ochtervelts look as terrified as Ruth, and they never notice that their party has swollen in number by two.

Iris glances about for Margarethe, but she isn't to be seen. Instead a devil's garden of blossoms: women in high color, flaming cheeks and gowns, fantastical combinations that war against each other like the worst patch of summer weeds. All the town regents: portly men in black with colored sashes and ceremonial swords and chestsful of ribbons, medallions, and lace. The ruffs are so high and stiff that the goatees look ready for harvesting.

The room is the loftiest Iris had ever seen except for the Grotekerk of Saint Bavo's. It stretches up two and a half flights, with a balcony one level up supported by marble pillars all around the perimeter. Many of the partygoers have taken refuge in the relative anonymity along the margins of the room, underneath the balcony. They're packed like fish in a crate.

On either side of the main room, doors lead to other salons, in which food is arranged on tables. Peacocks baked in crusts. Crabs nestled in each other's arms. Prawns, turkeys, oysters, and chestnuts. Pies, golden lemons, hams studded with cloves. Beans, cider, ale. A whole table of cheeses, brown, white, and yellow. Fish, venison, rabbits, as well as yeasty bread and flat bread and pots of butter. No guest has yet dared approach the tables, though rural children stand by with glazed, disbelieving looks, waving flies away.

Iris takes Ruth by the hand, and they weave their way through the crowd, scrutinizing the guests, who are as colorful as the food, and almost as delicious. "Master Schoonmaker!" says Iris in her most cordial voice, and the Master turns. His face broadens and brightens.

"What a surprise, some real people here," says the Master. "Can you guess how many of these people have asked my prices for portraiture and then have gone to hire my competitors instead?"

"Always working," says Iris. "What's this evening to be like, do you know?"

"Never seen a tenth of this splendor, and hope never to see it again. I think we have about an hour of waiting for the great she-elephant to come in," says the Master. "Her royal majesty is in a reception room upstairs with the Pruyns and with the other guest of honor, her godson. Eventually someone will tell us it is time to eat and drink ourselves into a stupor. Then music must whip us into a frenzy of anticipation until she sees fit to grace us with her presence. Near to the midnight hour the Dowager Queen and her godson will be escorted into the next hall, where there are eighteen paintings on display. I think we're expected to follow in devotional silence and look on the paintings ourselves. She will yawn and slip out through a side door, and I suppose that will be the sign for all of us to race away and undo our girdles and belch ourselves comfortable again."

"Only eighteen?" says Iris. "I thought there were to be forty!"

"The Dowager Queen asked the Pruyns to make a smaller selection. She's a noodly old thing, and she has a romantic attachment to moonlight. She wants to look at the paintings as they appear in the dusk of lamplight. That's when she'll enjoy her portrait most, as she claims many hours of insomnia to her credit. But she's also a crotchety old woman, and she has said she'll be tired of paintings if there are too many. So after all that fuss, this afternoon seven painters were eliminated entirely, and of the rest, only one painting for each artist was permitted."

He's too glib and sanguine to have been rejected, guesses Iris, though she hardly dares suggest so. "The Young Woman with Tulips is in, isn't it," she says.

"It is," he admits. "You've helped keep me in the consideration by your sage advice, little girl." He looks pleased, guilty, and sullen all at once.

"It's the most beautiful painting of the year," she says.

"Hah!" he replies. "What do you know of paintings?"

"Enough," she says.

"Not enough," he answers. "You only know mine. It may be my most perfect work, but it needn't be the best painting of the year or of the exhibition."

"I am confident of you," says Iris. She smiles at him, and he colors slightly, and in that moment she realizes she is very near to being an adult, for he needs her approval as much as she needs his.

"My friend," she says, and reaches out and takes his hand. "It's an important night for you."

"It's a social affair, nothing more, and I hate social affairs," he says.

"You're embarrassed, so you're avoiding what I'm saying: Your painting, Young Woman with Tulips will be seen by everyone tonight. If even a little local fuss for you isn't enough, by the time the night is over you will be recognized as a major painter by guests from Holland, Utrecht, as far away as Gelderland."

"True enough, everyone will see," he groans, slightly mocking himself but somewhat in earnest too. "And then what? Either I get the commission or I don't. If I don't, the more public failure I become. If I do, I may be unable to surpass Young Woman with Tulips. It may be that my best work is behind me already. In a way, I wish I had never done it. I wish I had ruined it and still believed myself capable of better. Now I am not sure I can ever do better. I look at it hanging on the wall, and I wish it were gone."

"That's nonsense."

Ruth reaches out and pats the Master's shoulder. She's never touched him before; in fact, she rarely reaches out to any person, only animals. Iris says, "Look, even Ruth knows how silly you are being."

"I don't expect you to understand," he says. "If it's a kind of madness, it goes with the work of painting. I wish Caspar were here."

Iris doesn't speak of Caspar to the Master. She merely says, "Have you seen Margarethe?"

"No. Didn't you arrive together?" says the Master. He looks as if he's trying to control himself from making a further remark, and failing, for he goes on, "Perhaps Margarethe is off relieving herself in the outhouse. She's no longer the person I would care to engage in conversation in an evening of pleasantries."

"She is my mother," says Iris with dignity.

"Indeed she is, and welcome to her," says the Master.

"You're annoyed because she wouldn't marry you," says Iris.

"I'm relieved that she wouldn't marry me," says the Master. "I'm annoyed because I think she drove her husband to ruin."

"She's not responsible for the crash in tulip values," says Iris.

"Why are you defending her?" says the Master. "Because she's your mother?" He peers at her as if seeing her for the first time, and then relents. "Oh, well, I forget; you're still young. Come, let us speak of something else. Which fresh new thing will sweep this Philippe de Marsillac off his feet?"

"The wealthiest, whatever she looks like."

He laughed. "So you're not all *that* young, to view the world in such terms!" he says. "Then, if you were a man, what woman would you fancy, in all this flump and finery?"

"How can you compare one beautiful thing to another?" says Iris the Ugly.

"Good question. Is there a relative value of beauty? Is evanescence—fleetingness—a necessary element of the thing that most moves us? A shooting star dazzles more than the sun. A child captivates like an elf, but grows into grossness, an ogre, a harpy. A flower splays itself into color—the lilies of the field!—more treasured than any painting of a flower. But of all these things, women's grace, shooting stars, flowers, and paintings, only a painting endures."

"But words endure too," says Iris. "You quote the Bible text about the lilies of the field. Those very lilies that Christ taught about are dead for centuries, but His words live. And what about the kind act, as my mother said? My mother the crab, the irritant in the oyster, what about what she said? The small gesture of charity? Isn't that sort of beauty more beautiful than any other?"

"And equally evanescent," says the Master, "for small charities cannot this wicked world amend. But perhaps charity is the kind of beauty that we comprehend the best because we miss it the most."

They look out over the swaying garden of beauties, rustling in their silks, pattering with their slippers, glinting in their jewelry, sweating finely in the press of the crowd. They look for charity, which is hard to see; they find much handsomeness instead.

* * *

The music has gone from being a novelty to being faintly repetitious when suddenly the strings and woodwinds are augmented by the leveling notes of some golden cornets. The noise of the guests increases for a moment, and then drops to a hush, as the doors at the far end of the hall are thrown open, and liveried footmen march out and stand flanking the doorway.

The Dowager Queen of France comes in on the arm of her host, Heer Pruyn. She looks bored by the ceremony of it, and nods grumpily left and right. Heer Pruyn escorts her to a chair—simple yet suitably ample—and he settles the guest of honor in it. There is the sound of wood taking some weight on it, creaking, as well as more than a mumble of human complaint. "Never heard of cushions, what, you think I'm supplied enough with my own natural cushions?" she is heard to bray. "After all these decades they tend to wear out, you know."

Cushions are found. She is elevated by several of the servants, cushions inserted beneath her, and then she is replaced. She smiles wanly, as if a little human comfort for her rear end is the best that she can hope for in her old age. It's only when she's been supplied with an Oriental fan and a small table supporting a crystal goblet of port—which she never sips the whole night through—that she looks about and says, "Philippe!" and it becomes apparent that her nephew or godson or whoever he is has been proceeding behind her with tact and discretion.

"The Prince of Marsillac!" cries the Dowager Queen of France, and raises her glass. The good people of Haarlem freeze, as they don't know the protocol.

"To the Prince!" exhorts Marie de Medici, waving her right arm about in an enthusiastic motion.

"To the Prince," weakly reply those nearest her, and others farther away say more boisterously, "To the Prince!"

He steps forward four or five inches, gives the tiniest little bow, which might as well have been a stretch to aid in the digestion of some lumpen bite of pork pie. All heads crane, including Iris's, to see the catch of the day.

He is strong enough to look at, a bit willowy in the thigh, but perhaps that's the odd French cut of the trouser or the unmasculine shade of the material—or is that kind of green a royal color? His nose has the Gallic lift and heft, like the rudder of a boat. His fleshy upper lip puckers in a way that will cause hours of argument—some say weak, others say winsome. But his eyes make up for any other deficiencies; the irises are stone-gray and brilliant, like marbleized paper lit from behind.

Heer Pruyn and his wife quietly organize a display of femininity for Philippe de Marsillac. Dame Pruyn selects a girl, much as she might select a ruddy apple or a pungent fish at the market, and ushers the chosen morsel forward, where Heer Pruyn then takes over and makes the introductions. The Prince stands like a true chevalier, with one hand turned nicely at the small of his back and his palm out. With his other hand he reaches to take the hand of the maiden being brought forward, to raise her hand to his lips for kissing, and to return her hand to her. The crowd around the Prince is silent, listening to the polite and stilted exchanges, until the Dowager Queen belches without apology and begins to chatter with those near her, by which the partygoers learn again how to talk and buzz and gossip, and leave the Prince and his string of possible brides alone.

"I'm worried about Margarethe," says Iris after a while. "Shall we go to find her?"

"You go," says the Master. "I don't want to find her."

"Come, Ruth," says Iris, "let's take a stroll and see what we can." She puts her arm through Ruth's, which comforts the older girl immensely. They begin to make their way behind the small orchestra, peering over shoulders and beyond headdresses, looking for their mother.

But before they've found her, Dame Pruyn is suddenly at their side. "I need the two of you," she says gracelessly. "You'll be perfect next—"

"We don't really want to meet him," says Iris. "There's no need. We're just here to observe—"

"Oh, it's the price of admission, didn't you know?" says Dame Pruyn. "I'm doing my job as a hostess, so let me at it—don't look so alarmed! I know who you are, the young thing who neatens up the studio of Master Schoonmaker there! Some pretense at talent, they say? Well, I see color and form myself, and I arrange it as in a ballet, and the contrast of you and your sister is just what I need right now. You may come as a pair if you like, if your sister is that awkward, but come you must, for I won't be denied."

"Please," says Iris, "we're looking for our mother—"

"The new Dame van den Meer, yes," says Mistress Pruyn dryly. "She was muttering something about her eyes, and seeing imps and scalawags from hell wherever she looks. I sent a serving girl upstairs with her to put a cold cloth on her forehead. She is resting her bad eyes, and for all I know she's snoring the party away. I'm not going to make it my business to wake her. There's plenty of time for all that."

Mistress Pruyn won't allow Iris to dawdle, or Ruth to shrink away. There's nothing to be done but follow their hostess across the floor to where Philippe de Marsillac is looking fatigued, and the Dowager Queen behind him is picking nuts from a tray.

"Straighten your spine, look him in the eye, speak when spoken too, and curtsey when he says good evening," mutters Master Pruyn. "The rest is up to you. I'll bet a single sentence is all you get. He's not the chatty type."

The gush of pink silks and flutey laughter ahead of them is dismissed, and the floor opens. Philippe de Marsillac has the good breeding not to drop his jaw or wince at the sight of Iris or Ruth, though there's just the faintest twitch at one side of his face—a stifled yawn is the kindest notion, but perhaps it's a grin kept in check.

"And, Your Highness, allow me to present the sisters van den Meer," says Heer Pruyn. "Newly residing in Holland after their childhoods in the lowlands of England."

"Sisters," says the Prince, as if he's never encountered the concept before.

Iris nods briefly, not knowing if Ruth and she are being addressed or assessed.

"I didn't catch your names, Misses van den Meer?" he says.

"This is my sister Ruth, if you please, and I am Iris."

In English he says, "And you two English girls are here at a ball in Holland to meet the Dowager Queen of France?"

In English Iris replies, "We are part Dutch, if you please, and we are here to meet the Queen Mother's eligible godson, whether we want to or not."

He throws back his head and laughs—a short, stifled laugh, but a laugh nonetheless—and conversation for twelve feet in every direction comes to a halt.

"You must be as grateful to speak a little English with me as I am to speak it with you," he says. "I can wag my tongue in French, Spanish, Latin, and English, but all those flapping syllables you find in Dutch give my tongue a headache."

"I do not mean to be impolite," says Iris, flushing. "You find a rude English country girl before you, sir; please forgive me. I don't know the ways of this land."

"You are new enough here still to find Dutch ways peculiar?"

"I am young enough to find life peculiar," she replies.

"And your sister? You speak for her?"

"She doesn't speak."

"She's very smart, then, for the woman who doesn't open her mouth to speak can't be discovered to be a shrew, a harridan, a gossip, or a grump."

"Are those the only careers open to us?" says Iris. "If so, I should end the conversation myself right now and consider myself ahead. A vow of silence does no one harm."

"Until your hem catches on fire and you need to call out to someone to bring a bucket," he says, finding himself amusing.

"My hem isn't often enough near the kitchen fires these days," says Iris truthfully. "My sisters tend the fire."

"Your sisters? You have more than the one?"

"There's another, a stepsister—"

"Where is she? Let her come forward—"

"She couldn't come. Someone needed to stay home and tend the master of the house, who is ill."

"Ah," says the Prince. "And how do you busy yourself while your sisters work their fingers to the bone?"

"Oh, sir, I've been trying to learn to draw, with the hope of apprenticing to a studio—"

The Prince raises an eyebrow. Seen this close, his remarkable eyes are hazel and gray, with a corona of green at the outer edge of the iris. With interest he comments, "So what they say of the Dutch is true! Every fishmonger and farmer must have paintings on his walls, and even the gentle sex must try her hand with the paintbrush! You are no doubt talented—"

"Not talented yet, but maybe a little brave." She feels brave to say this.

"I like to study paintings myself," says the Prince. "The worlds they show, the inner and outer worlds. It is what binds me to my illustrious godmother. I had not hoped to meet a young woman of merit—"

"You have probably not met such a young woman yet," says Iris, and corrects herself, "that is, I am a fledgling, a novice. But I love to look and see what is shown."

"What is shown, and what is hidden."

Iris doesn't know how to see what is hidden. She makes a gesture of uncertainty. The Prince begins eagerly, "It is my belief, and wouldn't you agree, that every painting of interest features a dark reservoir, a shadow, a pool, a recess, and that ground of shadow stands in for—"

The growling voice of Marie de Medici rises behind him in a cough. He sighs and catches himself. "I believe I'm being encouraged to continue my examination of the most beautiful women of the land. I hope you won't be fleeing the party anytime soon? There is dancing, once I've endured the introductions. You are very charming, and I should like the chance to keep practicing my English."

"You should practice your lying, for I am not very charming, and your English is more elegant than mine. But as you wish," says Iris, lying herself, for the last thing she will ever do in this life is dance with a Prince in a public gathering. "There are far more beautiful women than I awaiting your inspection, I believe, so I will say good evening now."

"More beautiful perhaps," says the Prince, "but so very Dutch."

"Some of them speak French," says Iris. "You must have learned that."

"French reminds me of home," he says. "I want to be neither home nor here, but someplace else. At least English is a language that has the catch of otherness in it. And I like England."

"You know England, my England?" says Iris. She has been about to turn away and lead the fiercely blushing Ruth with her, but suddenly the notion of the Prince knowing anything about that space behind her blank memory is riveting, painful, necessary to pursue. The dark shadow he sees in paintings . . .

"Green fields, hills you can climb; the forests, the fens; I know England almost as well as I know France, I think—"

"Hills!" says Iris. "Oh, to climb a hill again—!"

Master Pruyn is prodding Iris in the back. She makes her curtsey.

"The chalk downs, do you know them? I shall count on continuing the conversation—" says the Prince.

"My own daughter, Gabriela Pruyn," begins Heer Pruyn. And Iris sees that she and Ruth in their ugliness have been displayed first to provide the greatest possible contrast to the Pruyns' own daughter, coming next. Heer Pruyn pushes forward a dumpy youngster made up to look something like a stuffed swan.

The Prince's cheek muscle twitches again, but he hasn't managed a word of greeting when there is a small but palpable gasp from the crowd, and his head swivels along with the others to see.

"Oh," says Iris, safe and anonymous once more in the crowded sidelines, clutching Ruth's hand, "she's here!"

Clarissa of Aragon

The hush gives way to a small excitement of whispering as Clarissa Santiago of Aragon—Cinderella—their own Clara van den Meer—takes two steps into the hall.

She has told Iris that she hopes to arrive without notice, but there's nothing Clara can ever do without notice, even being as disguised by a veil as she is. The candlelight on all sides of the room makes a glowing golden background as she pauses. She tries to drift behind the ranks of townspeople, but they keep shifting aside, as if they have a duty to reveal this stranger to their honored foreign guests.

In the end her steps falter, and though she stands with her head down, as far back in the alcove as she can keep, she is no less than radiant.

Even before Iris can whisper to Ruth, "Remember, we don't say a word to her!" the murmuring begins. Clara is easily the most beautiful creature in the room. Heer Pruyn straightens his back and throws his shoulders into alignment, and as he makes his way across the floor, his wife follows behind him with her hands clasped respectfully. His words of introduction are quiet and lost in the buzz of gossip, no doubt because he's trying to conceal the fact that he doesn't recognize this most bewitching of guests. But he's a man of the world and, it seems, of honor. If he has determined that Clara is an uninvited guest, he doesn't reveal it. He takes her small white hand in his, and he leads her across the floor to where the Dowager Queen of France and the Prince of Marsillac are waiting.

"Clarissa of Aragon," he says.

"I know of no Clarissa of Aragon!" says the Queen Mother, her sagging face suddenly looking beaky with the pleasure of being suspicious.

Iris watches Clara struggle to gain control of her voice. At last she says, "I know of you, Your Highness." She curtseys with a deliberate, slow gesture. "Mine is a small family and a dying one, and I have been raised in the Lowlands following the struggles."

"You appear to be blond as a Dane behind that veil, or am I giddy on port?" says the Queen Mother.

"My mother was northern," says Clara. "I'm more comfortable here in Holland, where I can speak in her tongue."

Iris maneuvers to see Philippe de Marsillac. The Prince seems thunderstruck. All the ease and comfort he has just demonstrated in his conversation with Iris—which is the longest exchange he has had since entering the room—has fled him. He isn't so much flushed or pale as he is golden; his face seems to reflect the arcs of regal material in Clara's gown.

"You've bewitched my nephew," says the Queen Mother. "Remove your veil, my good miss, and let us have a proper invitation."

"I may not," says Clara.

"Pray tell," says the Queen Mother. She leans her chin toward Clara, which seems to be a sign that she wants her spine to follow, but since her spine is weak, valets rush forward and gently take hold of her elbows and tilt her forward. "I am *nothing* but interested."

Iris can't hear the answer that Clara gives, but she knows what it must be: "I am paying a penance," or words to that effect. A suitable excuse for wearing a veil in a warm room, and a message that Clarissa of Aragon is Catholic. Clara van den Meer, of course, is Calvinist by birth, so this is to throw curious townspeople off her train in the event someone should suspect her of being a local woman . . .

"A face so young and pretty, even hidden as it is, can't be the masque of iniquity," says the Queen Mother. "One needs to be old and gnarled as a boiled leg of mutton like me to deserve such a penance. I can see your hair is ripe as Croesus' gold even behind your lace. You are a Diana before us. Pray, let the veil drop!"

"I should not discuss it further," says Clara.

"Then shall we have a dance? Let us see you dance! Since the boy is tongue-tied for the first time tonight!" cries the Queen Mother, and she elevates a plump hand. Heer Pruyn makes a motion to the lead violinist of the small orchestra, and a vivid gigue is struck up.

"Please," says the Prince, "do me the honor."

"Nothing would please me more," says Clara, "but I may not."

"More penance?" murmurs the Queen Mother. "How fascinating. I myself am quite addicted to sin. It does keep my confessor busy, negotiating with heaven on my behalf."

"A . . . a turned ankle," says Clara. "I fell on the path alighting from my carriage. It is still recovering. I should sit down—I will remove myself now—" Her voice is beginning to race; she isn't up for this charade.

Iris can follow no more of the conversation then, for a tap on the shoulder causes her to turn. Caspar is standing there, in rumpled but decent clothes just barely distinguishable from servants' garb.

"How did you get in here!" says Iris, as alarmed as she is pleased.

"I passed myself off as La Principessa's boy-in-waiting. Wait'll I tell you!"

"Tell, do tell—"

"The odious Nicholaes van Stolk arrived at the house just as Clara was mounting into the carriage. He caught sight of the hem of her golden skirt as she pulled the door closed. He called out to her familiarly—Clara! he called, *Clara!* In his guttural voice, all like a husband, possessive and tender. I bade the driver move on, and I climbed on the back board to attend to Clara. But I could hear her heaving softly through the carriage, one sentence, over and over—" He leans toward Iris. "She said, 'It is the crow! It is the crow!'"

Iris doesn't understand at first, and Caspar can't explain. But suddenly—as she sees van Stolk at the door of the room, arriving without invitation, the cad!—she knows what Clara thinks—that he is the spirit bird, the one who caught her and made her a changeling.

That's what Clara thinks. She may be wrong. It was ten years ago or more—how can she remember a voice for ten years? And though overbearing and smug, van Stolk is a solid burgher in sober Haarlem. How could it be he?

Accusing van den Meer of profiteering, then collecting the spoils himself . . .

Clara may be wrong, thinks Iris, but she must be frightened nonetheless. Iris turns and casts her glance across the hall. Clara is trying to withdraw from the Prince; she is curtseying a second time, a third, and drawing her veil the closer about her face. The Prince sees it as a game, and is teasing her with courtliness and respect. Iris approaches as near as she dares, and passes her without facing her, but manages to whisper near Clara's ear, "Dear brave one—Van Stolk has arrived—you mustn't be frightened—"

Clara whips around, and she does the unthinkable: She reaches for the Prince's hand and murmurs something to him. Without a word the Prince of Marsillac escorts Clara to the side of the room. He opens one of the salon doors and ushers her inside. The door shuts firmly behind them both.

Iris looks about for Caspar again. Van Stolk has been surveying the room; with the crowds, he may not have seen Clara and the Prince. But he catches sight of Caspar and begins to make his way through the throng to him. Iris gets there first.

"He's bearing down on you," she says. "He will pester you to find out if that was Clara! He mustn't know. You better leave."

"I can't leave her here alone," he says. "Quick, let's dance; they're about to begin."

"I can't dance!" she says.

"Of course you can, easiest thing in the world. I have legs like ninepins and I can dance, so just follow and do as I say."

"Caspar!—" she cries. But he has tugged her into the center of the hall, and they fall into their places in the parallel lines, men and women standing opposite each other. Van Stolk falls back, partnerless, waiting.

Twisting about, Iris sees that the Dowager Queen has been removed to a far corner of the room, and Master and Mistress Pruyn stand on either side of her, holding elegant beeswax tapers in matching silver bowls. The Pruyns resemble a pair of human candelabra. The Dowager Queen caws, "A set of playing cards, a table, and a partner!" and all are found for her within minutes. The musical introduction draws to a close, and the instrumentalists watch for a down-beat. Then the dance is begun, and it takes all of Iris's concentration to follow the lead of the woman next to her.

Iris sees the Master at the shadowy end of the hall, spinning poor gallumping Ruth around in the shadows under the stairs. Ruth has no sense of rhythm or grace, but her face is broad with glee and she seems the most natural dancer in the room.

The figures are difficult to pick up, but they repeat themselves, and while Iris doesn't have anything in the way of athletic prowess, at least she's able to keep up. When she gets used to the steps, she finds she can observe the other dancers. With chagrin she realizes that the dancers are largely guests

from the Hague or elsewhere; most of the stolid Haarlem folk stand on the sidelines, scowling with dignity.

Iris also manages to observe Caspar, who is grinning at her whenever their eyes meet. She's not entirely sure what their campaign is all about, but at least they're working at it together. She remembers his remark, perhaps to Clara—"I trust you won't marry the wrong man." What man is that? Has he possibly meant himself? But if Margarethe is to be believed, he isn't interesting in marrying any woman. So why is he even dancing with Iris? Because she's so ordinary-looking that she's more like a plain boy than anything else?

How hateful the thoughts that can spring in her heart, even in a room of candlelight, music, and dancing! Iris can't even glance at Caspar now, not so much out of anger or remorse but out of a shame at her own hot jealousy.

She thinks instead of Clara, sequestered in a side room with the visiting Prince Philippe de Marsillac. And Iris is flustered. She feels the surprise and delight at Clara's competence—Henrika, bless her, had done a great deal for her daughter, even while keeping her in seclusion like a hothouse flower! But Iris also feels a pang of something else, for she hadn't expected either to meet the Prince or to like him. Does she really enjoy his company, or was it the speaking in English, or just talking about painting, or the sudden strain of homesickness that lurched up in her when he mentioned the fens?

The flooded fens, the dead man floating, unburied, unshriven . . .

The cries in the night, the knocks on the door, the words in the dark . . .

Fleeing by flatboat on black glassy fields, Margarethe hooded and faceless in the moonlight . . .

She can't, she can't. She won't allow those memories. She thinks with sudden fury at Clara. What a change! Clara's much vaunted shyness hasn't kept her from being led to the Prince, or kept her from addressing the Dowager Queen with cleverness and courtesy. And then Clara disappears like a courtesan behind pretty doors painted in white and picked out in gold.

I have been duped, thinks Iris. Indeed, I stumbled upon a small chance at happiness, and in a single evening I set my own trap for myself and caught myself there. Who could have guessed the Prince might find *me* amusing? But Clara is capable of charity toward no one but herself, as always was the case.

The music doesn't end a moment too soon. Iris tears away from the hand of Caspar and loses herself in a throng of laughing neighbors. Let Caspar handle van Stolk as he will. Iris never thought she would even talk to the Prince, but she had, and he had liked her—*liked her!*—and she is losing the Prince, just as she is losing Caspar, to the prettiest girl in Holland.

She says to herself, *Oh, beware, that Margarethe herself should rise in your breast!* And suddenly the absence of her mother all this while seems more than peculiar—it is unsettling.

She sees that the Master is still tending to Ruth. So that is all right. With boldness Iris mounts the stairs to the gallery, and asks a maiden where she might find Margarethe, who is resting her eyes. The maid tells her that Margarethe had indeed tumbled into a deep sleep, troubled by twitches and fits. But she has just awoken and has wandered down the servants' staircase—at the end of this corridor—to look in at the exhibition hall, though none were to go in until the visiting Queen Mother of France flung open the main doors and entered the room.

Iris explains that her mother is illish and needs minding, so she will follow down the back stairs and take her mother safely where she belongs.

The exhibition hall is narrow but long, and the long opposite walls are punctured on each side by three high windows hung with velvet. There are candles fixed in sconces at intervals, but they're not lit yet, so most of the paintings— on walls and on easels, and a few propped up on low tables— are merely patches of blurry shadow. But toward the end at the right, one painting gleams in a spot of amber light.

There is Margarethe, standing before the painting of Young Woman with Tulips, holding a candle up to it, peering through bleary eyes.

"Are you trying to set the thing on fire?" asks Iris.

Margarethe turns. "Oh, it's the Queen of France herself," she says huffily.

"Mama," says Iris. "What are you doing?"

"I am looking to understand what is the truth of this painting," says Margarethe. "Can it be that my eyes have become so crusty with the ugliness they have been exposed to that I don't know how to appreciate the beauty that everyone tells me is here?"

"Do you mean that honestly?" says Iris.

"I don't know what could be wonderful about this painting," says Margarethe.

"You've taken against Clara, so how could you love her portrait?" says Iris.

"You don't understand what I mean," says her mother. "I'm trying to tell you. What perturbs me, in the few quiet moments I have when not worrying about feeding myself and my ugly daughters, is that life has wrung from me any ability to respond to the beauty of the world. I'm not sure I ever had the ability in the first place, even as a child. Whether it be Young Woman with Tulips," she goes on, holding her hand up high, "or this portrait of a burgher, or that study of a sleeping housemaid, or, for that matter, the moon that spills its cold light on this floor. I derive no pleasure from any of these effects. I look on them coldly and without interest. Is it my eyes, I wonder, or is it my soul that is bruised?"

"Mama," says Iris.

"Doesn't it occur to you sometimes to kill yourself?" says Margarethe. "If you have lost the ability to respond to what makes other people giddy and silly, are you the stronger for it or the weaker? I could for many months, even years, draw up my spine because life was against me, and I refused to be beaten by it. But what is the point, if the very daughters one is working to protect are up in arms against me, and the very husband one has struggled to marry has become a blithering idiot? The world rocks on around me, and the noise of it is louder as the sight of it deteriorates. And I see minor demons in the corners of the room."

"Mama," says Iris. "We are not up in arms against you—"

"And here," says Margarethe, turning back to the painting, "here is the foolish Clara, and any Dowager Queen who sees this bundle of physical splendor will ask about the model. We'll have emissaries of mad Prince Philippe at the door within the week, to invite her to come and bed the Prince before he dies of consumption or whatever it is he has—"

"What nonsense is that?" says Iris.

"Do you really think that such a highborn fop needs to go trawling for brides among the daughters of Holland merchants?" says Margarethe. "For all your love of how things look, are you really so blind that you never *think*? There isn't a woman of his rank who would marry the man, however pretty his brow or however satisfying his technique in the bedroom! The Dowager Queen is playing a game with the likes of us desperate souls, knowing she can dangle a certain amount of wealth and privilege to get a bride capable of bearing a child before the poor dim prince falls off his rotten legs and expires! Having a husband predecease you isn't such a bad thing, Iris, assuming he is well stationed to keep you provided for—"

. . . Jack Fisher wasn't a *poor* man, exactly, and the family had their cottage, but still they had to flee. . .

"—and a prince of de Marsillac's rank who has the sense to die an early death might be the most glorious marriage a headstrong, resourceless maiden could hope for!" Margarethe grins.

"You are truly mad," says Iris. "You are lying. No one would be so callous."

"Look at me," says Margarethe, holding the candle up in front of her face, "and paint what you see here, my dear. As the mother, so the world. Alas."

"You are here to burn the painting," says Iris, "and you are standing here getting up the courage to do it. Give me that candle. I've done what you told me to do. I have talked to the Prince. He is not mad. We even talked about England. I even liked him. It's you who are mad, making stories of such crabbed scheming. Get away from that painting. Give me the candle, I say."

"He is a handsome enough thing, I agree," says Margarethe. With a sigh she hands the candle to her daughter. "It would be hard to do better, my dear. You could bear his child and take care of your baby, your bruised sister, your mother, your addled stepfather, even your reclusive stepsister. You could do all of this. I give you the light. You see with it as best you can."

Walking away from the painting, Margarethe says, "I stood and looked at it for as long as I could stand it. I can know nothing of it at all. Is it my eyes or my soul that is bruised, I ask you again? I would murder the girl if it would do us any good. I would murder myself for the same reasons. I am too tired of this difficult life. And the damn writhing goblins under my feet at every step!"

Midnight

So the clock tolls on, toward the hour in which the Dowager Queen of France will examine the work of Haarlem's best artists, and maybe select the man to memorialize her on her deathbed.

Iris has snuffed the candle out and left it on a side table just inside the doors to the salon. Then she has followed her mother out into the ballroom.

In a side room with doors left slightly ajar, the Dowager Queen has ensconced herself with the Pruyns. She chatters in a desultory way and picks at a plate of nut meats.

Nicolaes van Stolk is gone, and Caspar seems to have disappeared too.

Of the room in which the Prince has repaired with Clara, the doors stay closed, except for once, when a footman approaches with a tray bearing two crystal glasses and a decanter of something golden. Iris isn't able to see over the shoulders of the people who peer in, but it's only moments before she hears the remark that the Prince has removed one of the maiden's white slippers. He has been seen on his knees before her, caressing the pretty ankle that has suffered from twisting. News of such indecency thrills the Haarlem towns-people, since the maiden guilty of such license isn't a local maiden and so can't impugn their celebrated Haarlem morals.

Iris goes looking for the Master and Ruth. They're sitting outside in the warm air, watching the stars.

"I found Mama, if you believe it," says Iris. "She was star-ing at Young Woman with Tulips by candlelight."

"I hope she sets it on fire," says the Master. "Though there are storks' nests on the roof here to protect against lightning, arson, and the random baking accident, so I sup-pose fire wouldn't take."

Ruth's mouth drops open in alarm, and spit spills off her rotund lower lip. Iris snaps, "Stop saying that, you annoy me! You don't want the painting destroyed!"

"Maybe I do. Ah, who knows what we want? We're all mysteries, even to ourselves. You grow to learn that, my girl. You do. You will."

And Iris feels she has learned this, the mystery is in herself. The imp of the episode is herself. After all, it was she who urged Clara to break out of her prison and come to the ball, so to entice the Prince and save the family, whether she admitted as much to Clara or not. It was she who served as the well-intentioned agent of hope. And now it is she who is punished, as much by self-knowledge as by the loss of the Prince.

"What do you want, my dear? I noticed your friendly conversation with our guest of honor. You were all set to be the most roundly cursed girl in Haarlem until the stranger

from Aragon came in the room. Now she seems to have captured the prize. I hope you aren't too disappointed, Iris."

"Disappointed?" Iris had hoped it didn't show.

"*Are* you disappointed?"

"He was modestly amusing," she says, shrugging.

"Look at how everyone is still eyeing you."

"Surely not!" She's horrified.

"Why so surely not?" he replies. "Look what they see. The girl most unlikely to interest anyone, being only part Dutch, and only recently arrived in this tight, smug little city. Yet you hold your chin up high, you answer him in a language few of your neighbors can understand. You are mysterious and alluring. Besides, you do what few other young women have done: You're an occasional apprentice to the painter who may be the last portraitist of Marie de Medici, Dowager Queen of France. Are you still so young that you can't see you have some cachet of your own?"

"I with my nose like a spring carrot, I with my arms like awls, my bosom small and indistinct—"

"You, you, you," he says, "aren't *only* what you look like. Aren't you enough of a painter yet to realize that? Even Caspar seems taken by you."

"Oh, Caspar," she says dismissively. "Who can know about him!"

"What's to know about him?" says the Master sharply.

Iris feels beside herself—she feels irate—she feels to be her mother's daughter. "It's said he has no eye for girls, for one thing," she states, her words running together.

"Who publishes such nonsense about my Caspar?" says

the Master. "That would make me into an even more inter-esting scoundrel than truth allows."

"Who cares who says it, it's common knowledge," says Iris.

"Not common to me, and the lad has lived in my house these several years," says the Master, "and boy's blood being what it is, I doubt I would have overlooked such a matter. Now answer me. Who tells you such tales?"

Iris mutters, "Margarethe, for one."

"Margarethe, and Margarethe alone, I'll warrant," says the Master, and on reflection, Iris has to admit that this is true.

"So you've been falling in love with Caspar?" asks the Master. "I should have seen it. And our ever scheming Mar-garethe wouldn't consider such a match in your best inter-ests, since Caspar is only a poor boy, an apprentice painter, dingier than dung. Do you think she wants you attached to someone with such dismal prospects? Isn't that a good enough reason for her to spread scandal and rumor about a boy too innocent to defend himself?"

"You are a painter," says Iris, oddly furious at him. "You don't know how to see how things are, only how they look."

"And is it true you're angry at him for admiring the beauty of the blond-haired maiden of Aragon?" says the Mas-ter. He bobs his chin at her and his ginger beard bobs too. "Think things through, Iris. If you really believe him to be interested in boys, why should it bother you that he, like everyone else in the room, followed the mysterious beauty with his eyes? Is that why you flung yourself away from him at the end of the dance? He chased after you and couldn't find you again. He's left in dismay and, I might add, no small amount of disappointment in you. He's afraid he has lost you to the Prince."

"He hasn't lost me, for he never had me," says Iris. "Besides, the Prince seems bewitched by Clarissa, as you say."

"Ah, Clarissa, is that her name?" says the Master. He looks at Iris. "Clarissa, the blond-haired stepsister of Iris van den Meer?"

Ruth, sitting nearby, claps her hands over her mouth, which gives the whole thing away. "You fool, Ruth," cries Iris. "Now, not a word, Master Schoonmaker, or all will go poorly with you!"

Ruth is dismayed by the rebuke, and gets up and wanders away. For once Iris doesn't follow her to mind her. Let her mind herself.

"Who would I tell, and why?" he says. "It'll come out sooner or later. How the townspeople will gossip, though, when they realize it was your own stepsister who attracted the handsome Prince Philippe de Marsillac just when he had begun to focus on you."

"Did I ever tell that I hate you?" she says. "For all your splendor of realizing things in paint and canvas, you are a cold man. You only want to see and to capture, and you pay no attention to making anything better for anyone. Margarethe is right: You chase the wrong beauty. I found that I had some chance of interesting that Prince in myself, and you laugh at me and mock me for it."

"You have some chance of interesting Caspar the painter's apprentice, and you pay no attention to that," says the Master. "I won't be accused by you, Iris. You're too young for your criticisms to sting. Let the story happen the way it will."

"I don't know what will happen; stories don't tell you how things will turn, really," says Iris. "Paintings and stories are different. Paintings are steady, unchangeable; stories convulse and twist in their revelations."

"We never know what's about to happen. Maybe the Prince truly will be smitten with love for Clara, your own Cinderella!—and maybe the Dowager Queen this very evening will see the painting of Young Woman with Tulips and choose me to do the most significant work of my career. If I can bring myself to paint something better than Young Woman with Tulips, I will do a work worthy of the ages. Steady, unchangeable, and perfect. I should be able to die a happy man."

"The painting of Clara stands in your way," says Iris. "You won't be able to paint better than it."

"Now you're being even more cruel than usual," says the Master complacently.

"Than usual?" she says.

"You're your mother's daughter, I say," he goes on, "though you try vainly and remarkably and honorably to escape it."

"There's no escaping that," says Iris.

"There's no escaping the torment of having painted Young Woman with Tulips, and having it dog me for the rest of my life," says the Master. "But still, we must try."

Iris rises to her feet and turns away. "I am not cruel," she says.

"And I," he replies, "am not blind."

* * *

The clocks of the hall strike the third quarter of the eleventh hour. The food tables have been descended upon. The wreckage looks like the sacking of Rome. Marie de Medici seems almost to have fallen into a sleep, and the puzzled guests are unsure: Is it more polite to leave quietly, or are they expected to stay until she awakes and can bid them good-bye? The hardworking merchants aren't accustomed to keeping such late hours, and more than one droopy-lidded wife tugs on the coat of her husband to beg for home and bed. But this evening will never come again, and most families have brought unmarried daughters or nieces in tow. No one wants to leave without seeing the spectacle to its end.

Besides, the Prince and the mysterious maiden from Aragon have never emerged from the private salon. There are rumors that a hidden staircase must lead to a bedchamber upstairs. What the French get up to! The scandal is more delicious than the food.

Therefore it's something of a relief when the Dowager Queen rouses herself from her catnap and requires to be lifted to her feet. The orchestra lurches into a sarabande, but the Dowager Queen frowns and the first violinist cuts off the music with a chop of his hand. Marie de Medici steadies herself by holding onto the back of a chair, and she lifts her rotund chins and speaks in a Dutch tinged affectingly with a French accent.

"My godchild and I are in your debt," she says, "for the hospitality of Haarlem, in the form of the Pruyn family, is worthy of note. The affairs of state and the affairs of the sanctuary and the affairs of the heart, I believe, are all related. You have given me much to brood about in my dotage. But now I am an old woman and I should repair to my chambers, to pray and sleep, passing first before the paintings assembled in the long hall adjacent. Don't bother me with farewells; let me say au revoir to you all and thank you for coming. I won't soon forget this night."

The guests nod their heads slightly, and the young women standing nearest the Dowager Queen have the presence to curtsey. She pays them no mind, but turns and heavily walks the length of the hall. She entered the room with Philippe de Marsillac, but she is leaving it on the arms of Heer and Dame Pruyn. The implication is lost on no one, and feeling runs high. Surely the Prince should reappear and escort his famous godmother through the gallery? Is all the fuss this evening for nothing, that a veiled maiden should arrive and sweep the eligible gentleman right out from under their noses?

But before the surprise can develop into murmurings of disapproval, the doors to the gallery are thrown open. The Dowager Queen stands still, suddenly looking a bit more awake, and it is her voice that says the word in their minds: "Smoke."

At once the room descends into chaos. Many of the men surge forward around and past the Queen Mother, to force themselves through the doorway and assess the problem; the women fall back, some of them hurrying out into the night, forgoing their cloaks and shawls. Iris looks about and, through the crowd, sees Ruth lurking massively against a pilaster, bit-

ing her fingernails. Iris races up to her sister and says, "Come, Ruth, don't dawdle now. Move those clumsy feet."

Ruth moans the sound that, in recent months, has come to mean *Mama*. She repeats it urgently: *Mama!*

"She'll be outside, for sure; she'll have gone home," says Iris, making things up, "we aren't to worry about her. Quickly! If there's fire and it catches on the timbers of the ceiling or the floorboards, this could be an inferno in minutes. The oils themselves in the paints will flare—"

Mama, says Ruth, and then the sound that means *Clara!*

Iris slaps her hand and says roughly, "Even now, hush! Now hush!"

But Ruth bolts across the ballroom floor to the closed doors of the small salon. The servant who has been guarding the door has left to help with a bucket brigade setting itself up. Ruth doesn't wait for an answer; she puts her broad shoulder against the door, and she pushes. By the time Iris has reached Ruth's side, the older sister has forced the lock and splintered the door's frame, and flung the door open.

"No!" says Iris.

The Prince is standing there, looking somewhat rumpled and glazed, but he takes the measure of the situation at once. He glances from Ruth to Iris and back again, beyond them into the broad chamber, sees the panicking guests crowding, hunting for family members, reclaiming their wraps, calling advice. The Prince darts across the room to the side of his aunt. The Queen Mother has fallen back into a chair and is being fanned by Dame Pruyn, who is rather hopelessly shrieking, "Madame! Madame Marie!"

"Just what I need. The Dowager Queen will expire tonight before I can do her death portrait," says the Master, suddenly at Iris's side. "Come, get out of here while you can, girls."

Clara appears at the door, fixing her veil in careful drapes over her face, and looking this way and that. "Get on, get on, get out of here, all of you," says the Master. "How can they save the paintings when there's all of you people to worry about first?" He shoos them toward the door, but Clara seems reluctant to get caught in the press of guests. She turns and disappears back in the small salon. Ruth moans in worry and follows her, and Iris, cursing, does the same. They are in time to see the edge of Clara's golden skirts disappearing over the ledge of a windowsill.

"She's gone out through the garden," says Iris. "Now shall we follow her?"

There seems little else to do. The Master has turned and joined the other men pushing into the long corridor. Antiphonies of alarm and instruction. The smell of fire is rich, rancid, and already the sound of the roar is louder than the music had been.

At the end of the garden an iron gate leads to the front courtyard and the carriage drive. There Iris and Ruth join the other guests of the party, a safe distance from the Pruyn manor house. Sleek greyhounds leap and tumble and snap at each other's heels, and the horses hitched to carriages are skittish and need removing from the courtyard at once. Margarethe van den Meer is wandering about on the edge of the crowd, stumbling over herself, pawing in the shadows, calling for Ruth and Iris. The strengthening orange glow of the flames—already beginning to devour the roofline of the wing—illuminates the men carrying paintings out through the broad windows.

Suddenly Caspar is at their side. "The Master's work?" he says. "Young Woman with Tulips?"

"Where did you go?" says Iris, clutching his sleeve.

"I suspect the painting is gone," murmured Margarethe, looking into the shadows. "I suspect it is."

Ruth bursts into tears, as if they have just said that Clara herself had disappeared for once and for all.

"A most unholy night," says Caspar. His face is tight, his eyes unreadable. He hurries to learn the worst of it, and to help where he can.

Without speaking, Margarethe and her daughters begin to walk along the drive, looking for their carriage to take them back to Haarlem. Iris and Ruth keep to either side of their mother, and link their arms with hers so she will not stumble. For the first time in a long while, Iris feels the imp again, nearer than ever. But now she knows she doesn't need to peer in the hedges. Perhaps—behind a tumble of branches and tossing leaves—she might see the Queen of the Hairy-Chinned Gypsies. Or it might just be a shrub shaking in laughter at how human lives are so easily ruined.

Any imp to be found is nestled snug in the pocket of her heart.

And it's a cold place, the world, especially when warmed by arson.

A Most
Unholy Night

I ris can't help but imagine the sound of the fire as she tries
to sleep. The Pruyn estate is miles out of Haarlem. But Iris
is caught by the hissing and crackling sounds that come
from the embers in the kitchen hearth; in her head such
noise turns into the ruin of artwork and houses. Beside her,
Ruth moans, dreamy woes and maybe gas pains from all that
rich food.

And Clara hasn't returned at all, though Margarethe,
mercifully, never thinks to look in on the girl in her nest of
blankets by the hearth.

Where can she have gone, a panicked girl-child in a gown
suitable for wearing at any court in Europe? All those miles
outside of town? And abroad, on her own, she who hardly
knows where the end of the street goes? Several times Iris
racks herself up on her elbows, out of dreams, because she
thinks she hears a latch rattle, a floorboard creak. But always
it is nothing, and down into her moiling anxieties she sinks,
again and again.

Finally she falls into a sort of waking dream, a drumbled dream that unfolds even while she can feel the frame of the cold kitchen around her. The long, flat water, the moony night, Ruth in shudders, Iris staunchly poling the flatboat, and Margarethe with a dark shawl over her head . . . And the echo of the accusations the villagers were making as they pounded on the door. Witch, they called, Witch.

Witch!

Iris starts up again, and she realizes that she has been stirred by a real sound, not just by dream panic. She hears a footstep in the hall, the rustle of cloth.

"Clara!" she hisses, and she thrusts a poker into the hearth to stir up the fire so that the girl can see her way.

The brightening light reveals Clara entering the house in her gown, ruined beyond repair, and Margarethe approaching from the hall opposite, in nightdress and shawl, rubbing her bad eyes and peering in a sleepwalker's stupor.

Iris thinks for a moment it's merely another gust of dream. If she treats it gently, it might transform itself into something milder than it threatens. "Come to bed, sister," she murmurs to Clara, whose face, she now sees, is raw with weeping.

"I am a ghost in my own household," mumbles Margarethe. "Who is this who hovers here? Some tenant who buys the property when we sell it to pay our debts, and we repair to the poorhouse to die? Is this years on? Who are you, in your golden raiment, dripping rainwater onto the clean floor?"

"Mama," says Iris, now sitting bolt upright. Might this

yet be salvaged? "It's a dream. You're only having a dream. Come back to bed."

"Could it be Clara?" says Margarethe, but her voice is dim and faltering, as if she thinks it might indeed be a dream. "Clara turned into an angel? Or is it Henrika? Come to plague me for my sins?"

"Henrika, then," says Iris, moving forward, as if Margarethe is a wild beast to be caught . . . the fox in the trap . . .

"Henrika come back from the grave, to assail me with tales of my wrongdoings, is that it?" says Margarethe. Her eyes are squinting against what little light there is. "Or is it the sad and beautiful daughter left behind, who is out to ruin our lives?"

"Let me be," says Clara, "let me out of these terrible clothes, let me back to my ashes where I belong—"

"But the clothes are as angel garb," says Margarethe, and only then does Iris realize that Margarethe, probably alone of all the guests at the Medici ball, didn't see the arrival or departure of Clarissa Santiago of Aragon. Margarethe mutters, "So Henrika returns to the scene of her murder, to accuse a poor housemistress of poisoning her, but why should she complain? Look at the vale of tears I released her from! I have sprung her from her trap, I have taken on her burdens, a little spoonful of the right strength of the right tincture at the right time, and her indenture to this mortal struggle is paid, and her shackles unlocked! If she has come to accuse me, let her agree to exchange places with me! For if her lodgings are now in hell, she's put herself there by her own actions, and if mine are to be the same, let me drop there at the earliest opportunity and claim a comfortable place among the ashes and cinders of that hearth of Lucifer! There are enough of his minions pestering me at my heels and in my eyes already."

Iris says, "Mama, you ramble in your sleep, you mustn't say such things—"

"Is it the day of fire and brimstone? It's the day that rains glowing coals. I saw the face of Young Woman with Tulips wreathed in flames!" cries Margarethe, not so much with triumph but with terror. "Henrika, I assisted you to your grave, but I didn't consign your daughter to the flames. Another hand than mine burned *that* beauty."

"I am not Henrika," says Clara, shaking loose her mantilla. It drops, a fringey heap of wet lace. She struggles with the buttons on her gown and snarls at Iris, "Are you going to help me, or do I need to sleep standing up tonight?"

"This can't be Clara, she disappeared in flames," says Margarethe.

"She escaped for one night," says Clara. "She left her place at the hearth, and look where it brought her! My parents were right to train me close to home, for that is all I am suited for!" Iris is at her side then, working at the buttons, kissing Clara's wet neck, soothing her, before more is said than can ever be taken back.

"Clara did not break my wishes and escape to the ball?" says Margarethe. "It can't be possible."

"Clara went to look at the world once more, and once more she pays the price," says Clara coldly.

"It seems to be the girl herself, emerging with damp limbs

from a dress of impossible splendor," says Margarethe. She is crooning to herself as if drifting on an opiated dream. Soon Ruth will awaken and be terrified at the sound of Margarethe's unmusical humming. "Where could you get such a dress, I wonder?"

"I prayed to the spirit of my dead mother," says Clara, "and she came out of the linden tree in the form of a green finch, and dropped the parcel down."

"To avenge me," says Margarethe, eyes closed. "A green finch. A bird with the face of a woman. In the practice of distributing herring, I should have been more generous to the cats."

Clara steps out of the gown, which crumples into a sodden mass. With a sudden shriek she bundles it up and throws it into the hearth, but instead of burning, it douses what is left of the fire. The room falls into blackness.

"And how could a Cindergirl make her way to such a ball?" asks Margarethe with tempered syllables.

"The spirit of my dead mother told me collect a pumpkin from the garden, and with the magic that comes from beyond the grave, she changed it into a coach," says Clara.

"It's a capable spirit that can coach an autumn pumpkin from a garden not yet planted with spring seeds," says Margarethe. "And I suppose she made coachmen out of the rats that gnaw the last of our tulip bulbs?"

Clara doesn't answer. She stands with one white slipper and a disarrayed rumple of undergarments. "You have lost a shoe," says Margarethe, "and I see the track of red in your smalls. It is not a smear of oil paint, I believe."

Clara kicks off the remaining shoe. "There are some walls that, once broken, can never be rebuilt," says Margarethe. "A glass slipper, once shattered, can't be resoled. A mother once poisoned can't be revived. The chalice of virginity, once emptied, can't be refilled. Ah, to cage a finch in a linden tree, and twist its wings off, even if the human face on it continues to shriek!"

Iris finds she is biting her knuckles. She can't be hearing this. The shrieked accusations of her mother's being a witch are so close to true. In the shadows Iris reaches a hand back to the wall to steady herself.

"I am nothing," says Clara, as if talking to herself. "Leave me alone." She removes the last of her clothes and stands shivering in the dark, naked as a child, but no longer a child. "I don't want to be touched, nor held, nor scolded, nor remembered. I just want the ashes to hide me. I want nothing of princes and public, I want nothing of household and hearth. Leave me alone. Let me perish with some dignity."

"She is already perished," says Margarethe, turning from the room. "I put her in the grave myself. Why can't the dead learn to hold their tongues?"

The Second Slipper

The sisters sleep together, when they sleep at last, and the dreams that earlier have plagued Iris meander to a halt. All her nightmares have come true. No word is said about the Prince, or about the whispery scent of alcohol that Iris could smell on Clara's breath. Not a word about what had happened in the small salon, or about the hours since Clara fled the Pruyn house through the side window.

The only remark Clara makes is that the old dame with the walking sticks saw her safely home.

When the dawn light is coursing through the slats in the shutters at last, making thin stripes on the floor, Iris, tossing, decides that for every human soul there must surely be a possible childhood worth living, but once it slips by, there isn't any reclaiming it or revising it. Even by the act of painting, she thinks. Even by turning it into a fairy tale to bewilder a sleep-befuddled old mother, there is no revising the saddest of the truths that greet us daily when we awake.

So there she is, and the nub of the day upon her again. Ruth stirs and moans, hungry for the animal contact of warm skin that Iris has long outgrown. Upstairs, Cornelius van den Meer is calling for the pisspot to be emptied. Clara is up at the hearth already. She has retrieved the gown and hung it on a hook, but there are a half a dozen singed blotches on its skirt, to say nothing of soot and soil. "We're down to the last few soft-hearted potatoes," says Clara in a voice without emotion. "But the final heap of flour for a morning loaf has been untroubled by mice, for they've already left the house to find better prospects."

"It's a fine morning," says Iris. "Grant it that."

"Oh, no one will take fineness from a morning," says Clara. "The beauty of the day is the only thing that doesn't fade in time. Day after day, such beauty revives itself."

Before Margarethe comes downstairs, to begin whatever campaign for their survival she might next invent, Clara hides the golden gown in a wardrobe and kicks the white slipper under a chest. The pearls and pendants that Caspar pawned for the loan of such a gown are now irretrievable. Without a word between them, Clara and Iris behave as if the night before has not happened—neither Clara's amazing visit to the ball, nor Margarethe's sleep-throttled interview with them both.

So they all eat a small breakfast together. Margarethe seems more herself, though she is stingy with remarks, for once. The four women sip hot water with a modest dripping of honey stirred into it, and Margarethe says at last, "We have only a short time before our creditors descend upon us for payment. If you're to accept van Stolk in marriage, Clara, you must be ready. Or if we are to go to the almshouse, we go looking like decent people. Clara, I want you to wash yourself and put on a decent skirt. No, don't argue with me. The time has come to pay what we owe. Iris, you see that Ruth is well scrubbed and her personal things tucked into a scarf. I will bring myself to the bench in front of the house, for I won't have it said that I met adversity with any less courage than I met success."

Iris can't look at Clara. There is Gerard van Antum the clothier to pay, and worse, the dreadful Nicolaes van Stolk to surrender the house to. Margarethe has implied that each has been singled out as a possible suitor for Clara. Is Iris to be offered to whoever is the loser? No matter Clara's willingness—what about her suitability for marriage now? If she isn't still virginal, will that make a difference? Does Margarethe intend to pester Clara with questions about last night?

They have scarcely nodded their glum acceptance of their tasks when a rapping is heard on the door. Margarethe straightens her spine and adjusts her cap on her head. "Iris," she says, "the door, please."

"I haven't had time to put on suitable morning clothes—"

"Throw on a cloak, and quickly, let the visitor in."

Iris does as she is told, setting her face to betray no interest in the triumphant arrival of van Stolk. When she unbars the door and opens it, she blinks in the sunlight. Only after a moment does she make out that it is Caspar standing there. It's hard to recognize him at first, not just because of the sun, but because he isn't grinning at her. His face is oaken with seriousness. Iris feels a chill run over her shoulders and fold into spectral fingers at the base of her neck.

"Good morning," says Caspar, and he stands aside. Behind him is Philippe de Marsillac, in a red gash of a cape, his cheeks flushed from a brisk walk. "Let us come in," says Caspar, almost rudely, and he pushes through. Iris is reduced to holding the door and, pressed up against the wall as she is, manages to make only a small, ineffectual curtsey.

"We weren't expecting visitors this morning," says Iris, in crosscurrents of feeling about seeing Caspar and the Prince together.

"Delighted to be here," says the Prince. "Delighted to accept your hospitality."

There is nothing to offer in the way of hospitality, nothing at all—even the last browning potato has been mashed and eaten. "I will call my mother," says Iris. "Please, if you will wait in the salon . . ." With that she flees into the kitchen. Her mother never laid eyes on the potential suitor the night before. Iris is able to derive some small pleasure in saying to her, "It's just the Prince."

Margarethe is up on her feet at once, whirling about. "Clara! Run to the neighbor and beg a basket of bread and cheese! Bring back a flagon of ale and whatever else they can spare! He has come, he has come, and all is not lost! Hurry!"

For once Clara doesn't stand against her stepmother. She stumbles across the flagstones of the kitchen floor and barrels out the door without a backward look.

"Girls," says Margarethe, "come now, come quickly with me to the hall."

"We're hardly dressed to entertain royalty," sputters Iris.

"Every second counts. Do as I say." Margarethe is like a

ship whose sails have just caught the wind again after a month of listlessness. She courses into the front of the house with her shoulders back and her chin high. Ruth tucks her hands behind her back and whimpers slightly. Iris can't stop to be kind. She just grabs Ruth's elbow and pulls her along.

"There is no surprise like a complete surprise," Margarethe is saying, in something of a blather. "We're honored beyond our capacity to express it. To what purpose do you come calling so early on a spring morning?" She offers the Prince a chair, but he doesn't accept it. Instead he walks across the room in a state of excitement, while Margarethe backs up against a sideboard and rests her hands behind her to keep them from shaking.

Iris watches the two men in her life: the prince who deigned to chat with her like a person, and the painter's apprentice who danced with her despite the disapproving looks of the townspeople. She finds herself lost in conflicting desires, but the presence of each man tends to calculate against the other. In the end it seems only tiring that they are both there at once, not thrilling. It is that Caspar is so hard of face today, so brutal-looking and wary.

"There are secrets in this household," says the Prince. "These very walls harbor the hidden answers to many questions. This, my young friend here, has promised me. But I have no talent at investigation, so I must ask you outright: Have you any knowledge of the owner of this slipper?" He nods to Caspar, who pulls out of a leather sack the slipper that Clara has left behind in her flight.

Margarethe says, "My eyes are not what they once were.

Give me that, so I may understand it." She takes the slipper and looks at it closely, and says, "But of course, this is my own. How did you come across it?"

The Prince doesn't answer her. "Does someone in your household choose to wear it from time to time?" he asks.

"They might," says Margarethe, "if it were to please a prince for her to do so. Shall my Iris model it for you? Iris, put your foot in the slipper and show the Prince how delicate an ankle you have."

"There is no need," says Iris.

"Do as I say," says Margarethe.

Iris takes the slipper with too abrupt a gesture, and sets her foot in it, but though the shoe fits from toe to heel, Iris's foot is too narrow. It won't give form to the shoe, or fit it snugly. "You see, it doesn't fit, Mama," says Iris. "Such an exercise! I'm not made for delicate slippers such as these."

"Then Ruth shall try, if it's a wearer of slippers you seek," says Margarethe. Ruth is hard pressed to obey, but finally she squats on the floor and accepts the slipper. The Prince is watching with careful eyes and an inscrutable expression. Ruth's feet are huge, and the whole exercise is pointless and insulting. But Ruth tries to fix the slipper on her foot, grimacing at the effort—not because the slipper doesn't fit, but because her fingers are sore.

"Ah," says the Prince. "Look at the maiden's hands."

Ruth put her hands behind her back, and the ill-fitting slipper falls off.

"Let me see," says the Prince. "What I have come to see, let me see."

Ruth won't obey.

"What kind of misbehavior is this?" cries Margarethe. "Ruth, show the good man your pretty fingers, or I'll thrash you soundly!"

Weeping suddenly, Ruth thrusts her hands forward. Two of the fingers on her right hand are raised in white blisters.

"How did you come by such a burn?" asks the Prince.

"She can't answer you," says Margarethe. "She is shy."

"She is mostly mute," says Iris. "Her tongue is twisted at the back where it connects with her mind."

"A kitchen accident?" asks the Prince.

"The very same," says Margarethe. "The sores will heal nicely."

"Or did a lighted taper drop its untrimmed wick upon you as you set out to burn the painting by Master Schoonmaker?" says Caspar.

Margarethe gasps, and Iris feels her heart tumble into a chasm. All now is lost, even more, it seems, than the night before. Every creature with blood in its limbs is a traitor, one of God's mistakes. Has Margarethe given poison to her employer?—Ruth, *Ruth*, set alight Schoonmaker's masterpiece?—Has Caspar cast suspicion and the weight of law upon his terrified friends? And Iris herself has collaborated too, by encouraging Clara to attend the ball without permission.

There's no one left to stand and act in contrast to betrayal, to give the help so sorely needed. No one.

Ruth drops her face into her hands and weeps with loud animal snortings of phlegm. "I told you their iniquity is profound," says Caspar. "They are drunken with odd tales of malice, the whole lot of them. For their jealousy they've ruined my Master's greatest work, and likely his career as well. To say nothing of broken his heart."

"You will be held accountable, and you will pay for it, and suffer," says the Prince. "I have alerted the Haarlem schout of the suspicion that attends this household, and I will testify to the governors of the prison of this girl's confessional wailing. The damage done! Not just to your own household, to the honor of the Pruyns, to the nerves of the Dowager Queen of France, but also to the painting itself, which by all accounts was a masterpiece. I only wonder," he continues, "how can one be jealous of a painting? Who could have planted such severe rage in your breast?"

No one speaks.

Behind them, a step across the kitchen floor, and then Clara comes forward into the salon with a basket of bread. "What you have asked for, you have received," says Clara, setting the basket on a table. "Bread, and a small pot of butter, and some conserve and some cheese."

"Another maiden in the house," says the Prince, and then, looking back to Iris, remembering, "your stepsister, the one who minds the hearth."

Iris nods.

"Let her try the slipper," says Margarethe wildly, perhaps to shift the attention of the Prince from the sniffles of Ruth.

"There is no need; the slipper was merely a ruse to get you to open the door to me," says the Prince. "A ruse, I see, that I did not even need to enact." But Clara has come forward and taken the slipper from where it has fallen. She puts it on, and stands and lifts her chin.

Iris guesses that in Caspar's anger at the destruction of the Master's painting and possibly his career, Caspar hasn't bothered to tell the Prince that Clarissa of Aragon is really Clara van den Meer. Iris watches the Prince look at Clara with surprise. More than one story comes together.

Outside, a bank of clouds slides sideways, and more spring light advances into the room. It falls upon Clara as always it will, as if it has traveled the thousands of miles from the sun just for the benefit of illuminating her beauty. She is ill-kempt, raw-eyed, nearly slatternly in her robe, and more splendid to see than any painting. The Prince says, dubiously, "*Clarissa!*" and he takes a step forward.

Clara moves a half step backward—but only a half step. Her hand goes up to block the Prince's accusatory finger from Ruth's cowering form. Clara's is a gesture of charity, the only beauty that has consequence. It is the oniony heart finally delivering up its goblet blossom.

"Shield my family from harm," she says, "and let everything else follow as it may."

Stories Written in Oils

So now children play our family's shame as a story in the streets. And Clara, our Cinderella, our Ashgirl, is dead, and all these old dilemmas awake in my mind as if they happened yesterday. What no one tells the young is to be careful of their childhoods. The memories from those days are the most compelling paintings in the mind—to which, with nostalgia or dread, you must ever return.

Caspar has heard the tale and he has told it back to me, and as he tells it I play a small and stupid part, and this is as it should be. But I wasn't as insensible as he portrays me. I was silent but not dull. I was slow but not vacant. The night of the ball I didn't lie snoring in the hearthside, but weeping silently from the pain to my burned hands. This is how I overheard the conversation between Margarethe, Clara, and Iris, in which Margarethe betrayed herself.

Clara came forward to save me, just when my treachery was likely to bring our family down. I hadn't seen that she would do so. I don't believe I would have set her portrait aflame had I known the turn that events would take. Cinderella—girl of Cinders! I never saw the ruined canvas once I had lit it—I turned and fled—I never saw the most beautiful girl in the world become char, ashes. A real cindergirl.

Maybe with the destruction of that perfect image of her, Clara was released from one of the many spells that bound her. There she was, for all we knew, pregnant with the Prince's child, perhaps in love with him or not—who could tell what that meant, when we were so young and foolish?— certainly she was eager to escape the household in which she had learned, the night before, that her mother's death had been murder. Clara's understandings about the world, never easy to ascertain, were even more veiled from that day forward. But she was removed to the protection of the Pruyns by the end of the day, promising, with cold tears, to take care of Iris and me from a distance. How we chose to tend to our own mama, poor evil Margarethe, was our own affair, and she never once inquired after her, in letter or in person.

If you ask me why I set the painting alight—I'm not sure I can answer with honesty. I think I knew the Master was terrified of his masterpiece. And I had my share of pride and jealousy. My ears worked! I could hear Margarethe call me an ox! And there Clara stood, preserved for eternity as an angel. In the end I probably despised the glorious canvas, but, give me credit, I also could see that Clara hated it too. Hated it, and also was afraid it was an emblem with which the horrendous van Stolk might possess her. What is strange is that we may remember what we have done, but not always why we did it.

Caspar was always in love with Iris, from the first day he met us. He took his revenge on our family only when he learned from the Master what Margarethe had been saying of him. Clara's forgiveness of me went a good deal to soften Caspar's rage on behalf of the Master. And Caspar was right to be patient with himself. In time he made Iris a good husband, while she painted at his side, and sometimes under his name.

Now Caspar dutifully cares for his ugly sister-in-law. He continues to bring me along to the chapel when I require it, to the meadow when I need it, to the studio when he wants my company so he can keep from sinking into a melancholia, missing his Iris.

She is in my mind, gray dawns to mothy dusks—she is as often Iris the fanciful child as she is Iris the struggling, arrogant, angry daughter-of-her-mother she could sometimes be in her adult life. And the stronger for it too, I might add, the richer life lived for it.

Iris was burdened by her fancies. For years she insisted that she could remember the night we left England. The villagers had come marauding to our cottage, at the town's end, where we lived little better than milking cows. They had pounded on the door and accused Margarethe of savage witchery. They said she had called forth the full moon, she had called up the high tides, she had broken the dikes by her own malice. She was a witch, and wasn't it clear?—look at the ugly daughter she bore, as large as a slab of granite, and dull, and mute. Iris was slow to realize that when Margarethe talked about our family being saddled with an imp, she meant *me*—her curse, her burden. Iris was too good-natured to take this in. She invented an outside imp, a distant cousin, when she already had a sister.

She liked to look, but not at the harsher side of things. She rarely remarked on my part in our family story. I had abused Margarethe's eyes with red pepper, I had burned the painting, I had sulked and held myself back, pretend-dumb as the beast they likened me to. No, I wasn't evil, but I was jealous of everything: Clara's incredible countenance, Iris's talent, Caspar's attentions to them both. Iris never saw that, in some ways, I belonged in the gallery of God's mistakes.

Iris claimed to recall how we fled those flooded fields of our childhood, heading back to Holland, where Margarethe's family might take us in. But how could Iris recall this? It was night, and we were asleep, and dreams pester children.

"You want to find out for sure?" said Iris to me once. "Approach our old mother before she dies. Ask her one question. Ask her how she knew that Jack Fisher was dead. She only heard the villagers boasting about it. She never waited to hunt for his body. She didn't bother to bury him if he needed it, or to nurture him back to health if she could. She pushed off from England without a single moment's hesitation. For all we know he didn't float there, a bloated corpse in the flooded fenlands. For all we know he's still alive, and she named herself a widow out of fear and desperation. Don't ask her if she was a witch, or if she is one now, or if she remembers that she poisoned Henrika so she could marry

van den Meer. Just ask her how she knows for sure that Jack Fisher was dead on the night we fled for our lives."

I never asked Margarethe that, and I won't. The old thing is a thousand years old, and refuses to die, though her own imps still writhe at her feet and chew on her corns. I do know that Margarethe confessed to murdering Henrika, but that famous night Margarethe was partly asleep, in a state of dreamy agitation. Was Margarethe really capable of such a crime? I have no doubt. Did she actually do it? I don't know, and don't care to know. Probably she did, but what good would it have done any of us to be sure? Neither Iris nor I ever mentioned the midnight confession to Papa Cornelius, and the business marriage between him and Margarethe saw only quiet times from then on.

I won't ask Margarethe about those ancient times. Nor will Iris ask such dirty questions. Iris died long ago. Died fairly young, but not without some notice. With money that Clara supplied, Iris paid to apprentice at the studio of Pieter van Laer. She would have liked to apprentice with Judith Leyster, Haarlem's brave woman painter, but then Judith Leyster married Molenaer and they moved to Amsterdam. Iris's talent perhaps was not in painting as she always thought. But she loved to look—that never changed—and she talked a great deal, and told stories. I can't think of a single painting of hers I admire. I only admire that she did them at all.

Margarethe neither admired nor scorned Iris's work, being blind.

* * *

The Master didn't recover from his shock. In the end, with the loss of his *Young Woman with Tulips*, his reputation was indeed diminished. He is still better known as the Master of the Dordrecht Altarpiece than as Schoonmaker, genre painter. When he died, Caspar took over tenancy of his house and studio. I believe the paintings in the Gallery of God's Mistakes were all thrown onto a bonfire. Face down, so that no one could see the sight of these miserable creatures tortured by flames, as surely their lives must sometimes have seemed. May they have their rest in some anonymous corner of the garden of Paradise!

The Dowager Queen of France, to Dame Pruyn's relief, rousted herself from her own fit and went on to live a good few years.

To our surprise, Papa Cornelius's health also recovered, in direct proportion to the recovery of his income. For one thing, Clara kept her word, and found ways to channel money from France to restore at least some of the money her father owed in debt. Also, the canny Dutch learned to regulate the tulip industry and to protect what few assets were left for those whose finances were imperiled. At length the market improved, and Papa Cornelius again prospered, but not wildly, being bound by government constraints on the tulip trade.

The Prince of Marsillac did succumb to some pox or consumption, as Margarethe had predicted—the lone example of her reporting gossip accurately instead of inventing it for her

own ends. He left Clara with two children and a secure income from estates in France. Clara outlived her magnificent beauty, as women must, and in another one of her fits of sudden anguish she took herself off to New Amsterdam, on the other side of the gray Atlantic. Who knows what bumblebees, crows, or she-elephants lurked there to pester her! It was from New Amsterdam that the letter came, from a predikant of the colony, to tell her relatives she had died and was buried in the churchyard, in view of a substantial harbor that is home to ships from the Netherlands and all of Europe besides. She died of a complaint of the heart.

Of van Stolk? The memory here fades. He never did possess the van den Meer house, of course. I suppose he aged and moved in with relatives. And it was always unclear to me whether he had been an abductor of young Clara, or had this only been a fancy of hers, a crystallization of her terrors about the dangerous world? And regardless of the outcome, was that kidnapping a premeditated affair, after all, arranged because of the wealth of her family? Or was it the inspiration of a moment, because the child was known and loved, and had wandered away from her family? And because, money or no, she must have been splendid to see, as children can be. At the age of three or four, a treasury of smiles, a dancing wreath of light. All that quicksilver attention to the world! Children, like artists, like to look.

Crows and scavengers at the top of the story, finches at the top of the linden tree. God and Satan snarling at each other like dogs. Imps and fairy godmothers trying to undo each other's work. You might be born as the donkey-jawed Dame Handelaers or as dazzling Clara van den Meer, Young Woman with Tulips. How we try to pin the world between opposite extremes! And in such a world, as Margarethe used to ask, what is the use of beauty? I have lived my life surrounded by painters, and I still do not know the answer. But I suspect, some days, that beauty helps protect the spirit of mankind, swaddle it and succor it, so that we might survive. Beauty is no end in itself, but if it makes our lives less miserable so that we might be more kind—well, then, let's have beauty, painted on our porcelain, hanging on our walls, ringing through our stories. We are a sorry tribe of beasts. We need all the help we can get.

Before leaving for the new world—another new world!—Clara returned to Haarlem once, to see her father a last time. Margarethe wouldn't descend from her room, claiming that the presence of Clara might restore her eyesight, and in her old age she preferred her blindness. Papa Cornelius, however, took great pleasure in Clara's highborn position. He delighted in his grandchildren and showered them with kisses.

The children loved to run in the sheds where the new tulips were being cultivated. I remember seeing them one morning. They were playing a game of hide and chase. They were oblivious of any imps in the shadows, or hairy-chinned spiders in the rafters. The children tore up and down the long corridors made by rows of rough tables supporting great artificial fields of flower. The new plants were abundant, ranks of

spears poking up through the soil. You could barely see the blond heads of the children in a blur as they raced along.

It would have made a nice painting, were someone to choose something as lowly as that to study. Another story, a story written in oils rather than one painted on porcelain. But to be most effective, the faces of the children would need to be painted in a blur, the way all children's faces truly are. For they blur as they run; they blur as they grow and change so fast; and they blur to keep us from loving them too deeply, for their protection, and also for ours.